Advance Praise

"During the midst of the madness of the pandemic, Dr. Chanté DeLoach has created and held space for mental health professionals seeking to 'make way outta no way.' Her superbly crafted text is at once both accessible and relevant to various mental health practitioners grappling with service, purpose, and meaning. Her insights, grounded in relevant research and blended with sound clinical judgment, are sprinkled with real-world applications that makes for easy reading, understanding, and application. Her pragmatic approach to keeping therapy relevant to increasingly diverse sets of consumers, all while the rules of engagement are undergoing seismic shifting, will help this text continue to be a necessary resource in the coming decade. As an old African proverb states, where there's a river, you must build a bridge. Thank you, Dr. DeLoach, for your study bridge to better mental health practices."

—**Taasogle Daryl Rowe, Ph.D.,** Professor Emeritus of Psychology, Graduate School of Education and Psychology, Pepperdine University

"*How We Practice Therapy Now* is an incredibly timely, useful, and comprehensive book. This book explores everything from teletherapy practice, the changing face of ethical considerations when using various technologies, multicultural issues, as well as individual therapist identity and values and the impact these factors have on current psychotherapy practice. The book is accurate, engaging, and right on point for today's experienced and psychotherapists-in-training. I would highly recommend this book for clinical supervisors, practitioners, and psychology graduate students."

—**Katherine Helm, Ph.D.,** Director of Graduate Programs in Counseling, Professor of Psychology, Lewis University

"*How We Practice Therapy Now* is not only relevant, it is vital. Dr. DeLoach does a skillful job of integrating historical and current thinking about nontraditional delivery of therapy services and the adaptations necessary to respond to the global pandemic. This volume uses a conversational tone, examples, and personal experiences to present technical aspects of virtual and teletherapy, making the content accessible to both novices and experts. Every practitioner should have this book on their shelf."

—**Erica Holmes,** Associate Program Chair, Director: Psychological Trauma Studies Specialization, Antioch University, Los Angeles

HOW WE PRACTICE THERAPY NOW

HOW WE PRACTICE THERAPY NOW

CHANTÉ D. DELOACH

W. W. NORTON & COMPANY
Independent Publishers Since 1923

This book is intended as a general information resource for professionals practicing in the field of psychotherapy and mental health. It is not a substitute for appropriate training, peer review, and/or clinical supervision. Standards of clinical practice and protocol vary in different practice settings and change over time. No technique or recommendation is guaranteed to be safe or effective in all circumstances, and neither the publisher nor the author(s) can guarantee the complete accuracy, efficacy, or appropriateness of any particular recommendation in every respect or in all settings or circumstances. All case subjects described in this book are composites.

The author is not a lawyer, and nothing contained in this book should be construed as legal advice. For advice about how to comply with HIPAA requirements and prepare legally appropriate informed consent documents, or for any other legal advice or legal questions related to your therapy practice, please consult an attorney with relevant expertise.

Any URLs displayed in this book link or refer to websites that existed as of press time. The publisher is not responsible for, and should not be deemed to endorse or recommend, any website other than its own or any content that it did not create. The author, also, is not responsible for any third-party material.

For information about permission to reproduce selections from this book, write to Permissions, W. W. Norton & Company, Inc., 500 Fifth Avenue, New York, NY 10110

For information about special discounts for bulk purchases, please contact W. W. Norton Special Sales at specialsales@wwnorton.com or 800-233-4830

Manufacturing by LSC Harrisonburg
Production manager: Katelyn MacKenzie

Library of Congress Cataloging-in-Publication Data

Names: DeLoach, Chanté D., author.
Title: How we practice therapy now / Chanté D. DeLoach.
Description: First edition. | New York : W.W. Norton & Company, [2021] |
    Series: A Norton professional book | Includes bibliographical references and index.
Identifiers: LCCN 2021011720 | ISBN 9780393714708 (paperback) |
    ISBN 9780393714715 (epub)
Subjects: LCSH: Psychotherapy—Technological aspects. | Telecommunication in medicine.
Classification: LCC RC475 .D45 2021 | DDC 616.89/14—dc23
LC record available at https://lccn.loc.gov/2021011720

W. W. Norton & Company, Inc., 500 Fifth Avenue, New York, N.Y. 10110
www.wwnorton.com

W. W. Norton & Company Ltd., 15 Carlisle Street, London W1D 3BS

1 2 3 4 5 6 7 8 9 0

To all the therapists holding space through it all.

Contents

Acknowledgments

Writing this book during a pandemic was a massive undertaking; I have benefited from the support, wisdom, and generosity of spirit of many people who I want to acknowledge.

I am grateful to have a loving and supportive family. First, I am appreciative of my husband and life partner, G., for sharing me with the world. He has given me the space to write, shared insights and provided constructive feedback, wine, and tacos. Many of the pages of this book were written either before dawn or with my then four-year-old daughter climbing up my back. Her joy made a pandemic as well as racial uprisings more bearable. My hope is that I have written something she will be proud to one day read. Thank you, Mom and my late father who both gave me the space to express myself, even as a young child. All of that time expressing myself was apparently beneficial! I gained additional parents through marriage. Thank you, Dr. Victor and Catherine Blankson for loving and supporting me as your own. Your pride extends continents. Space does not allow me to individually name everyone in my family, but please know that I appreciate all of you. I want to extend a special thank you to Tawn. You have been a steady presence every day of my life. I wouldn't be where I am without you. Thank you to Harold for giving me laughter and for reminding me that we don't give up in this family. Thanks to Tracey; Devin, Cameron, and Cassius (aka "the boys"); and my aunts Velma and Joyce. Every text message, FaceTime, and family Zoom call gave me needed joy and allowed me to write another page.

I am also blessed to have "chosen family" through my circle of friends. Drs. Taasogle Daryl Rowe and Sandra Lyons-Rowe, the parents I adopted, I give thanks for your love, support, and professional mentorship. I am a better therapist and educator because of you. My friends: Jannis, Bree, Analena, and Shaifali were consistent with text support and laughter. I would not have finished this book if not for the life-sustaining memes and GIFs. Naomi, Torrey, and all of my friends who do not allow distance to get in the way of support, I value you. Thank you for each sharing in the joys and pain of life. I have several mentees who have become my sister psychologists. Thank you, Marissa, Sujata, Ayanna, and Shena. I hope that my work makes you proud. I am honored to be engaged in this life work with you all. My LA Mocha Mom friends extended much needed love and light as did my backyard pod. The Leimert Park pod gifted me with a few additional daylight hours to write. Thanks to Ki and the Mama Bears for needed space and vegan donuts. My SMC colleagues and friends were a much-needed source of light. Special thanks to: Tyffany, Sherri, Edna, Erin, and Steph. Thank you to Baba Falokun Fasegun and Iya Fayomi Williams for spiritual support.

I want to acknowledge my editor, Deborah Malmud at W. W. Norton & Company, for her encouragement of different versions of this project. Her support and helpful feedback were invaluable. This work is better because of the input and incisive feedback of the editorial team.

I did not become the psychologist that I am on my own. I give thanks to the Divine for guidance. I have been inspired by and stand on the shoulders of the work of therapists and healers across traditions. My hope is that your work is honored and reflected in my words. Finally, I am grateful to all of the people who have trusted me to walk with them through some of the most difficult moments of their lives. I have learned and grown from their commitment to being better versions of themselves. Their resilience continues to inspire me. Throughout this text, I have shared case examples that are composites of clients. I have changed identifying details to protect the confidentiality and sanctity of our work.

Introduction

March 15, 2020

"I hope you are all healthy and managing to stay informed yet centered right now. A lot has changed in the last week since we met, and things are evolving by the moment. We are all being encouraged to practice social distancing to protect our own health and to promote the public health of all. While this is a disruption to our lives, it is also an unexpected opportunity to spend time with loved ones and center our health and wellness practices. Please know that I remain a source of support through the madness. For now, I will be meeting with clients remotely via video (or phone if necessary). Current guidance is that our sheltering at home orders will be in place for 2–4 weeks, and then hopefully we can safely resume meeting in person."

I sent that email to clients one year ago; we continue to meet via video and are primarily sheltering at home with no definitive path of what is next. Multiple times per day I hear the word *unprecedented* to describe virtually every aspect of this time. In many therapists, the shift to sheltering at home and providing teletherapy provoked mixed emotions. While for some this was an opportunity to work from home and not have the stressors of a commute or the expense of an office, it was abrupt, startling, and even disorienting for many of us, therapists and clients alike. For many, the sudden shift to 100% video therapy was like being forced to drive a stick shift when you are accustomed to driving an automatic, then being forced into traffic with stops on multiple hills! The learning curve for some therapists has been steep and the adjustment slow. I was fortunate—I had been offering video-based therapy to a select group of clients for a few years, so I was prepared and knew what to expect. Most therapists were not set up with the infrastructure, equipment, or necessary training to effectively engage in long-term teletherapy with their entire client load from home. Many of us may not have even had a home office, or if we did, it may not have been useful because there was no privacy or soundproofing. For many clients, this shift was just as shocking and unsettling. So many of us told ourselves and our clients that teletherapy would "just be for a short time," yet the pandemic continues and we have had to work to adapt to changes of the world even as we discern what is next.

There has been a necessary emphasis on physical health during the pandemic: curbing transmission, effective treatment, and developing a vaccine. Yet, the mental health effects of months of fear and uncertainty and the total upheaval of life as we know it are only now coming into view. There is a historic wave of mental health problems currently unfolding, including depression, substance abuse, post-traumatic stress disorder (PTSD), and suicidality (Czeisler et al., 2020; Panchal et al., 2020). Recent research found that more than 50% of people feel that their mental health has been majorly impacted by the pandemic (Panchal et al., 2020). These numbers have increased as the pandemic continues. Calls to emergency hotlines and online therapy companies have skyrocketed. For example, the online therapy company Talkspace reported a 65% increase in use of their services within the first few months of the pandemic (Associated Press, 2020), and a federal crisis hotline reported ten times the number of calls since the beginning of the pandemic than the number of calls prior to COVID-19 (American Psychological Association [APA], APA Task Force on Race and Ethnicity Guidelines in Psychology, 2020). Early data about the effects on private practitioners is different. Many therapists (59%) have reported a decline in client load (Sammons et al., 2020). Some clients lost their jobs and couldn't afford to continue therapy. Other clients were just doing their best, mentally and emotionally, to survive and couldn't focus on therapy. Some therapists reported an increase (6%) in new clients, which may include the return of old clients (Sammons et al., 2020). The reported increase may also be attributable to existing clients who previously needed sessions on an as-needed basis suddenly requiring weekly sessions.

"Hey Doc, I know we haven't talked in a while. I think it's been about a year or so. I would like to return and jump back in . . . The world is a lot right now. I hope you have the time and space with everything going on. And I hope you are safe."

This message, from a former client of mine, is one that many of you may recognize. Many of you may, like me, have been unable to say no despite already having a full load. The stress and strain on family relationships and partnerships has been palpable. I have lost count of the number of clients who have contemplated breakups or terminated relationships during the pandemic. The loss has been and continues to be overwhelming. Clients lost (and are losing) jobs, income, opportunities, and loved ones. And so are we. Equally if not more difficult is that therapists are experiencing this crisis alongside our clients. We are all navigating health fears and concerns for ourselves and loved ones, negotiating children being home from school and their needing support with online classes, bearing witness to a racial justice movement, all while holding space for clients who are experiencing the same struggles. During times of collective trauma, such as traumatic events in a workplace, natural disasters, or mass shootings, it is standard practice for external therapists to come in and provide support for the affected community, including the local therapists involved. Here, there are no external therapists to bring in: we are it. This is *unprecedented*.

Consider Sam, a therapist with a small, but thriving private practice focused primarily on supporting parents of children with ADHD and autism. Sam is also a single mother of a four-year-old son. When the pandemic began and schools closed, she had to transition her practice to fully online and scramble to figure out a plan. She could not work from home and have no one there to watch her son and help with his virtual preschool lessons. He was too young to be left unsupervised. As a single parent, she could not afford to take a leave from her practice, nor did she feel good about just abandoning her clients during a pandemic. She considered hiring a babysitter or asking a friend to help while she was in sessions, but she was too afraid of the COVID-19 risks. Approximately three weeks into the shelter at home orders, Sam knew that something had to change. After multiple discussions with friends and family, Sam decided to temporarily move in with her sister, who lived a few hours away, so that she could have some help. Even though her sister was working and had a daughter of her own, she felt it was the only viable solution. Due to the cramped living quarters with two children and multiple adults in the household, most days Sam is set up to engage in her sessions in a small corner of the bedroom. During the early days of the pandemic, Sam's son barged into multiple sessions looking for her or his toys. It became commonplace to hear background noise from the household, the neighbors, or just life happening for her and her clients. The setup was far from ideal, but it was real and human, which her clients got to witness. Although Sam was embarrassed and felt completely unprofessional, they often laughed about it. This setup allowed her to continue to engage in her work, support her clients, and not be alone in supporting her son through the pandemic. Sam's clients have struggled a lot during the pandemic. Parents have been stretched thin, and even more thin for her clients with children who have challenges with regulating their emotions, focusing, and concentrating and who thrive with structure. This has been a difficult time for all of her clients. Sam has noticed that working with her clients remotely, in their home environment, has improved her ability to coach parents in real time and provide needed support and affirmation. In some cases, remote therapy has been even more effective than her in-office work with clients. Despite the severe challenges of this shelter-at-home period, Sam has begun considering the ways that teletherapy could become a permanent service that she offers. She has also come to appreciate the flexibility that it allows her for coordinating with her son's schedule, which is especially beneficial to her as a single mother.

Like Sam, we are all adjusting and figuring things out alongside our clients, many of whom are continuing to struggle even now. What many of us are seeing and feeling in our private practices is just the nascent stages of this mental health crisis; we are only just beginning to identify the severity and range of mental health effects and the massive economic depression that has ensued. It is clear, however, that many people will continue to struggle for years to come. Prior to COVID-19, rates of psychotherapy utilization had been steadily declining for the past decade or more (Gaudiano & Miller, 2013). Reasons for this decline are complex, but it appears to be related in part to the challenges clients experience in finding and connecting with a therapist that feels like a good fit for them (Gaudiano & Miller, 2013; Owen et al., 2014). For years, therapy has been fraught with premature termination or early dropout rates, which can be higher in clients belonging to racially minoritized groups* (Anderson et al., 2019). Also, the cost of therapy has long been a factor related to access and premature termination of therapy : many people leave therapy because it costs too much, and a growing number of therapists do not accept insurance. Approximately 30%–60% of private practices are now fee-for-service and have moved away from insurance (Babayan, 2015). Practicing therapists can attest that the movement to primarily fee-for-service is in large part due to the painfully low reimbursement rates of insurance companies and the bureaucratic challenges and barriers specific to mental health within managed care. These systemic issues are valid and shape our decision making about our therapy practices. Fee-for-service also contributes to the long-standing perception of therapy as a luxury and its association with privilege. It makes sense, from a client perspective, that high out-of-pocket costs coupled with not feeling that the therapist is a good fit or that the style of therapy is meeting one's needs would call for discontinuing therapy.

Even before the pandemic, many therapists had been working to re-brand therapy and their approach to services to bring it into greater alignment with the needs of today's clients. This is evident in the increase in wellness-based approaches and out-of-office therapies. Therapists are increasingly identifying the practice of psychotherapy as a healing science and art within both

---

* Language matters, particularly in reference to oppressed people who have often been disempowered in the naming of their identities. Where possible, I will use terms that point to a person's ancestry or heritage (e.g., African American, Mexican American) in lieu of generic terminology that centers normative whiteness. The term "racially minoritized" is used intentionally, to refer to the active process of *minoritizing* people and to those groups' lived experience, instead of "minorities," which describes their personhood and identities (Vidal-Ortiz, 2008). The terms People of Color and BIPOC (Black, Indigenous, and People of Color) are also used, not for their culturally nebulous phraseology but as an acknowledgment of the power that arises in the solidarity of racial coalitions.

healthcare as well as wellness spaces. The wellness industry has ballooned to an estimated $4 trillion industry (Global Wellness Institute, 2018), so the identification of psychotherapy as a wellness practice has the potential to increase the visibility of therapy while shifting the view of therapy away from being solely grounded in the medical model. The evolving view of therapy as a wellness practice can also be seen in the rise and increased acceptance of mindfulness and complementary approaches to health. The integration of yoga and body-centered approaches within therapy are now common, particularly among trauma therapists (Boyd et al., 2018; Brom et al., 2017). Many therapists have moved toward a more wellness centered orientation, and it is also more common to see therapy moving beyond the confines of the therapy office to nature-based settings and home environments. In these ways, therapy has been evolving and continues to evolve into a practice that is no longer restricted to or defined by place and that is capable of reaching more people by being in the service of public wellness instead of the service of an elite few.

The face of therapy is also changing. There have long been cries for the field to diversify to better reflect the demographics of the United States, but the mental health field has remained persistently white (Lin et al., 2018). While there are slow increases in the racial diversity of new professionals, it is perhaps equally, if not more, troubling that white therapists in private practice overwhelmingly see white cis-heterosexual clients (American Psychological Association [APA], 2016). This data makes visible the continued failure of the mental health field to meet the needs of marginalized groups, especially racially minoritized people. This failure is particularly significant not only during the COVID-19 pandemic but also amid the mass global racial protests against racism and police violence against Black people. The Movement for Black Lives[†] has prompted many professional counseling and psychological organizations to acknowledge these failures and challenge themselves and their members to more fully embody and

---

[†] The most recent racial justice movement, commonly referred to as the Black Lives Matter movement, builds upon and extends the multigenerational Black protest and freedom movement. Throughout the text, I use Movement for Black Lives to broadly refer to the ongoing global movement for Black liberation and the coalition of more than 100 community and social justice organizations working together to advance racial justice.

actualize the ethical imperatives around social justice (American Counseling Association [ACA], 2020). Generation Z is the most racially and ethnically diverse generation, and both Millennial and Gen Z individuals agree that this country has issues with racism, particularly anti-Blackness (Parker & Igielnik, 2020). These generations also support LGBTQ+ rights and view change as a whole as being beneficial to society (Parker & Igielnik, 2020). It makes sense, then, that many of today's clients, across racial identities, seem to want therapy and therapists who resemble their lives, values, and politics, and they seek these therapists out on social media. To that end, today's therapy must be intersectional in its approach to understanding clients' multiple identities and the multiple interlocking social systems that shape and impede the full expression of those identities (Crenshaw, 1989; French et al., 2020; Collins, 2000). Therapy must also be decidedly antiracist if we therapists are to truly live up to the ideals of our professions and meet our clients—especially our most marginalized clients—where they are. Put simply, if we are unable to validate all of our clients' identities and their oppressive realities and provide a therapy that is at once affirming and in pursuit of liberation for them, are we actually providing a therapeutic environment? Similarly, if we allow whiteness to go unexamined in therapy with our white-identified clients, are we really engaging in meaningful work about any other aspect of identity and life in today's world?

These shifts are important and signify arguably necessary movement away from the "blank slate" value neutral therapy of the past. Many of the shifts that we see are not just in reaction to the COVID-19 pandemic or even to the racial justice movement; they appear to be also related to the evolving landscape of healthcare, increased consumer choice, and cultural shifts in how people—especially millennials and Generation Z—think about healthcare. Research on these demographics demonstrates that almost three-quarters of millennials prefer seeing a doctor through telemedicine (APA, 2018). As digital natives, they are more tech-savvy and health conscious consumers who want convenience and have their needs met (Accenture, 2019; APA, 2018). They appear to be more comfortable disclosing mental health struggles than previous generations, and over a third of them report having received therapy (APA, 2018). These generational shifts, coupled with the changes necessitated due to COVID-19 and its aftermath, have forged new pathways for psychotherapy.

Psychotherapy has changed because the world has changed. To be honest, we therapists have changed as well. It may be a long time before many of us feel safe in an enclosed office with closed windows with unmasked clients sitting across from us. Yet most of us would not want to provide therapy to clients while wearing masks, either. Many of these changes are here to stay for the foreseeable future yet provide fertile ground for further expansion of services or acceptance of others. Some therapists cannot wait to meet face-to-face again. But, there may be some therapists and clients who will want to continue using virtual therapy, and these therapists will no longer provide traditional face-to-face therapy at all. Research initiated after the pandemic began suggests that psychologists are projecting that they will continue to see 35% of their clients via teletherapy after the pandemic is over (Pierce et al., 2020). Many of us may be reevaluating the need for physical office space. Therapists who have grown tired of the barriers to treatment and who seek to provide more individualized treatment might be interested in a boutique style concierge practice or in integrating some concierge clients into their traditional practice. This may come with internal conflict over the ethics of exclusivity during a time when more people need access to care. COVID-19 may have prompted some therapists to make their services more accessible, particularly those traditionally underserved by the mental health field. There are multiple possibilities during this time of change. These changes may elicit myriad emotions for some therapists—uncertainty, fear, loss, excitement, and so many more.

Along with the benefits of and potential excitement about the evolution of private practice, there are several persisting questions and potential challenges. As stated, some of these shifts continue to unfold in real time. There are distinct ethical, legal, and clinical concerns, especially in practicing in digital environments and outside of the office. During COVID-19, some laws and regulations were temporarily relaxed. Therapists must be aware of which laws remain applicable, of relevant insurance regulations, and of ethical requirements. Therapists must also consider the distinct clinical needs of each client and conduct a thorough clinical screening and assessment to ensure that a client's needs can best be met using emerging approaches. Issues such as privacy and confidentiality, especially when using technology or engaging in out-of-office treatment, can emerge frequently. Clinicians must also assess if this model works for them personally and if it is aligned with their philosophy of care and the types of clients and issues they see in their clinical practice. As previously mentioned, it is unprecedented for therapists to continue to provide support and care for clients for months (and potentially years to come) even as we endure the very same stressors and traumas. Engaging in new and emerging models of therapy is complex, and therapists need resources to navigate this evolving terrain. This necessitates more intentional engagement in radical self-care (Lorde, 1988) during these unprecedented times.

In the pages ahead, I aim to engage in an ongoing conversation and share a series of reflections with you, as fellow therapists. My hope is, as we sit with poignant questions about our work during this historic moment that together we lean into the change that is occurring and begin to intentionally reimagine a therapy that is a reflection of the times and needs of our clients. Together, we might craft a personal approach to therapy that leverages technology in service of client well-being and acknowledges that justice is essential to wellness. In so doing, this might necessitate we accept that therapy and our therapeutic style may no longer be aligned with the current moment and clients' expectations of us. I want this book to be at once easily read and unsettling. Even as we all desperately hope for normalcy amid this protracted time of uncertainty, I implore us to avoid retreating back to what we know. The long-standing decline of psychotherapy use and high premature termination rates demonstrate that what we were doing was not entirely working—not for us nor for the public good. Most therapists can list multiple ways that the U.S. mental health system needs to change to better meet the needs of clients. We can also easily identify the areas in which our clients need growth and adjustment. Yet, are we as easily able and willing to identify the ways that we, as therapists, need to change? Young adults are wellness oriented and open to a psychotherapy that meets their needs. We must consider what it means to be prepared to practice in today's world and also the knowledge and skills we need to elevate ourselves to remain relevant and effective.

Using clinical research and integrating diverse case examples, this book is an invitation to actively engage in shaping the evolution of the field instead of being a passive recipient of it. Together, we will engage in critical reflection about the current state and direction of private practice and our own evolving identities as therapists. In each chapter, I will provide critical resources for you to use for navigating the complexities of your practice in a rapidly evolving world.

In Chapter 1, I provide background on teletherapy and other forms of remote and virtual therapies. Here, we will also consider the effectiveness of teletherapy and multiple ways to integrate teletherapy and virtual therapies into practice.

In Chapter 2, I walk through the necessary steps to get properly set up or to elevate the experience of teletherapy. We will consider the required equipment and infrastructure, demystify the different online platforms for providing teletherapy, and contemplate ways to set up a warm and inviting online office. We will also consider business and practice management issues, such as what to include in an informed consent for teletherapy.

Chapter 3 focuses on clinical issues in practicing teletherapy and virtual therapies. We will discuss how to screen and evaluate appropriateness for teletherapy. Through case examples, we will also discuss the best ways to develop therapeutic rapport and to intervene in a crisis when working virtually.

In Chapter 4, we will discuss wellness approaches and out-of-office therapies. Here, we will think critically about holistic models of therapy and provide some practical models to ground and guide therapists in this work. We will discuss the benefits and potential pitfalls of working outside of the confines of the therapy office.

Chapter 5 introduces concierge therapy, an individualized approach to therapy in which clients often pay a retainer or membership fee to receive greater access to their therapist as well as quicker appointments and response times. Through case scenarios, I will illustrate the benefits of providing flexible services to fewer clients as well as the challenges that may arise with this approach.

In Chapter 6 we will discuss race, intersectionality, and justice in teletherapy and emerging therapeutic practices. Readers will be invited to critically reflect on their own identities and comfort in discussing the challenging issues of race, power, and privilege in clinical work. We will move beyond early cultural competency models to ground ourselves in cultural humility and intersectionality and to engage in antiracist praxis. Challenges and considerations in social justice-oriented work will be discussed.

Chapter 7 is focused on the legal and ethical issues in practicing in online environments, out-of-office therapies, and other emerging practices. Through case scenarios, we will reason through the complexities of ethical decision making, discuss how to navigate virtual threats to security and confidentiality, and of legal issues, such as licensure and HIPAA. Social justice and antiracist counseling as an ethical imperative will also be discussed.

In Chapter 8, I conclude with a focus on the therapist. We are experiencing shared trauma and high risk for burnout and compassion fatigue. We will discuss self-care as a critical aspect of personal and professional development and sustainability. As we reimagine our clinical identities and the field of psychotherapy amid an ongoing pandemic and an emerging mental health crisis, there is an increased need for mental health and fewer boundaries between work and home, and there are heightened amounts of screen time and limited physical connections with people. Resources will be provided for assessing your self-care needs in light of a world of accelerated change. Readers will be guided through the development of a self-preservation plan that promotes our own wellness as we support others'.

Let us begin with this brief reflection to make visible and focus on what it has been like to practice during the pandemic.

Pause | Reflect

- What has it been like for you to provide counseling during the COVID-19 pandemic? What was different personally and professionally practicing during the pandemic than prior to COVID-19?
- How are you different, if at all, as a result of your personal and professional experience during this time?
- What changes do you see in psychotherapy (both pre- and post-COVID-19)? How do you feel about these changes?

HOW WE
PRACTICE
THERAPY NOW

1

TELEMENTAL HEALTH AND VIRTUAL THERAPIES

Communicating through technology used to be akin to talking through paper cups on a string: a lot was lost in transmission. While constructing paper cup phones as an arts and crafts activity with children can be fun, the idea of relying on paper cup phones as a method of providing therapy is frightening. Thankfully, communication devices and teletherapy options have evolved far beyond cups on a string. For some, however, teletherapy might still conjure the same image and fears of how much will get lost in transmission. Early in the pandemic, I had a conversation with my mother describing how I would now be teaching and providing counseling online. After a long pause she responded, "So, do you mean on TV?" I immediately laughed and clarified how and *where* online teaching and counseling occurs. While humorous, some readers might relate to my mother's response or have clients who might respond in similar ways. To be clear, many elders embrace technology and some surpass young adults in their knowledge and usage of it. My mother is not one of these elders. She safely holds on to a time that was comfortable and less complicated, but a time that has passed. My

"Hold on, I'm calling tech support."

Source: www.CartoonStock.com

mother's reaction is not far off from some people's reactions to the thought of teletherapy. The transition to and acceptance of any form of remote therapy by some therapists (and clients) is hard. The familiarity of in-person therapy feels safe and comfortable; it is what we know and how we have been trained to provide therapy. We may have difficulty envisioning how anything happening via video could even come close to the power of what happens in the therapy room. Our fear of the cups on the string emerges.

As discussed in the Introduction, modern therapy has been evolving and is now expected to be offered remotely by phone, video, text, or through various virtual means as a method to provide counseling to more people. The technology is not limited to therapy. It is versatile and has been extended to virtually all aspects of behavioral health services, including the delivery of treatment, education, assessment, supervision, and consultation (Luxton et al., 2016). Because of COVID-19, most of us have likely been providing teletherapy to clients in their homes. But, the flexibility of teletherapy means that the client's location can also vary, from clients' homes, hospitals, clinics, prisons, and nursing facilities. Even before COVID-19, many of us had begun using technology for: 1) the administrative aspects of therapy work, such as practice management software and 2) for adjunctive tools, such as electronic self-monitoring devices and smartphone applications.

Certainly, the necessity of widespread usage of teletherapy during the pandemic has increased the population's awareness and knowledge of teletherapy as a therapy modality. Yet, it is not new; teletherapy dates back to the 1950s when the first documented telemedicine consultation took place (Bashur & Shannon, 2009). In the 1960s and through the 1970s, telemental health (TMH) began to increase and expand, particularly in the military and in rural mental health, to include greater diagnostic services as well as to provide different types of individual and group therapy and substance abuse treatment (Luxton et al., 2016). Despite this expansion, early views of teletherapy varied; many providers saw it as effective but qualitatively different than in-person treatment. Teletherapy was looked down upon. Some might have argued that it was not deemed to be as good as traditional in-person therapy. This seems to parallel early judgments of online education and online dating: "It's just not the same." Our views have slowly evolved in all of these areas as they become more normative. Yet, some judgments remain. Just observe an intergenerational conversation about dating apps to hear the lingering judgments. While some perceptions of teletherapy have shifted over time, early judgments have had an impact on its reputation and the public's openness to engaging in teletherapy. Prior to COVID-19, there was a disconnect between therapists' reported interest in teletherapy and their actual use of teletherapy to deliver services (Glueckauf et al., 2018). Most therapists reported being interested in teletherapy but did not actually engage in it. Now, because of the necessitations of COVID-19, most of us have had first-hand experience using different forms of teletherapy. It is unclear how this may have shifted therapists' personal experiences and perspectives of teletherapy as a viable modality, but most of us have now tried it. In this chapter, we will discuss the brief (and complicated) history and evolution of TMH, its clinical effectiveness, and some models of integrating different forms of TMH into a traditional practice.

HISTORY OF TELEMENTAL HEALTH/TELEPSYCHOLOGY

As mentioned earlier, TMH has only recently become part of popular discourse, yet it has been around for decades. Let's take a moment and discuss some of the different nomenclature because language around TMH varies. TMH is referred to by many names, including telemental health, telepsychology, teletherapy, telebehavioral health, and virtual therapy, to name a few. This different terminology is often used interchangeably in popular media as well as in the scholarly literature, yet for the present discussion, the terms teletherapy and TMH will be used to refer to any counseling or psychological services provided through the use of technology. A range of providers* participate in TMH, such as psychologists, marriage and family therapists, clinical counselors, nurses, and substance abuse counselors (Luxton et al., 2016). There are also myriad choices in care delivery systems, necessary technologies, and available data across these areas. In these ways, TMH is broad in scope, in technological options, and in potential providers

---

* There are a range of providers that provide counseling, therapy, and the range of mental health and wellness services. The term therapist will be used as inclusive terminology to refer to this interdisciplinary group of practitioners, whose work centers on the mental health and well-being of clients.

and consumers. I will talk more about the range of options and how to make an informed decision in Chapter 2.

While TMH has been around for some time, the technology has evolved tremendously, and early teletherapy was not delivered to clients in their homes (Ryu, 2010). Early models of TMH were primarily based in remote clinics. Clients were required to go to a host site (typically a remote clinic accessible by the client) that had the necessary secure video equipment and personnel to assist and monitor clients. Therapists would call into the videoconferencing system and provide teletherapy. If technical issues arose or if the client needed support, the therapist could contact a staff member at the host site for additional in-person assistance. This model, often referred to as the hub and spoke model, is still used within some rural hospitals as well as the military and Veterans Affairs (VA) systems (Bashur & Shannon, 2009; Luxton et al., 2016).

TMH has always been of particular use in the VA system, which continues to lead in its use of teletherapy to meet veteran health needs (Pierce et al., 2020). It was not until recently, in the 1990s, that TMH expanded its global reach. With the international spread and evolution of TMH came recognition of the ability of TMH to increase access to mental health care. Indeed, an early goal of TMH was fostering mental health care access to populations with barriers to treatment, such as rural communities and specific ethnic communities (Luxton et al., 2016). This expansion also provided a broader base for researchers to begin evaluating the effectiveness of TMH as well as comparing TMH to in-person treatment. In the 2000s, armed with emerging and continuing research on the effectiveness of TMH, more mental health practitioners became aware of teletherapy.

As previously mentioned, early views could be described as curious but skeptical and judgmental. In a study of mental health professionals, many expressed lower acceptance of therapy provided using technology in favor of traditional in-person therapy (Pierce et al., 2020). These attitudes also varied based on client diagnosis and presenting issues. Many of you may have held or may still hold these beliefs. It is important to locate these perceptions of TMH within the larger context of the times. The 1960s through the 1970s, when TMH was getting started, was also a time in which there were many challenges and changes in the fields of psychology and counseling. The field of psychology was diversifying, there was a rise in applied- and practitioner-oriented training programs, and there were increased challenges to the cultural hegemony and heterosexism of the field that led to the establishment of the APA multicultural guidelines (APA, 2003) and ethnic psychological associations.

I want to pause here for a moment because these changes to the field sound a lot like the wave of change that is occurring now. While it wasn't a pandemic that created a sense of urgency around those previous changes, there were multiple social factors that contributed to them. Those changes were not always welcomed with open arms. In fact, there was outright resistance to those changes. Take a moment to consider your response to the questions at the end of the Introduction. How did you respond to the question of how you feel about the changes you see unfolding in the field of psychotherapy? If you were practicing during the 1990s, when there was an articulated struggle over these changes in the field, what was that like for you? Some of us may have been part of that change or cheered it on. Others may have been ambivalent or even opposed to it, favoring more fidelity to a traditional model. The same may be true now. Consider what it means to hold on to tradition as the world calls for something different.

Teletherapy is fundamentally intertwined with the development and expansion of widely accessible technology, particularly the advent and rapid rise in popularity of the smart phone. The smartphone dates back to the 1990s, first with IBM's text-capable phone followed by the rise of the Blackberry (Anderson, 2018). Remember those? It was the debut of the iPhone in 2007, however, that many people associate with the smartphone revolution, given its vast capabilities and quick international rise and adoption (Anderson, 2018). Whether we are an iPhone or Android user, most of us can remember the first iPhone and when we got our first smartphone or iPhone, specifically. It was that revolutionary, and it has, quite simply, changed life as we know it. In 2018, the Pew Research Center estimated that 95% of Americans had cell phones of some type and 77% reportedly had a smartphone (Pew Research Center, 2019). Undoubtedly, much has changed in the past few decades both in available technology and in our relationship to technology. This is the resulting primary tension: we have grown more dependent on technology over the years and this is unsettling for some. The

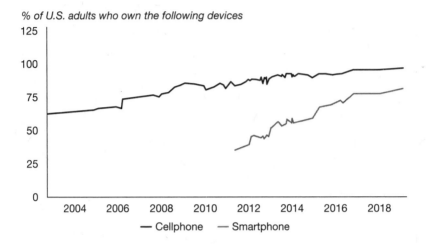

Figure 1.2: Mobile Phone Ownership
Source: "Mobile Fact Sheet." Pew Research Center, Washington, D.C. (2019) https://www
.pewresearch.org/internet/fact-sheet/mobile/

collective dependency on technology has also prompted an array of questions about effects on health, relationships, and interpersonal communication. Regardless of where we fall in our personal technology use, technology has allowed some form of life and connectedness—including therapy—to continue during the COVID-19 pandemic.

Despite widespread use of technology for many aspects of modern life, skepticism and even criticism of teletherapy has continued to vary (Perle et al., 2013). Despite criticisms, TMH has been a major area of growth in mental health. While there is no data yet on any changes to therapist's perceptions of TMH during or post-COVID-19, the widespread and long-term use of different forms of TMH may already have provided practitioners with more personally informed perspectives, based on their recent clinical experiences. Because teletherapy is here to stay, let us discuss the different forms of TMH, their effectiveness, and the different ways they might be integrated into private practice.

TELEMENTAL HEALTH MODALITIES

> **Client:** *Hey Doc, I'm running about 10 mins late. See you soon.*
> **Therapist:** *Ok, thank you for letting me know.*

These text messages are an example of a common way therapists and clients used technology for simple communication even before COVID-19. TMH can be synchronous or asynchronous and can be facilitated using multiple forms of technology. Synchronous communication refers to parties communicating live, in real time, whereas asynchronous communication does not necessarily occur at the same time, such as in emailing and texting (APA Joint Task for the Development of Telepsychology Guidelines for Psychologists, 2013). Other psychotechnologies for engaging in TMH include phone (landline or mobile), interactive videoconferencing, chat, and various smartphone applications (commonly referred to simply as apps). Psychotechnologies are technologies that are particularly useful in the delivery of mental health care (Maheu et al., 2012) and that may afford the opportunity to offer services beyond what was previously practical or possible in the provision of in-person psychotherapy. Any of these technologies may be used as a singular method for providing therapeutic services and/or to augment traditional in-person therapy.

Synchronous Modalities

Therapists use synchronous TMH modalities more often than asynchronous ones (Glueckauf et al., 2018). This makes sense, as therapists are trained to engage with clients live, in real time. The most familiar synchronous TMH modalities include phone and videoconferencing (VC) (Glueckauf et al., 2018). Many of us can relate to this; at the beginning of the pandemic, most of us likely transitioned clients to video-based therapy. Video can be used for direct service provision, including initial consultations and screenings, therapy, and assessments. In addition to clinical work, VC can be used for psychoeducational purposes, including the delivery of continuing education content, other didactic training, and even telesupervision (Glueckauf et al., 2018; Maheu et al., 2012). Given how long we have been primarily home-based, many of us have likely participated in webinars and trainings for continuing education and license renewal. Many therapists are also now using audio and video pod-casting to provide psychoeducation and information related to mental health.

Two-way interactive video remains the most commonly used modality for teletherapy because it has a number of benefits. First, it most closely approximates the traditional therapeutic environment, in that therapists and clients can see one another and interact in real time. This may help fos-ter therapeutic rapport, particularly with new clients, with whom therapists have not yet met in person (Luxton et al., 2016). This format also allows us to observe visual cues, such as body language, and to assess some aspects of the client's physical environment and background. An additional benefit of VC is that it is more often reimbursable by insurance than other forms of TMH (Luxton et al., 2016).

Telephone is another commonly used synchronous method of TMH. Therapists commonly use the phone for administrative functions, such as scheduling, as well as screening and initial consultations with clients (Glueckauf et al., 2018). The phone can also be a quick and reliable alterna-tive during times of internet disruption or technical difficulties with video.

> Client: . . . Uh oh. Can you hear me? Can you see me? It looks like you are frozen.
> Therapist: I can see you, but you're now muted.
> Client: [*clicks a button*] How about now?
> Therapist: [*typing into the chat box*] I still cannot hear you. You can try logging out; or perhaps I should just call you if that does not work, so that we don't lose any more time in our session.

Many therapists (and clients) found, during the sheltering-at-home phases of the COVID-19 pandemic, that talking privately with a thera-pist was difficult with others present in the home. Some clients were able to access therapy and be more open by meeting by phone in a car or while going for a walk instead of having a video session at home where there was a lack of privacy. Also, some clients may experience the phone as a less emotionally intimidating form of engagement, given not having to engage in the obligatory eye contact nor having to visually attend to the therapist as well as their own internal experience. Moreover, there is a conversation emerging about the rise in self-consciousness—even for therapists—as a result of viewing oneself in teletherapy sessions. Since the pandemic began, many of us have likely found ourselves noticing more often how we look, or perhaps even changes in how we look. None of us are accustomed to being able to see ourselves during sessions. Given the distraction this can cause for clients (and therapists), phone appointments may be preferred.

Phone is perhaps the most accessible teletherapy option, yet it has some limitations. First, while the majority of people in the United States have access to a phone, many rely primarily on a cell phone or wireless device (Pew, 2019). This trend is even more pronounced with adults under 34 years old, adolescents, and low-income communities (Vogels, 2019). Understanding patterns of access and the types of devices clients most readily use is important in therapist teletherapy decision making. Checking with clients about their TMH preference, their internet availability, and the types of devices they have access to is recommended. This allows clients to have agency in the therapeutic process and may prevent connection issues or interruptions to TMH sessions. Consider this case:

Mike is a 43-year-old African American man in counseling due to a long history of depression and social isolation. For several years, Mike has reported low energy, emotional numbing, indifference, and detachment from his family. Mike works long hours as an attorney, throws himself into his work, and has little time or energy for a social life. When the pandemic began, Mike's firm immediately supported employees working from home. Mike felt safer being at home because being diabetic placed him at higher risk for COVID-19 complications. Spending long hours in Zoom meetings and having little movement outside of his home began to exacerbate his depression symptoms. When counseling sessions transitioned to video Mike noticed, during the first session, that he was not able to attend to counseling in the ways that he normally would. It was hard for him to look at himself on the screen and to look the therapist directly in the eye; it didn't feel therapeutic. Because Mike needed movement and air, we discussed trying to have some of our sessions by phone while he stretched or moved indoors or took a walk, safely, outdoors. Mike jumped at this opportunity. During the first session by phone, Mike noted that he felt a little freer to think and talk as he walked. Because he walked at a leisurely pace, he was never winded or out of breath. He learned which streets or paths were quieter and had fewer people on them so as to avoid others overhearing him or having external noises interrupt the session. Mike found this approach worked better for him than video, and because it allowed him to move, he also felt better about it physically.

Overall, because the majority of people have access to a phone of some type, this remains a highly accessible, inexpensive, and reliable teletherapy choice. Despite these advantages, engaging in teletherapy by phone does not convey the subtleties of body language and other visual cues that are important to the diagnosis and treatment of complex psychological conditions. Moreover, though some phone sessions have been covered during the pandemic and during times of crisis, phone sessions are largely nonreimbursable by third party payors, such as insurance and Medicare (Luxton et al., 2016). The financial implications of which TMH technology to use must be discussed with clients who rely on insurance or insurance reimbursement. Also, like in this case with Mike, when clients are accessing services using a cell phone, there may also be concerns about phone reception and privacy/confidentiality if the client is not in a private location.

Other synchronous TMH choices include live chat or text options. These are often employed through the use of psychology and wellness-centered smartphone applications, such as Betterhelp and Talkspace. These sites/apps are popular and widely accessible, as they provide 24/7 instant access to a therapist. These sites/apps often include features such as mood and emotion tracking, within-app journaling, and connection to literature based on client-endorsed issues. Notably, this is a low-cost alternative to in-person therapy (Maheu et al., 2012; Truschel, 2020) and may also be a welcome option for people who are unable to privately communicate by phone or video at home. With the proliferation of so many apps, the American

Psychiatric Association, among other professional groups, now provides guidance to therapists. They rate apps on metrics such as safety and privacy, empirical evidence that supports its use, and ease of use, including ability to share information with the therapist (Truschel, 2020). Many therapists rightfully have concerns about providing "therapy" via live chat or text without visual or voice cues to aid in assessment and proper treatment. The type of "therapy" provided may be quite limited. While this kind of therapist might be able to provide general support and a listening ear, more severe or crisis issues may not be appropriate for this setting, especially if the person is not also in some other form of therapy. Consider for example, engaging in live chat with a client who expresses statements that may have garnered, based on tone and body language within an in-person or video session, further questioning and assessment of their risk for self-harm.

> **Client:** Yeah, this week has been really hard.
> **Therapist:** Hard, in what ways?
> **Client:** [*long pause. . . looks down and away and has slow tears*] I just haven't felt like this before.
> **Therapist:** I noticed the change in your body as you reflected on the week. You look scared.
> **Client:** Yes, I got to a scary place.

In this example, the therapist is able to glean more from the client's pause and shift in body language than from their verbal response. If this were a live chat, the client's choice of language alone may not have elicited the same response from the therapist. In this situation, the therapist may have asked about what was hard about the week, but this may have elicited more of the content or triggers for the week. While the client *might* have eventually disclosed what was scary in a live chat, this could have been a missed opportunity to engage with the client in a potentially critical moment. In this case, a therapist working through live chat would not have had the necessary information upon which to make informed clinical decisions. This is a clear limitation of synchronous chat and text forms of support. Some therapists may fear that apps may eventually replace the need for therapy with a professional. While apps are still developing, it is clear that what they offer can be helpful but not the same as what is offered in professional in-person counseling (Truschel, 2020). Moreover, it is helpful for therapists to consider ways that apps may augment what they offer during the course of therapy or after termination of therapy (Maheu et al., 2012).

Asynchronous Modalities

Asynchronous methods of TMH are most often used for nonclinical services, such as scheduling. An increasing number of therapists also allow clients to communicate with them via text message to cancel or schedule appointments as a convenience. Some therapists may also use online or smartphone apps to complement in-person therapy, phone therapy sessions, or VC sessions (Maheu et al., 2012). For instance, a therapist may be working with a client on issues of anxiety and may recommend a meditation or story time app to help support mindfulness-based practices at home. This is a good way to leverage technology in support of client goals, especially when trying to support clients in practices that are new or where there may be some hesitation.

Some forms of technology, such as apps, can be used synchronously or asynchronously (e.g., chatting, texting, and video messaging). There are ways to schedule times to be online or available to text or chat (synchronous). For example, recently a client of mine was on voice rest for a medical condition and wanted to schedule time to engage in synchronous chat to check-in. There are also a growing number of therapists who engage in "therapy" or respond to more clinically oriented questions via asynchronous messaging, such as email and text. It is not uncommon for a client to send a message to the therapist between sessions, such as:

> Client: After our session, I tried to talk to my partner, and we got into a big fight. It's just like we discussed. I'm not quite sure how to handle this. I'm so over this situation.

In this situation, an existing client sends an email to the therapist between sessions. It appears they are not only wanting to inform the therapist of what happened but also to receive support. While there are theoretical differences in how we approach between session contact, it is important that, however we respond, we are not providing "therapy" by email. Many of us may wish to provide support or affirmation and still maintain a boundary in what we provide via email:

> **Therapist:** I am sorry to hear about the big fight. I'm sure that is upsetting. We will have to delve deeper into this when we meet next.

Some therapists might add an additional note that if the client needs to meet sooner to please let them know so that they can schedule a session. In the response above, the therapist has affirmed the upsetting nature of what is happening but also has maintained the boundary that the processing of information is limited to scheduled sessions in whatever modality the therapy occurs for the client. Even with existing clients, with whom a therapist has a relationship, the ethics and limitations of engaging in text and email "therapy" must be considered. If a therapist chooses to proceed (with caution) in this manner, the client should be clear about the purpose and limits of asynchronous communication. This should be outlined in initial paperwork and discussed with the client.

More recent developments in asynchronous TMH have occurred primarily within psychology or therapy-oriented apps. In addition to the synchronous services that these apps provide, asynchronous services, such as emailing or chatting with a therapist as well as voice and video messaging between therapist and client, are also frequently offered. App users can also connect with helpful literature that is based on applicable issues, that has information about tangible coping strategies, or that walk them through guided meditations or relaxation exercises. While these sites provide instant support and consumers largely experience them as helpful (Truschel, 2020), they also have some limitations. First, it is important to note that there is insufficient research on the effectiveness of text-based treatment (Luxton et al., 2016). Thus, while they may be supportive and widely accessible, they are not a substitute for professional treatment. This is particularly important relative to consumers who have more severe presenting issues and those in need of a greater level of stabilizing support. Consumers who grow accustomed to 24/7 access to live chat with a therapist via an app might also have unrealistic expectations of a therapist if they begin to work with someone professionally, in-person or using a different form of teletherapy. Moreover, while there are times where consumers might be in crisis and require immediate access to a therapist, many clinicians would argue that there is value in a client accessing other internal and external resources in addition to or instead of reaching out to a therapist, such as in the case above where the client has had an upsetting disagreement with a partner. Thus, a concern might be that 24/7 access to a therapist on an app may foster dependency instead of psychological autonomy.

Virtual Therapies

Virtual therapies (VTs) are also gaining popularity. VTs typically include gaming and virtual reality devices and platforms. Gaming apps gamify, or create a game out of, the process of unlearning negative thinking and behavioral patterns and learning to engage in healthier thoughts and behaviors (Maheu et al., 2012). For example, in the popular gaming app SuperBetter, users must employ positive behaviors to defeat symptoms, such as maladaptive habits, which are villainized by the app as a so-called "bad guy." Gamifying the pursuit of mental health goals may not only make learning and practice fun but also foster creativity and a competitive determination to "win." This platform may be particularly attractive to adolescents, clients who are gamers, and those who might clinically benefit from more play.

Virtual reality technology works similarly, creating realistic environments in which clients can be immersed. Therapists can use virtual realities (VR) or augmented realities (AR) to create immersive (virtual) therapeutic experiences (Maheu et al., 2012). Readers who have worked within the VA system may recall that VR has long been used within the VA system to treat returning veterans with PTSD (Luxton et al., 2016). VR and AR have now become more widely available to other clinical and nonclinical populations. Bravemind is an example of a VR that allows a clinician to control a virtual world and implement exposure therapy within a clinical session. Evidence supports the therapeutic benefit of using VR with clients experiencing anxiety disorders, including specific phobias (Ugolik, 2019). Gaming apps and virtual reality technology do not provide therapy or connection with a therapist and therefore might best be used as an adjunct to traditional in-office therapy or other forms of TMH.

Instagram "Therapy"

Related to teletherapy is what many refer to as *Instagram therapy* (Carman, 2020; Chandra, 2019). Instagram therapy refers to therapists using social media, specifically Instagram, to advertise their services and offer advice or guidance to followers. Some Instagram "therapists" offer workshops, invite and/or respond to private messages, and offer live individual and group virtual "sessions." Some Instagram therapists also partner with influencers to promote their services and increase their overall visibility. Others are now offering membership communities in which they provide curated psychoeducational materials, virtual gatherings, and even one-on-one coaching.

Most Instagram "therapists" make it clear that what they offer on social media is not therapy, but the lines likely begin to blur, especially for people who have never been in therapy. Proponents of Instagram therapy argue that the popularity of these therapists destigmatizes mental health discussions and brings therapists out from behind closed doors, making therapy and therapists more visible and approachable. This may be beneficial for the field as a whole. Many followers may experience this as positive and largely supportive. Yet, there are many areas of concern about this emerging discipline. For instance, some research has associated Instagram with negative effects on mental health (Royal Society for Public Health, 2017). There are also troubling ethical concerns about the offering of virtual sessions, live on social media, and conflating therapy and other wellness and spiritual practices, considering the ethical guidelines and legal regulations that licensed therapists are bound to adhere to.

Clearly, there is a wide array of teletherapy and virtual therapy options available for therapists to use in work with clients. These options are only increasing. For now, it is important to distinguish between Instagram therapy and TMH. Let's discuss some of the advantages as well as the challenges and clinical considerations of TMH.

ADVANTAGES OF TELEMENTAL HEALTH

Advantages of TMH for Therapists

- Reduced need for office space lowers overhead costs
- Potential expansion of availability or extension of hours/ schedule
- Client-centered schedule may result in increased clients
- Follow ups between office sessions may be easier
- Increased involvement of other family members = collaborative and supportive treatment
- Helps facilitate integrated care
- Allows for a mobile lifestyle

Many of the advantages of teletherapy became clear during the COVID-19 pandemic. Specifically, it was because of teletherapy that continuity of care was possible when meeting in person became unsafe. Beyond emergency need, many therapists may have identified or experienced some of the other benefits of teletherapy during this time. For therapists who practice online, there is a reduced need for office space, which can reduce overhead costs. For therapists who want to transition to fully remote operation, there would be no need to rent an office, which is often the primary expense for therapists in private practice. Even therapists who may not decide to only practice online could significantly reduce their overhead expenses by subletting office space or renting an office only for the few hours or days that they want to be in the office. For some therapists, this might allow for a more mobile lifestyle. This might be particularly attractive to therapists who are nearing retirement or who want to work from a vacation home part of the time. With the reduced need for commuting to an office, some teletherapists may be able to offer a more client-centered schedule with expanded or extended hours of availability. For example, some therapists may not have been able or willing to offer evening or weekend appointments in the office but might consider limited after-hours availability for teletherapy. In addition, the use of teletherapy may expand availability, allowing therapists to follow-up between scheduled sessions with greater ease. One of most significant clinical benefits of teletherapy is the ability to include others, such as family members, who may live in different households or locations as well as those who may have been unable or unwilling to come to the therapist's office. While teletherapy has long been an option and therapists have had the ability to include family members virtually, many therapists and clients might be more open to this modality now that they have had months of experience engaging in treatment in this way.

In addition to the benefits for therapists, there are also multiple benefits of TMH for clients.

Teletherapy Advantages for Clients

- Effective, patient-centered clinical treatment
- Increased access to mental health care
- Increased access to specialists and wider range of therapists
- Convenience: reduced travel time and cost of therapy
- Access to continuity of care
- Possible reduction in stigma
- Modernized care delivery

Perhaps the greatest benefit to clients is the increased access to effective therapy. Therapists and clients alike benefit from the convenience and elimination of barriers to care. This is of particular importance during an ongoing pandemic and the ensuing mental health crisis. When services are accessed remotely, we are only limited by jurisdiction, which means that clients may be able to access therapists who live in different parts of the state or even a different state (but who is licensed to practice in the client's state). This can make available a far wider range of therapists across specializations, racial and other social identities, or styles of practice. Given the amount of widespread racial stress, many clients are likely seeking support in these areas. Because of the reduced travel time, TMH requires less time to access therapy due to not having to drive to the therapy office. This may also reduce the overall cost. For example, clients may not have to use sick time or leave work early to drive across town to have a therapy session, or they may not have to arrange childcare. Because a stigma remains around therapy, especially within certain communities, teletherapy may also allow access to therapy in a more comfortable way, from the privacy of the home. For clients with unpredictable work or travel schedules, teletherapy may also enable continuity of treatment, whereas if one is reliant solely on traditional in-person therapy, this might result in multiple cancellations or longer gaps between sessions. Lastly, teletherapy modernizes mental health care delivery in a way that aligns with the way many people—especially digital natives—have come to expect (Maheu et al., 2012; Vogels, 2019). Teletherapy offers a reimagining of a therapeutic system developed largely during a pretech-nological era and brings it into alignment with the twenty-first century. It also leverages technology to the benefit of both therapist and client in ways that are far more egalitarian than traditional in-person medical models of therapy.

Challenges and Limitations

While there are many benefits of TMH for therapists and clients, there are also several challenges. First, it is important to note that teletherapy—especially video-based therapy—requires access to consistent broadband internet. While many clients have access to smartphones and/or computers with WiFi, it is important to assess access and quality of access. Therapists must be aware of the "digital divide" and digital obstacles to teletherapy. The *digital divide* refers to the gap between people who have full access to technology and those who do not. Lack of full access to technology is very much racialized, with pronounced racial gaps between white and Black and Latinx households as well as along social class and age lines (Vogels, 2020). Therapists must be aware of these issues. For example, we should go beyond asking if a client has a cell phone or computer and ask what type of phone and what quality and speed of internet connection. Second, it is important to acknowledge that technology alters relationships (Luxton et al., 2016) in ways that are not often well-understood. This is particularly important to note for relationships that do not exist offline because there is no point of comparison. Establishing new relationships via video may be different than working with people in person and then transitioning to teletherapy.

Because technology is necessary to access care, the therapist must be skilled in and capable of trouble-shooting technology issues for the client and themself. Anyone who has used technology in any capacity can attest that technology problems do occur and can disrupt a session. Therapists must plan for these issues. While these interruptions can be challenging, being prepared and having a plan can help you navigate these frustrations. Other clinical challenges and considerations include:

- TMH may not be covered or fully reimbursed by insurance or third-party payors
- Licensure and regulations limit therapists to working within their scope of practice and state of licensure
- Confidentiality, privacy, and security issues using technology
- Challenges with remote crisis response
- Distinct screening and assessment process and considerations for clients with severe mental illness or recent instability

These challenges will be covered in greater detail in future chapters. I have now discussed different telemental health modalities and forms of technology to expand psychotherapy offerings. I have also introduced the benefits and challenges of these modalities for therapists and clients. Let us pause and reflect on this information. Consider the following questions:

Pause | Reflect

- What form of teletherapy resonates most with you? Why?
- What concerns do you have about engaging in teletherapy or a particular form of teletherapy? Why?
- During nonemergency times, how do you determine if or when you will employ teletherapy?

The answers to these questions may reveal thoughts and perceptions of teletherapy that were already evident and made visible some areas that may have been less clear. For example, it may be that you are not opposed to all forms of TMH, rather there might be some forms of teletherapy with which you are less comfortable or competent, such as the use of asynchronous apps or meeting by phone. Let's consider more about how and when therapists select particular forms of teletherapy.

CLINICAL EFFECTIVENESS OF TELETHERAPY

Most of what is known about the effectiveness of TMH is focused on video-based teletherapy. Overall, clinical research on the effectiveness of teletherapy using VC demonstrates that it is often as effective as in-person therapy for a number of conditions across diverse client populations (McCord et al., 2020; Perle et al., 20130). Further, teletherapy has been found to be a cost-effective treatment modality that fosters access to mental health care, particularly in populations historically marginalized by psychology and with low service utilization rates. So, while we must be attentive to and consider the digital divide, it is also important to consider how many more people we might be able to reach using teletherapy. In addition, TMH may be a way to increase access to and retention of populations with limited access to culturally aligned care, such as racially minoritized communities, the geriatric population, and adolescents. Overall, the research indicates that TMH is effective in:

- developing therapeutic rapport
- clinical assessment, diagnosis, and treatment
- effective treatment of an array of mental health conditions
- working with diverse populations

Teletherapy has been used in multiple settings, including hospitals, community clinics, private practice, and home environments (Luxton et al., 2016). Notably, patients have reported comparable satisfaction and clinical gains from teletherapy as they do in traditional in-person therapy (Jenkins-Guarnieri et al., 2015). TMH may also be the preferred service delivery method for geographically or socially isolated populations, adolescents, and veterans (Luxton et al., 2016). While many clinician's automatic response might be to assume that clients with greater needs or more severe mental illness are not well-suited for TMH, the research in this area is mixed and may not fully support this assumption. Indeed, there are concerns about being able to fully evaluate and respond to the complex needs of clients with persistent mental illness using TMH. Yet, the flexibility of teletherapy may better allow therapists to meet the distinct needs of these populations. For example, consider a young adult client with bipolar disorder who has a history of medication noncompliance and one previous hospitalization but who has recently demonstrated increasing consistency with medication and now has an openness and commitment to ongoing therapy. Prior to COVID-19, most therapists would likely argue that this client is inappropriate for teletherapy. While this may be true, it is important to make that clinical determination based on multiple factors. It also important to consider the potential for more frequent sessions, for reduced barriers to care, and for involvement of family in therapy when meeting with the client via video at home. Further discussion of clinical considerations and evaluation of fit for TMH is provided in Chapter 3.

The effectiveness of teletherapy is also supported by research on patient satisfaction, which has found high levels of satisfaction with TMH. Less is known, however, about client satisfaction with TMH when other options, such as traditional, in-person treatment, are available (Jenkins-Guarnieri et al., 2015). It makes sense that factors such as technical difficulties, discomfort with technology, and poor connection quality may negatively affect patient satisfaction. Interestingly, the research suggests that clients' presenting issues are not strongly correlated with their satisfaction with teletherapy. There are also differences between satisfaction between individual sessions and group therapy.

Therapeutic rapport is also important to consider. Quality of therapeutic rapport via teletherapy may affect a provider's willingness to use TMH and also subsequent patient satisfaction (Jenkins-Guarnieri et al., 2015). While the research in this area is still unfolding, there appears to be consensus that a strong therapeutic alliance can not only be established using teletherapy but is also comparable to the rapport established in person (Jenkins-Guarnieri et al., 2015; Stiles-Shields et al., 2014). This is perhaps one of the most compelling results of the research on teletherapy, given the centrality of rapport to our work. Rapport and TMH will be discussed further in Chapter 3. We should remember that there may be a difference between patient and provider perception of therapeutic rapport in-person versus via TMH. This is an important differentiation to make, in that it suggests that the therapist's comfort with and competence in teletherapy may be a factor in establishing rapport and in patient satisfaction. This is a reminder of the importance of periodically checking in with clients regarding their satisfaction. Moreover, we must be able to differentiate between problems or limitations of teletherapy versus limitations of our own therapeutic imagination and skill in using technology to connect and engage in the therapeutic endeavor. Training in TMH is not part of standard graduate education. In many locations, there are even prohibitions against training and supervision hours being accrued through TMH (Gluekauf et al., 2018). These findings underscore the need for training for clinicians to increase their familiarity with and competence in this growing treatment modality.

INTEGRATING TELEMENTAL HEALTH

To discuss the multiple ways that TMH can be employed, let's consider the following case:

Amy is a 27-year-old Mexican American woman working as a freelance writer. She is seeking counseling due to a long history of generalized worry and anxiety that she describes as typically manageable. Amy states that her anxiety usually gets triggered by writing deadlines, family issues, and relational stress. She comes from a small nuclear family with most of her extended family living in Mexico. Amy describes her relationship with her mother as close but complex. She often feels "weighed down" with expectations from her mother and is unable to communicate the effects of this on her in a way that her mother can understand without taking it personally. For two years, Amy has been in a romantic relationship that she describes as very loving but tumultuous. She describes her partner Ryan, a 35-year-old white man, as being "not the most responsible guy in the world." Amy and Ryan had just recently moved in together when COVID-19 began spreading in their area. Being suddenly confined at home together placed additional financial and emotional stress on their already tumultuous relationship. Amy's overall anxiety increased, leading her to seek therapy.

In this case example, there are multiple individual and relational issues that merit clinical attention. Amy has great awareness that anxiety is an area of concern, as are the relationships with her mother and partner. Established best practice for the treatment of anxiety includes weekly psychotherapy with the goal of reducing anxiety symptoms and increasing healthy coping mechanisms. In addition, extra attention may be spent working to foster insight into her familial and relational dynamics and to improve her communication skills. Special consideration should be given to culturally appropriate communication strategies within the family and to cultural differences within the interracial relationship. Now, consider for a moment what might be different if, by necessity or by choice, the work with Amy is conducted using teletherapy. What might shift, if anything? Why? Are the treatment goals different? Is how you typically work in-person different than when you are meeting with a client remotely by video? How are the processes of developing rapport and assessing of mental status and safety different? These are important points of reflection because our responses make us aware of the ways we think about teletherapy, the ways technology may alter the way we interact as therapists, and some of the subtleties that may not be captured or may be captured differently when modulated through technology.

Consider the different forms of teletherapy previously discussed. Consider the different ways that teletherapy could be employed with Amy either as a singular method of treatment delivery or to supplement traditional in-person therapy. There are multiple options and potential considerations. Certainly, video-based therapy could be used to engage in psychotherapy focused on anxiety management. Video-based therapy could be implemented to engage in couples and/or family therapy if Amy was interested in engaging in this type of work with other therapists in addition to the individual work. Other forms of teletherapy might also be beneficial. Consider, for example, that Amy and Ryan live together during a period of sheltering at home. Depending on their living circumstances, there may be a lack of privacy to talk openly about Ryan and her concerns about the relationship. In this situation, Amy may benefit from being in a different (yet safe) location, such as a car or nearby park, and to meet by phone. Meeting by phone would deprive the therapist of the opportunity to observe any visible signs of anxiety or any nonverbal shifts in affect that could be beneficial in diagnosis and treatment, especially with a new client. Meeting by phone, however, may allow Amy the emotional freedom to be more open in disclosing what she is experiencing than if she was concerned about the potential of Ryan overhearing her session. Alternatively, Ryan could leave the apartment (safely, of course) while Amy participates in therapy, at least for some of the sessions. Amy may also benefit from support or coaching on how to negotiate this discussion with her partner.

Another TMH option is the use of psychotherapy and wellness apps. Amy might find that connecting with a therapist using text, chat, or video messaging is helpful. If she has privacy concerns, this might be a way to engage with a therapist without the fear of Ryan overhearing a verbal or video conversation. In addition, it would not require that she leave their home, which might be a concern during a health crisis. Given that many people have less or no work during the health pandemic, finances might be an area of concern. Accessing services through an app is likely a more affordable option than weekly therapy with a therapist in private practice. Lastly, the use of apps could be used to supplement video, phone, or in-person therapy. Specifically, a mood-tracking app could be used to help Amy track emotions, mood, and triggers and to send that data to the therapist. Additional features, such as journaling and mindfulness practices, can also be used to help guide Amy in wellness practices that are known to reduce anxiety and foster well-being.

These options illustrate that there are multiple ways to integrate the various forms of TMH into clinical practice. It is clear that even if practitioners do not wish to continue with teletherapy postpandemic, the various forms of TMH provide therapists and clients with additional tools that can help support our in-office work. For those who choose to continue practicing teletherapy, it is important to remember that there are multiple forms of

TMH. VC may not be the best fit for all clients, given their unique circumstances. In addition, it is possible to use different forms of TMH with the same client to more completely meet their needs.

CONCLUSION

Prior to the pandemic, TMH was on the rise. The widespread practice of teletherapy during COVID-19 appears to have increased acceptance of its use: teletherapy and virtual therapy options appear to represent the future of psychotherapy (McCord et al., 2020; Pierce et al., 2020). Not limited to video-based therapy, TMH also includes interactive mobile phone applications, virtual reality, and electronic gaming (Maheu et al., 2012; Truschel, 2020). Despite innovation in these areas and the rise in popularity of TMH and virtual therapies, there remains a dearth of training and support for students and practitioners in these areas. Only recently has there been greater consensus in best practices and established guidelines to direct therapists practicing in these areas. This is imperative as we work with clients with a greater range of issues through teletherapy. There are a bevy of benefits of TMH for therapists and clients, particularly reducing barriers to access. Even in citing the benefits of teletherapy, we must not hold it up to be the holy grail of therapy because it comes with its challenges and limitations. It is also important to acknowledge that TMH may not be a good fit for all therapists. There are differences between working online for several hours and working in person for that same time period. Some therapists may not feel that TMH is the best modality for them based on their personality or approach to therapy. In the next chapter, we will discuss what is necessary to get started in TMH and how to get clients prepared for TMH.

2

GETTING SET UP
IN TELETHERAPY

In the previous chapter, I discussed the history of TMH and the different asynchronous and synchronous methods of employing TMH. As noted in Chapter 1, there are distinct psychotechnologies required and multiple choices and considerations in determining which form of TMH is the best fit for the client. Many of us may have been thrust into practicing TMH as a result of the crisis and may not have been adequately prepared or had the necessary infrastructure to thrive in TMH. Beyond the period of crisis, to establish a full or part-time TMH practice, it is important to know and invest in the necessary infrastructure to maintain the standard of care and expected quality of services. Infrastructure includes the knowledge, skills, and equipment to transition an in-person practice to a digital environment. There are also multiple technological considerations and associated legal considerations. Which videoconferencing platforms both work well and are HIPAA-compliant, and which features do I need to use? How should I set up my online office? What does my informed consent need to cover in this new environment? All of these are important questions to think about before to practice online. It is equally important that we prepare our clients so they can have a positive telehealth experience. In this chapter, we will delve deeper and demystify some of the technical options to clarify what is necessary for your practice. We will also discuss distinct and essential business and practice management considerations as you begin or expand your TMH practice.

GETTING STARTED IN TELETHERAPY

Let's start by considering some of the differences between an in-person practice and a TMH practice. In a fully TMH practice, everything occurs remotely, and therefore the therapist relies solely on technology for most, if not all, aspects of the business and clinical work. This means that the therapist needs the necessary infrastructure to ensure that all components of the business can operate remotely. First, all client documentation should be available online. Central in client documentation is the informed consent. While much of the consent process is the same required language about therapy and limits of confidentiality, there are distinct considerations for TMH. We will discuss more details about legal and ethical requirements of TMH and other emerging models of therapy in Chapter 7, but it is important to highlight some of the issues here given the importance of consent to beginning therapy in-person or online. Ultimately, a primary function of informed consent is for clients to be informed of the purpose and process of therapy as well as any risks or limitations (McCord et al., 2020). Therapists' traditional informed consent forms do not take into consideration the specific risks of teletherapy, such as the risks to their privacy that come with technology, nor do such forms address the steps that therapists can or should take to mitigate these risks (Shore, Yellowlees, Caudill, Johnston, et al, 2018). Resources such as professional associations that provide guidance are included throughout this book, but to ensure your consent is comprehensive and that you and your clients are protected, consider consulting a lawyer who specializes in healthcare law. In addition, the teletherapy consent should clearly describe what happens if there is a technical disruption, for example, if the internet connection is interrupted and a video session is unavailable, or if your cell phone dies. The consent also should articulate an emergency protocol that states what actions the therapist will take should an emergency occur during the session, such as contacting emergency personnel and/or patient emergency contacts. Lastly, the informed consent should clearly articulate that the legal, ethical, and clinical standards remain the same for teletherapy as for traditional in-person therapy. As with in-person therapy, if clients have concerns about the care they are receiving, in addition to being encouraged to discuss this with their therapist, they have the right to report this information to the appropriate state regulating board. The following checklist can aid therapists as they develop their informed consent.

Informed Consent Checklist

- ☐ Clear and accurate description of teletherapy, including the use of technology to deliver therapy services to the client at another physical location; same clinical standards of quality apply
- ☐ Network and security protocols to protect client confidentiality and private health information
- ☐ Benefits and limitations of teletherapy, including privacy risks
- ☐ Client technology requirements
- ☐ Client right to terminate treatment at any time without consequence
- ☐ Right of therapist to modify treatment plan to ensure best treatment and care
- ☐ Plan for technical disruption of service
- ☐ Emergency protocol
- ☐ Legal and ethical standards, and how to report concerns

Initial Paperwork and Obtaining Consent

Whether working remotely or in-person, verbal consent is insufficient (McCord et al., 2020). Working remotely requires a shift in how some therapists have their clients complete paperwork and document their consent to participate in treatment. Some clinicians may have transitioned to electronic or online form completion while still practicing in-person. For others, this may be new and present a whole new world. Once you have developed a comprehensive consent form, let's consider the available options to obtain consent from your clients. Some clinicians may prefer to email these documents to clients and have them complete the forms and return them via email to the therapist. While this may be the preferred option for many therapists who want to avoid more complex systems, it may not be the most secure unless you are using an encrypted program. Encrypted email and messaging programs are available and frequently used in banking and finance, for example, but may not be convenient or cost effective for people outside of these sectors. If email feels like the best fit for you or your client population, further research on encrypted email is warranted. There are multiple add-on encryption platforms that can be added on to existing email services such as Gmail and Microsoft. Given the rapid development in this area, therapists who are interested in these services should consult with or review recent HIPAA compliant technology sources.

Other options include setting up a secure client portal to access and submit paperwork on the therapist's webpage or using a web-based electronic health records management system also known as EHR. Use of online and cloud-based EHR systems has grown tremendously in the past decade as therapists have sought secure technological solutions for clinical documentation, record-keeping, and storage of files. More recently, comprehensive practice management systems (PMS) have also emerged. These systems are popular due to their ability to streamline and manage not just clinical records but also many of the daily operations of a practice, such as scheduling, appointment reminders, billing, and other administrative tasks (Gluekauf et al., 2018). Because TMH therapists are working remotely, it may be prudent to transition to a web-based system to manage clinical records as well as the administrative tasks of the business. Many of these systems also have the added benefit of offering secure videoconferencing. Regardless of the specific platform or method you choose, if you are going to practice telehealth, you must think critically about secure ways to obtain consent and initial client paperwork, otherwise you will be violating your professional ethical obligations to your clients.

Insurance Coverage and Fee Payment

Another area of consideration in the practice of TMH is around insurance coverage and fee payments. As mentioned in Chapter 1, there has been parity in Medicaid and Medicare coverage of TMH and in-person therapy for some time (Luxton et al., 2016). During the COVID-19 pandemic, many insurance companies have also temporarily extended coverage to include video-based teletherapy (APA, 2020). Due to the emergency nature of TMH and increased need for mental health care, some insurance companies also waived co-payment requirements during the pandemic. While it is unclear if these temporary expansions of insurance coverage to include teletherapy will continue, there is mounting pressure for this coverage to remain in place. Moreover, there are few viable reasons for barriers to coverage for TMH. Yet, teletherapy practitioners—particularly those who accept insurance—must remain aware of coverage changes or limitations and how this will affect billing and reimbursement. You should be sure to verify each client's insurance before commencing therapy and specifically verify coverage amounts and any limitations for TMH. Notably, when billing insurance for TMH sessions, it is important to document session location indicators. Many therapists and medical billers may have the default location set to the "in office" location. This must be changed to "video or remote" in order to bill for remote sessions. Even therapists who do not accept insurance should remain aware of these issues as many clients who pay out-of-pocket rely on insurance reimbursement. Thus, we need to at least have minimal information about insurance reimbursement so as to understand and help support clients navigate these complexities and access our services.

Lastly, therapists practicing remotely must be set up to accept payments online, including co-payments for insurance clients. Compliance with HIPAA is important here, too. There are a number of secure HIPAA compliant online payment options. Many existing practice management programs and EHRs also offer integrated online payment. For convenience, however, many clients may want to use popular and easily accessible payment apps such as Venmo, Cash app, or PayPal. Before you agree to be paid through any of these systems, you should research whether that system is HIPAA compliant. Any system that does not offer a Business Associate Agreement, which is discussed below, is not HIPAA-compliant. A system that has social networking features most likely is not secure for healthcare purposes, since it will allow third parties to see who is paying you. Yet, many clients are accustomed to being able to easily pay in these formats and they may think that you are out-of-touch with technological advances in payment options if you do not agree to use them. If a client insists on using one of these methods to pay for services, express your security and confidentiality concerns to them in person and document the concerns in your informed consent, and document your communication about security and confidentiality concerns in clinical notes. Clearly, technology and security are central to practicing in digital spaces. Let's delve deeper into some of these considerations.

Technology and Security Considerations

A primary and ongoing consideration for clinicians in practicing TMH is with technology and security. First, let's discuss the minimum requirements necessary to ensure that client sessions are private, secure, HIPAA compliant, and contain the necessary features to offer teletherapy via video in particular. Many vendors of videoconferencing platforms use language that can be confusing or even mislead therapists. For example, many vendors use terms such as "HIPAA compliant" and "HIPAA secure" as marketing strategies for health professionals seeking to provide TMH services. Yet, it is not always clear what this marketing language means and whether such systems actually provide the features you need. So, let's first define a few of the terms that are important to understand in order to protect your business and your client's private health information.

The terms *secure, encrypted*, and *HIPAA compliant* are frequently used to describe videoconferencing programs and practice management systems. It may be helpful to think of the term secure as an umbrella term. Technology that is "secure" reflects and incorporates certain practices that are designed to keep data secure from unauthorized access or changes, both when it is being stored and when it is being transmitted from one device or physical location to another.

One method for keeping stored (e.g., clinical records) or transmitted data (e.g. video sessions or client messaging) secure is encryption. Think of encryption as a process of converting text or any other data into a secret code that requires a key to decode. This can be done in a number of ways, one of which is through a protocol called SSL (secure sockets layer) or through its successor, TLS (transport layer security). However, the encryption is achieved, the bottom line is that no one can read the data who doesn't have a key. Ideally, any videoconferencing platform you use should use some form of encryption. If it does not, find out what kind of data security it provides. If it's not clear from the marketing materials, call the company and get clarification.

HIPAA compliance is another consideration. HIPAA is a federal law that requires that health care providers "maintain reasonable and appropriate administrative, technical, and physical safeguards" to protect what the law refers to as our client's electronic "protected health information," or "e-PHI." While the law does not specify the particular technology that clinicians must have, it requires that we use the "technical, hardware, and software infrastructure necessary to protect e-PHI," "maintain continuous, reasonable, and appropriate security protections," and document what measures we have taken. Any "HIPAA-compliant" videoconferencing or other system should enable you to meet these requirements. You can find guidelines for HIPAA compliance in connection with telehealth at https:// www.hhs.gov/hipaa/for-professionals/security/laws-regulations/index .html. HIPAA does not give individual patients the right to sue you for violating the law, but you still may want to consult a lawyer who specializes in HIPAA to ensure compliance.

Another aspect of security and technology to take into consideration is the access that our "business associates" have to our patients' protected health information. A business associate refers to any individual or company that we use to support and manage our practice. The services that our business associates provide may include medical billing, IT services, and practice management software, such as EHR programs. Under HIPAA, every business associate that you use must sign an agreement that obligates them to safeguard any protected health information to which they have access in the course of providing those services. This agreement is referred to as a Business Associate Agreement, or "BAA." Many companies that serve as business associates have already developed custom BAA's for their organizations. While these may be satisfactory, you should not assume that they will be. It is important that therapists review (and possibly have a lawyer who specializes in HIPAA review) each such form carefully to ensure that it contains the terms that HIPAA requires and that it protects both the therapist and client health information. Among other things, the BAA should clearly state that the business associate will use appropriate safeguards to prevent unauthorized disclosure of your clients' protected health information and that it will monitor its own systems for security incidents and notify you of any security breaches.

From this background, it should be clear that to practice TMH, therapists should have all initial documentation available electronically and use a system or method that provides multiple levels of protection for stored and transmitted data, including video sessions. Now, let's consider what technology is required and capable of doing this.

Technology Infrastructure

There is a wide range of technology options to select from for engaging in TMH. When choosing a technology, select one that you consider to be secure, user-friendly, and easily accessible by clients (Luxton et al., 2016). Many clients have access to commonly used video calling apps such as Face-Time, Skype, and Google Duo. While these are often more convenient for many clients (and therapists), these do not meet the HIPAA security requirements for health sessions (see https://www.hhs.gov/hipaa/for-professionals/special-topics/emergency-preparedness/notification-enforcement-discretion-telehealth/index.html). During the COVID pandemic, the federal government relaxed these requirements to ensure continuity of client care (Pierce et al., 2020) Many state boards and regulating bodies also relaxed their own analogous requirements. Many therapists and clients may have taken advantage of these waivers and simply used these default platforms to continue therapy and avoid having to learn and/or invest in a new system of therapy provision. This may have been more common for therapists with little or no desire to continue teletherapy beyond the emergency period. Yet, these waivers most likely will not be permanent. For therapists who intend to continue TMH or further expand their online practice, choosing and investing in a secure, HIPAA-compliant videoconferencing system, including equipment, is necessary.

To offer video-based sessions, the therapist must have a functional camera, microphone, and monitor. Most laptop computers, tablets, and smartphones have these built into the devices. These devices are the most affordable option because they minimize the amount of additional required equipment and thus expense (Cooper et al., 2020). Given the extended amount of time that most of us have been practicing remotely due to the pandemic, many of us may have already determined that the camera or monitor on our laptop is insufficient for the volume of sessions we conduct. To practice remotely with a large number of clients, a webcam with better quality is necessary. In addition, therapists who have interest in offering webinars, recording podcasts, or other related online or digital activities may have determined that the default camera and microphone does not have the necessary quality. Ideally, a movable, tiltable camera with zoom capabilities provides the greatest range of function and allows the client to have the sharpest image of the therapist and their surrounding environment. Similarly, a monitor with high resolution provides the best image of the client and their environment, which is helpful for collecting information during assessments. Therapists engaging in high amounts of VC or other web-based work may benefit from a larger monitor than the standard 13" or 15" laptop screens. Larger screens may also help minimize eyestrain. Lastly, therapists will want to ensure that their computer is running the most up-to-date operating system, and they should minimize the number of open windows and other programs operating while in video sessions to optimize video transmission.

Therapists should also have strong broadband internet and the ability to plug into the Internet via an ethernet cable as a backup when the WiFi connection may be inconsistent. For personal use, many of us may be able to rely on slower internet speeds, but in order to stream video sessions multiple times per day, a therapist's home internet capabilities must be quite fast. For example, Zoom recommends a minimum connection of 1.5mps to 5mbps (megabits per second) to optimize video quality. The FCC defines fast internet speed as a minimum of 25 mps although many people advocate for a minimum of 100mps due to how many common devices and appliances rely on internet (e.g. smart home devices, television). In addition, many factors can slow our internet speed such as having multiple people working from home, taking online classes, playing games or streaming movies. Many people do not know the speed of our connection. There are multiple ways to test internet speed, including using some easy websites such as www .speedtest.net. It is also prudent to test your connection and setup before beginning teletherapy sessions with clients. Hopefully you can do this easily with family or friends, because testing this way allows you to check your connection speed, view your therapy space on video, and receive feedback on ways to modify the space.

Videoconferencing Platforms

The choice of VC software is also a critical decision. It must be functional, offer a secure connection, and be easily accessible by clients (Cooper et al., 2020; Luxton et al., 2016). The number of choices for HIPAA-compliant VC software has grown tremendously in recent years. Many of these options offer similar features that may overwhelm some new TMH practitioners who are unsure of the differences between the platforms. There are a few primary differences in the features offered in VC platforms. As mentioned above, the first criterion is that the platform offer a safe and secure connection. While technology continues to evolve, therapists should verify that at a minimum, the VC platform can provide encrypted storage of data as well as encrypted video transmission. Second, the therapist should ensure that the provider is willing to sign a BAA that complies with HIPAA. If the provider is not willing to do so, you should select another provider.

Other valuable features of VC programs may include customizable virtual waiting rooms, multiprovider use for clinicians in group practice, screen sharing, and/or file transfer capability. The screen share and file transfer features may be beneficial for therapists who use worksheets, mapping, genograms, or sharing of articles or resources during sessions. For therapists who see couples or families or who facilitate groups, it will also be important to evaluate if the VC platform they are considering allows video sessions with more than one client. If it does, is there a difference in video quality? It is important to consider this before settling on a product, because many platforms do not offer this feature or require an upgrade beyond basic membership for it.

Lastly, there is a wide range of costs associated with VC platforms. There are popular options that are free and may be sufficient for therapists who wish to offer occasional teletherapy sessions. These options may be beneficial when a client does not want to miss a therapy session but, for instance, is sick or lacks transportation or childcare. Some commonly used VC platforms also offer a wide range of other practice management services.

For example, in addition to secure VC, they offer electronic health record-keeping, including client notes, scheduling, billing, and online payments. Clinicians who primarily practice remotely likely need to invest in a robust VC platform that can adequately support their clinical volume. Remember, for clinicians who are practicing remotely, the costs for VC platforms are far lower than monthly office rent. Now that we have considered the technological needs for TMH, let's discuss the environmental considerations and where TMH will occur.

Videoconferencing Platform Requirements

- Easily accessed by clients on computer, tablet, or phone
- Secure encrypted transmission and storage of video and audio data
- BAA available
- Couple, family, or group sessions at fast transmission speed

Optional Features

- Customizable virtual waiting room
- Multiprovider or group practice access
- Screenshare and/or file transfer
- Comprehensive practice management system (notes, billing, scheduling)

VIRTUAL OFFICE AND ENVIRONMENT CONSIDERATIONS

With the abrupt transition to teletherapy and working from home, many of us may not have been prepared to work exclusively from home. Many of us may not have had a dedicated home office; we may have had other family members, including children, sheltering at home with us, and our environment may not have been optimal for therapy. Our clients likely experienced similar constraints. It was not uncommon to have children burst unexpectedly into sessions, have animals walk by the camera or claw for our attention, hear toilets flush or other noise from adjoining rooms, or see distracting items in the background! In such situations, it required all of us—both therapists and clients—to be flexible and adapt to the situation, even as we acknowledge how disruptive this can be to therapy. While these things are atypical for therapy environments, they remain highly human experiences and allow us to, in real time, bear witness to how clients adapt and manage the lack of environmental control. Similarly, our clients get to witness this in us as well; it presents an opportunity for the therapist to model this flexibility to the client.

There are several aspects of our environment to which we must attend to ensure that our home office space is set up to conduct teletherapy. When practicing at home, many of us may simply set up the computer and video and think we are done. Using the computer at our desk may be our default, and we may give little additional consideration to other aspects of our environment. Yet, thoughtfully considering the space where we see clients can go a long way in crafting an online experience for clients that is therapeutic. Let's start with privacy. Just as our in-person office is private, so should our home meeting space be—as private as possible. Ideally, we are meeting in a space where no one else is present and no one can overhear our session. This could be a home office with a door that closes and locks. For those who do not have a private home office, setting up a chair with a stand or table in the corner of a room with a door can also work just as well. In addition, a white noise machine or app might help to reduce the likelihood of others overhearing the session. The use of headphones can minimize external noise, ensure that others cannot hear the client, and may also help the therapist focus on the client instead of external distractions, such as a young child in online classes in the next room.

Minimizing external distractions is important. Distractions may include other people or pets in the home as well as electronic distractions. If there are other members of the household present in the home, you can notify them that you will be in a session, put up a "do not disturb" sign, and, again, use noise cancelling headphones and/or a white noise machine to create a quieter environment. Given the protracted nature of the pandemic, many therapists may still have children home from school and thus have parenting responsibilities and external noise in the home as a result. Thoughtful (and strategic) scheduling of sessions and, if possible, scheduling sessions so that they are not held at the same time as when noisier activities will be occurring in the household might be beneficial.

Seeing clients online also opens us up to technological distractions and potential technological interruptions. Many of us have notifications for incoming emails and also the capacity to receive text messages and phone calls on our computers. Remembering to disable notifications prior to beginning a session is imperative so that the session is not interrupted by any notifications. In addition, it is prudent to exit from or minimize any other open windows to reduce the temptation to view other things during a session. The vulnerability to technological distractions presents an appreciable difference from in-person sessions. Most therapists would agree that checking messages or reading something else during a session would be inappropriate. Yet, many of us are accustomed to multitasking while on our phones or other devices. It is easy to inadvertently fall into that same pattern of behavior even if we are using the device for a session. This may be even more tempting when we are experiencing fatigue or if we are in session with a client with whom we feel less connected. Thus, creating intentional practices to disable notifications and to enter full screen mode may help ensure that we remain fully focused on the client.

We also need to attend to how our virtual office looks and feels. Clients notice our office, including the art, photos, reading material, and overall decor. These elements all work together to create a particular aesthetic and contribute to the overall feel of our office. We should reflect and consider whether we put the same thought into crafting the feel of our online office. Lighting further contributes to how warm the space feels in-person and online. Yet, while minimal lighting is often preferred in the therapy office, this may not always translate well for VC (Luxton et al., 2016). Typically, for teletherapy sessions, the therapist needs a light in front of their face so they can be seen well on camera. Yet, background lighting is also important because the room should not appear dark. Because natural lighting changes throughout the day and based on weather conditions, therapists should be careful not to rely solely upon natural light and to have other lighting available in the space. Giving this amount of attention to lighting is likely foreign to many therapists. Most of us do not want to feel that we are setting up a mini production studio in our home office or living room. Yet, working on camera requires different considerations to create the same warmth as in our traditional office.

Sometimes a therapist may not be aware of the client's view of their work space. One way to identify what a client will see during sessions is to turn on the webcam when we are not conducting a session and observe what is behind and/or around us. Is the office or home unclean or disorganized? Is there clutter? Are parts of our home that we would rather our clients not see currently visible? Does the environment look as warm and inviting as our in-person office? If not, consider what needs to change. Often, moving the lighting, clearing clutter, or adding a plant might create the warmer environment you and your clients seek.

Some therapists may prefer to use a virtual background instead of exposing their actual living or home work-space. This is another distinct difference between meeting online and in person. Virtual background refers to the use of an image (or even a video) to use as the backdrop behind us during the video session. These options may be particularly appealing for therapists who do not have a dedicated home office and prefer to obscure their personal living space. If you choose to use a virtual background, it is important to intentionally choose one that will not be distracting nor take away from the session. For example, while a beach background might be beautiful, consider what it might feel like to talk to your therapist while they are on the beach or have an amusing or comic background. Using a virtual background could be perceived as unprofessional or inauthentic, since we are masking where we are. For therapists who choose to use a virtual background, it may be prudent or even comforting to use a picture of your actual therapy office or other professional meeting space. If you ordinarily show your actual background space and decide to begin using a virtual background, clients will notice this and may wonder about this decision. They may wonder if you have moved locations or if there is something to hide. In the same way that clients grow accustomed to routine and consistent behaviors in person, any deviation of our behavior or established routine online is likely to be noticed and may affect the client's experience. Therapists are encouraged to consider this and be prepared for how to talk about this or respond to client questions. For example, you might begin a session stating: "You might notice that my background is a picture of my downtown office. I am still in my private home office; I wanted to feel like we were in our usual meeting space today. Is the background ok for you?"

Online Office Checklist

- ☐ Private and secure
- ☐ Quiet (sound proofed or use a sound machine)
- ☐ Bright and warm lighting
- ☐ Clutter-free background
- ☐ Modern, minimal decoration
- ☐ Comfortable chair with back support
- ☐ Camera positioned at eye level
- ☐ Standing desk or shelf at eye level for longer days or to integrate movement into session

---

ADDITIONAL CONSIDERATIONS: WORKING REMOTELY

Seeing back-to-back clients online is not the same physical and emotional experience as doing so in person. For those who practiced online during the pandemic, you likely experienced this firsthand. Many therapists who are practicing online, especially those using VC all day, may experience what is being called "Zoom fatigue." This refers to the fatigue or exhaustion that may result from the increased cognitive load required to appear engaged, the heightened attention to words and incomplete availability of nonverbal cues and sensory data, and the energy required to sustain eye contact (Dodgen-Magee, 2020; Locke, 2020). It requires more cognitive and emotional energy to process and attenuate the effects of multiple hours of VC. In addition to Zoom fatigue, the effects of staring at a computer screen for long periods can also be taxing. The blue light from the screen can negatively affect our circadian rhythm (Harvard Health, 2020). There are also physical effects of sitting and staring at a computer screen for multiple hours per day, often in furniture that we may not have chosen for its ergonomic features. This can result in eye strain, back pain or related issues, and headaches. Many of us may have personally experienced these symptoms during these months of the pandemic.

A less tangible effect of seeing clients through VC is the otherwise atypical mounting self-consciousness associated with viewing oneself on screen for multiple hours per day. Therapists are unaccustomed to looking at themselves throughout sessions; this can be both distracting and stressful for some of us (Dodgen-Magee, 2020). While this may be difficult for some of us to admit, therapists are not immune to the negative self-esteem effects of viewing oneself for long periods.

The effects of long hours of teletherapy are real. We must think critically about our schedules and attend to the necessary changes for working digitally within a physical environment. There are some things we can do to better support ourselves and our online work. Consider the following recommendations:

- Change devices throughout the day: switch between a computer and tablet, for example.
- Use blue light filtering software to reduce exposure to blue light.
- Move between a standing desk and a sitting desk.
- Incorporate movement between sessions.
- Find the comfort zone for your schedule.
  - How many back-to-back sessions are you able to effectively manage for yourself and your clients?
- Schedule breaks between clients and actually take a break from technology during that time.
- Schedule clients intentionally.
  - Be mindful of which clients you are scheduling at which point in your day and of the need for breaks before or after clients who may need greater levels of support.
- Create a physical and mental boundary between home and work.
  - Create and maintain a separate designated area that you can disconnect from when not working.
- Create an end-of-work ritual to mentally and physically transition to personal time.
- Intentionally engage in less technology use during your personal time.

These strategies share a few things in common: they invite us to be intentional in our technology and device use, and challenge us to engage in movement, specifically, moving our devices, positions, and bodies. There may be some things we can do to reduce zoom fatigue, some that are within our reach and some that may compromise confidentiality. For example, one strategy is to change locations or to conduct a video session outside, though these options may be unavailable to us if we share a home with others or lack private outdoor space. Another strategy to reduce Zoom fatigue is changing from gallery view to speaker view or hiding the view of oneself to bring less attention to ourselves and reduce the self-consciousness associated with viewing oneself. It is most important to determine what *is* possible and begin with changes that are available to us. By focusing on our available options instead of what we cannot do (e.g., move outdoors if we do not have a backyard), we approach this challenge from an empowered position and may feel good about the changes we can make. Now that I have discussed some of the many considerations for therapists as we prepare to engage in TMH, I will now discuss how to prepare clients for teletherapy.

GETTING CLIENTS PREPARED FOR TELETHERAPY

Many of the technology and environmental factors I have discussed are also important considerations for teletherapy clients. Many clients, especially millennials and adolescents, have technology-centered lives and therefore are able to navigate teletherapy with ease. This is not the case for everyone, however, and is never a safe assumption, even with digital natives. To ensure that clients are prepared for TMH, we need to provide them with support and guidance (Cooper et al., 2020). We must also be prepared to troubleshoot when technological issues arise during a session. Prior to any teletherapy session, clients should be provided information about the chosen VC platform, the necessary technology, and how to access it. Emailing clients clear and succinct information will streamline this process and prevent any confusion or delays in the session. For convenience, it may be easiest to use the language provided by the chosen VC platform in a short email with a link to their site and FAQs, since these are typically updated regularly. Of particular importance is clearly communicating the type of device and/or operating system necessary. For example, clients should be told explicitly whether they need to access from a computer or if a mobile device is sufficient. If access from a mobile device or tablet and an app is required, the client should know this in advance as well as if there is an additional cost for the app. Consider the following modifiable template:

> *Dear Client, I am looking forward to our upcoming teletherapy session. For convenience and privacy, we will be using the Therapy-Video platform. This platform is easily accessed from any computer. You need only click on the link provided in your appointment confirmation and you will be taken to the secure video session. You will need to have a webcam and microphone and be ready to meet in a private space. The built-in camera on your computer or tablet are usually sufficient. If you will be accessing our session from a tablet or phone, a free app is required. Please take a moment to download it now. For any other questions or for more information, you can find out more about the video platform here. I look forward to continuing our work remotely by video.*

Relative to technology, therapists should be sensitive to what type of device clients are using to access and participate in sessions. For example, clients who primarily rely on a cell phone and cell signal might have frequent connection issues, especially for video streaming. In addition, many people who are accessing sessions from a phone may be stuck holding the phone throughout the session, which could become a distraction or may mean that they cannot have their hands free to completely express themselves. With a smaller screen, they may also have difficulty if the therapist is trying to walk them through body work or incorporate EMDR, for instance. It may be helpful to recommend a phone stand or something that allows them to position the phone and remain hands free to clients who must access from a phone. For therapists working with low income communities or with any client experiencing financial challenges, providing resources for low-cost internet, local hotspots, and other technological assistance might be helpful to maintaining continuity of care.

Like therapists, clients should be encouraged to schedule appointments at a time when they can be free of distractions and interruptions. While this is not always possible when sheltering at home with others or for stay-at-home parents, this remains a valid goal so that therapy can occur when the client is best able to focus on therapy. Some clients who appear to be unable to gain privacy may benefit from additional support or coaching around potential solutions. For example, some clients might be better served by leaving the home and meeting somewhere else or while going for a local walk. Others might need to move their meeting time to a different day or time, when they are better able to have privacy in the home, such as their children's nap time. While we typically consider other people and pets as distractions, therapists should also be open to clients having a well-trained pet or designated emotional support animal present during a session. This may provide comfort for clients in ways seldom possible when meeting in a therapist's office. Also, there may be times when a therapist wants to have a family member come into a session for a conjoint or family session. With the conveniences of being in the same home or attending remotely, this is far easier to schedule and negotiate.

Lastly, because many clients will be meeting at home, clients should be reminded that teletherapy remains a clinically oriented appointment. Some clients may be comfortable meeting in bed or in pajamas because they are in their home environment. Some therapists may feel uncomfortable with this casual attire and demeanor from clients. Other therapists may find that clients are better able to be open and vulnerable from the safety provided by their bedroom, which may allow the therapist to delve deeper into difficult issues in ways that a client may have previously been resistant to or to engage in mindfulness or somatic work in this kind of safe place. As the therapy environment changes, it is important that we reflect on our expectations of clients and consider whether our expectations have evolved with those changes. Moreover, we must consider what potentialities may exist from working in these different spaces. Holding firmly or even rigidly to the same rules in a new and different time and setting merits self-examination. If we find that we are being rigid, we therapists must engage in our own reflective work to examine whether maintaining this rule is a necessity for therapy or if it is just about our own issues. Many therapists have likely shifted how they dress or how formal they are after several months of working from home and enduring the ongoing stressors of the pandemic. While performing therapy in the home environment presents distinct threats to privacy as well as other challenges, there are many potential benefits.

CONCLUSION

The learning curve for getting started in teletherapy can feel steep for many therapists. There are multiple considerations. In practice management, we must ensure that our paperwork is available for clients to securely receive and submit. Our informed consent should be specific to the practice of and risks associated with TMH. We must also consider liability insurance to ensure that practicing virtually is a covered service. Technology considerations go hand-in-hand with issues of privacy and security online. We must ensure that any VC platform that we use protects our clients' private health information so that we are in compliance with HIPAA. Once we have the technology, we must work to intentionally create a therapeutic online environment in the same ways that we do for our in-person work. Part of our job also involves ensuring that clients have the necessary information to easily access and fully benefit from teletherapy. Engaging in these tasks before beginning teletherapy can ensure that clients have a streamlined process. The checklists provided in this chapter will help you navigate these complexities. A combined checklist is also provided for your use in Appendix A. While the start-up for TMH may require financial investment as well as investment of time and energy, this investment pays off through a successful teletherapy practice that is managed with ease. In the next chapter, we will discuss clinical considerations that come into play once your practice is set up.

3

CLINICAL ISSUES IN VIRTUAL AND TELETHERAPY

Chime notification sounds. A new client appears on the screen. She looks a little different than you imagined based on the initial phone conversation. The background behind her is strikingly beautiful; green and lush. It stands in such contrast to her sad affect that you instantly notice. She is up close to her camera, and you can almost see the wetness in her eyes.

Therapist: Hi Sara. It's good to see you and to meet . . . even on video.
Sara: Yeah, this is weird, but good. I need it.
Therapist: OK, let's go ahead and get started.

Some things stay the same. There is something comforting about that during this protracted time of uncertainty and ever-present change. There are fundamental aspects of psychotherapy that remain constant across treatment modalities. We still need to connect with our clients, gather information, provide support, and walk with them through challenging times. Practicing in a digital space does not change the importance of therapeutic rapport, emotional safety, and confidentiality. Similarly, many of the administrative tasks, ethical and legal obligations, and clinical goals remain the same. How we meet these goals and which resources are available may be different when working in a digital or out-of-office environment, which presents unique considerations in screening clients, establishing rapport through technology, and mitigating crises and emergencies. While many practitioners focus on providing the same treatment via teletherapy as they provided in-person, remaining rigidly committed to providing "the same experience" may result in a missed opportunity. With the shifting of modality or format of therapy comes the opportunity to disrupt the therapeutic norm and the specific practices that may not have best served many people, including therapists. With a change in format may come the possibility of a more forward-leaning and expansive version of psychotherapy. In this chapter, we will identify and reflect on some of the specific clinical considerations that arise in teletherapy. We will also consider the spaces and ways teletherapy might expand the ways we engage in psychotherapy.

SCREENING

During the pandemic, most clients have been seen remotely by necessity. However, we must still consider how to assess client appropriateness for teletherapy. As discussed in Chapter 1, clinical appropriateness for TMH should be informed by the clinician's expertise and background in addition to available clinical evidence, licensure regulations, and any relevant mental health practice laws (Cooper et al., 2020; Luxton et al., 2016). An important aspect of clinical competence for TMH practitioners includes the ability to determine which particular TMH services and treatment modalities are appropriate for each client. While some clients may benefit from asynchronous messaging with a therapist, some clients will need interactive VC treatment, and others will be best served by traditional in-person treatment (Cooper et al., 2020). Many clients may benefit from a combination of these services. These decisions should be made after carefully screening each prospective client to determine their diagnosis, their symptom severity, whether they are in crisis, the level of support available to the client, and the client's internal resources and motivation for therapy. Screening should also explore availability of and access to competent in-person therapy services and whether the client has access to a secure and private space for participating in TMH services (Cooper et al., 2020; McCord et al., 2020). Therapist competence is also a relevant consideration. Regardless of the treatment setting or modality, we are ethically required to practice within our areas of expertise. For therapists seeking to use TMH as an opportunity to expand their areas of clinical expertise, additional training and consultation are necessary to ensure that they have the required knowledge and skills (Cooper et al., 2020).

The following questions offer guidance and direction in clinical decision-making, including identifying exclusionary criteria for teletherapy:

- **Competence and expertise.** Does this client present with a background and issues that are within my area(s) of expertise?
- **Stability and severity of symptoms.** Is this client emotionally stable enough for an outpatient private practice setting? Does this client need greater support than I or my practice can provide?
- **Asynchronous versus synchronous telemental health.**
  - Asynchronous as a stand-alone treatment should be reserved for people who are high functioning and not in crisis. Asynchronous can also be used as a helpful adjunct to in-person or interactive video sessions.
  - Synchronous chat and messaging are best used with someone who is very high functioning and needs only periodic or low levels of support.
  - Synchronous phone contact is most appropriate when rapport and relationship are already established or when the therapist does not need continual visual observation for effective intervention.
  - Synchronous VC is appropriate for clients who are otherwise suitable for outpatient treatment (low risk for self-harm, adequate internal and external resources and support) and have a safe private environment for video sessions.

In responding to the questions above, if you answered "no" to either or both of the first two questions, this is a client who likely should be referred out. Not every treatment modality is appropriate for all clients and their needs. This remains true for TMH. Historically, TMH was presumed to be unsafe for clients in need of a higher level of care (Luxton et al., 2016). Yet, there is now research demonstrating its effectiveness even with clients with severe mental illness (Miu et al., 2020), and during the pandemic, more therapists have had to provide therapy remotely, even to clients they may not have previously considered candidates for teletherapy. It remains imperative, however, to consider the distinct needs and necessary resources to support clients with histories of hospitalization, multiple periods of emotional instability, low digital literacy, and limited access to necessary technology. Clients with low cognitive functioning may need the support of someone else in the home to be able to access services, for instance. Therapists who work with clients with more severe symptomatology, including suicidality or histories of aggressive behavior, may find that the ability to see the full range of nonverbal behavior is critical to treatment, thus in-person treatment may be most appropriate. Others may find that clients with emotional instability are not candidates for being seen only through asynchronous methods (e.g., email or text) but would be candidates for VC sessions, which allow the therapist to effectively observe, assess, and treat the client. In addition, it is important to consider for example, whether the therapist (or the practice) offers crisis or emergency services in-person or in a remote format.

Lastly, it is important to consider that some clients may have symptomatology that might be exacerbated by TMH, which would warrant special consideration or modification to treatment. For example, clients with codependent tendencies that might be intensified with greater access to the therapist or who have specific delusions of reference regarding televisions or internet may not be suited for telehealth. These clients may inadvertently experience an increase in some of their symptoms. Also, clients who live in unsafe or abusive environments may benefit from attending sessions outside of their home environment. The potential for an abuser overhearing a therapy session may place a client in danger. Some therapists may deem clients with histories of substance abuse or those currently abusing substances as inappropriate for TMH when in-person therapy is available (Cooper et al., 2020; Luxton et al., 2016). For clinicians who have expertise in working with substance abusing populations and the associated range of addictive behaviors, TMH may be an effective way to provide therapy, especially in concert with an online 12-step program or other support group for addiction. There may be challenges with therapy with clients still working through addiction, however, because it may be more difficult for a therapist to detect substance use or inebriation over video, it may be necessary to establish specific protocols for assessing and discussing sobriety or substance use (Luxton et al., 2016). Therapists would likely need to explicitly ask about any substance use or about engagement in the respective addictive behavior as part of the assessment within each session. Another option is having a client complete an objective measure assessing substance use and/or cravings, triggers, etc. on a weekly basis. As mentioned in Chapter 1, there are apps that can easily allow therapists and clients to track symptoms and progress. This approach would be one way to use an asynchronous mental health tool to complement the synchronous method of VC in work with addiction.

Clients' proficiency with technology may be an area of concern for some therapists. Some TMH therapists may deem that someone with limited technological skills is inappropriate for teletherapy. However, it is also important to consider that, through TMH, clients who previously had limited experience in this area are able to increase digital literacy and basic life skills that are likely to help them in other areas of life (McCord et al., 2020). Overall, clinicians should document their rationale for the treatment modality they decide is most appropriate for a client. The choice of treatment modality may also need to be updated if the client's circumstances or functioning changes. For example, if a client was previously stable with good social support, asynchronous methods of TMH may have been deemed appropriate. However, if the client's symptoms worsen or the client reveals that they need to work through more significant clinical issues, such as previously unprocessed child abuse or other trauma, this therapeutic modality may no longer be appropriate.

Ultimately, if a client needs greater support or more intensive intervention than what you can provide, the client should be referred to someone who is better able to meet their needs. Prospective clients who live outside of the therapist's local area and who, after careful screening, are deemed to be best served by in-person treatment should also be referred to other therapists. Referrals should be readily available to offer to clients who are either not candidates for TMH or are not a good fit with the therapist's background and expertise (McCord et al., 2020).

Screening for Teletherapy Checklist

☐ Client's presenting issues are within my areas of expertise

☐ Client's symptoms and health are stable enough for outpatient treatment
  - If not, what additional support does client require? _____

    _____

    _____

  - Are these supports available in the home or through collateral care?
  - If not, refer out for more intensive level of care.

☐ Asynchronous
  - Client is high-functioning, with no recent or current crises
  - Client is adequately supported
  - Client has access to and understanding of required technology

☐ Synchronous
  - Outpatient treatment is appropriate
  - Risk for harm to self or others is low
  - Client has access to and understanding of required technology
  - Client has access to a safe, private environment for teletherapy

Additional Screening Needed

☐ History of emotional instability, aggression, recent hospitalization

☐ Severe or persistent mental illness

☐ Low cognitive functioning

☐ Poor or inconsistent access to necessary technology

☐ Additional support/care needed: _____

    _____

    _____

INITIAL SESSION

The initial session—whether in person or by video—can be awkward and uncomfortable for many clients and for therapists. The scenario of the initial session with Sara at the beginning of this chapter revealed some of the therapist's thoughts about seeing the client and her environment for the first time by video. Across modalities, the initial session is important to gain essential background information about the client, including history of presenting symptoms, overall health information, goals for therapy, diagnosis when applicable, and initial treatment and wellness planning (Luxton et al., 2016). This process is largely the same for teletherapy sessions, however, a distinct difference in the initial TMH session is that it also provides an important overview and/or orientation to telepractice. Some therapists who offer teletherapy have previously required an in-person initial session. This has not been possible during the pandemic, and many of us may not feel comfortable conducting in-person sessions for the foreseeable future. Therapists who prefer an in-person intake session may feel more confident in their ability to evaluate clients' overall functioning in person or may feel that meeting in person helps establish rapport. Because the research supports the effectiveness of in-person and VC intake sessions (Glueckauf et al., 2018), which form to use can be largely based on clinician preference. Your preference may be grounded primarily in what is most comfortable for you as well as your confidence in your clinical decision-making skills in each modality. Therapists new to teletherapy may want to transition existing clients, with whom they already have an established therapeutic relationship, to remote or online versions of therapy. Beginning the transition to TMH with existing clients allows the therapist to experiment with different forms of TMH and leverage the trust present in those established relationships to ease the transition for them and their clients.

When meeting online for the first time, verification of identity is also necessary (McCord et al., 2020) and can be conducted in multiple ways. One option is for a client to submit a copy of their identification with initial paperwork. When meeting for the first time, the therapist can discreetly match the client's photo identification to the person appearing on video.

This is likely the least intrusive (and awkward) method of identity verification. Other therapists might request that a client show their identification on camera at the start of the session, and the therapist will manually verify this information. Notably, a client's photo identification may not match their current physical presentation, as can happen with trans clients or clients who have gone through significant weight loss or other personal appearance changes. These situations should be handled with care, and therapists should consider how identification requirements may be triggering or feel personally intrusive. You should consider ways to give clients agency in this process and to avoid perpetuating potentially oppressive and emotionally triggering processes for clients.

In addition to verifying identification, telehealth guidelines suggest that we should verify the client's location at the beginning of every session (McCord et al., 2020). This ensures that in the event of a clinical emergency, the therapist can respond appropriately and send emergency assistance to the client's precise location. For some therapists this may seem cumbersome, but for many sessions, this may be as easy as visually recognizing the client's home background. Localization can also be combined with the check-in. For example, asking, "Hi Martha, where are we meeting today?" Or a therapist can comment on the different background that they notice behind the client. For example, in a recent video session with a client who typically meets outside in her garden, I noticed that she was indoors in a room with a beautiful painting as a backdrop. By commenting on the painting and asking about the different location at her home, she was able to verify her location as well as describe the emergency work being done outside her home that had been disruptive and provoking anxiety due to the need to have workers in her space during the pandemic. My comment resulted in my receiving additional information about environmental stressors that my client had personally minimized and thus had not yet discussed in session.

Lastly, when engaging in an initial VC session, it is prudent to discuss the client's comfort with the technology used for the session, whether the client has consistent access to a computer or mobile device for sessions, and to ask any technology related questions. Teletherapists should expect and be prepared for technological issues. It is important to establish a backup plan to implement in the event of technology issues. For example, a therapist may state that if ever there are more than one or two interruptions in the internet connection, the therapist will call the client, and the rest of the session will continue by phone. Thus, therapists should have a backup phone number available to use if necessary.

Initial Session Reminders

- Verify client identity
- Verify client location and privacy
- Turn off or silence electronic notifications and messages

ESTABLISHING RAPPORT

The therapeutic relationship is paramount to the therapeutic endeavor. Some authors describe therapeutic rapport as the harmonious connection and healing alliance that develops between therapist and client (Norcross & Lambert, 2019). And, like any other authentic trusting relationship, it is rarely if ever developed in one encounter. Rather, rapport is something you begin establishing from the first phone call or email encounter with a client—it builds over time and experience. Geller (2020) argues that *therapeutic presence* serves as the foundation and helps to establish therapeutic rapport. Therapeutic presence refers to a way of being with a client that can enhance the therapeutic techniques we use in our clinical work (Geller, 2020). Rapport is essential to any therapeutic modality, as it has been demonstrated to be a predictor of treatment success (Norcross & Lambert, 2019). How to develop an authentic relationship while using synchronous and/or asynchronous technology may be a challenge for some therapists. As mentioned in Chapter 1, research suggests that therapeutic rapport in TMH can be just as strong as that developed in person. Geller (2020) suggests that therapists offer emotional and psychological safety through their embodied presence, even in teletherapy. Further, Geller (2020) states that physical distance is not antithetical to demonstrating a felt psychological presence. Practical strategies she recommends include:

- Consider sitting a little further back from the camera so that clients can see more of your full body, including your gestures.
- Therapists may need to focus their eye gaze on the camera and be more intentional about their facial expressions, since the face occupies most of what clients see.
- Therapists should stay attuned to their own experience to ensure that they are able to integrate sensory information to clients in session.

The therapist's presence relies heavily on the therapist's attunement with themself and their ability to use their own embodied experience within sessions. To remain centered and present, both while in sessions and while with our loved ones outside of therapy, therapists would likely benefit from increased mindfulness and self-compassion during this time in which therapists are experiencing many of the same stressors and traumas as their clients. Let's consider the nuanced complexities of demonstrating therapist presence and building rapport through technology.

Client: [*crying and blowing nose*]
Therapist: I see how difficult this is for you. And even on video, I can feel the weight of what you are carrying.
Client: Yes! This is just so hard, and everyone sees him as this good guy—the life of the [*expletive*] party.
Therapist: What is it like for you that I see you and witness your pain?

In this example, the therapist can observe and comment on the client's emotional experience while explicitly making their presence with the client felt even via video. Ensuring that our presence and empathy are felt and experienced through technology is critical. This is even more important for therapists working with trauma survivors or during periods when clients are more emotionally vulnerable. Nonverbal communication is central to establishing therapeutic presence and building therapeutic rapport (Geller, 2020). Attending to and mirroring the client's body language demonstrates that the therapist is with the client. This remains paramount even in teletherapy. While some parts of the body may not be visible in VC sessions, we can observe and attend to the parts that are within view or are observable in other ways. Other ways include tone of voice, choice of words, and other vocal intonations. Therapists can use nonverbal communication to demonstrate interest and empathy during VC. While clients should be able to see the therapist's facial expressions and hear their voice, clients may not notice or be able to see the therapist lean slightly forward toward them nor register other subtle movements. Because we are unable to observe body language in phone sessions, this method is more limited. The phone does, however, still allow the listener to notice voice, volume, tone, word/phrase choice, and even silences, which all provide important information for the attuned therapist. Consequently, the TMH therapist may need to be more intentional about their use of vocal or verbal minimal encouragers to connect and demonstrate care.

At its core, therapeutic rapport is about authenticity and trust. Let's briefly reflect on rapport.

Pause | Reflect

- Consider how you, as a therapist, demonstrate care and build trust with clients in person.
- What comes to mind? Did you come up with primarily verbal or nonverbal elements? How do these translate to a digital environment?
- Do clients without an in-person relationship with you pick up on these behaviors or practices in the same way as those who encounter you in person?
- If not, what might need to change?

Psychotherapy training teaches us that there are numerous ways to build trust, such as through active listening, by demonstrating empathy and curiosity, and by providing supportive nonverbal cues such as nods (Norcross & Lambert, 2019). Many of us continue to engage in these practices yet find that being more personable and allowing ourselves to be known also helps clients trust and value us (Hill et al., 2018). While therapists across theoretical orientations differ in their perspectives on self-disclosure, one of the most direct routes to an authentic relationship is humanizing and sharing oneself. Some therapists connect with clients and allow themselves to be more fully seen through small talk, humor, or other minor forms of self-disclosure. This often happens organically as the therapist is walking the client down the hall to the office or at the beginning of a session. While therapists practicing virtually do not have the walk to the office, beginning each session with some small talk and a check-in can be part of your standard practice. Connection may also happen organically when the therapist shares a story or anecdote with a lesson that is relevant to something the client shared. Again, there are differences across theoretical orientations regarding the appropriateness of self-disclosure, and even small talk, with clients. Regardless of theoretical orientation, it is important to critically reflect on the expectations of today's clients. The blank-slate therapist may not appeal to all clients, and some clients may want to feel that they know their therapist as a person. In contrast, others may find that knowing anything about their therapist creates an uncomfortable dynamic. Assessing the client's comfort and needs in these areas may be important. For example it is common, in an initial session, to ask clients if they have any questions about therapy or treatment. I typically take this further and empower clients to be intentional in their decision to work together. I ask, "Is there anything that would be helpful for you to know about me to inform your decision about whether we will work well together or that would make you feel safer?" Often, clients are pleasantly surprised at the invitation to learn something about their therapist. In my many years of practice, of the clients who ask a question, almost all of the questions were appropriate and personally meaningful for them. The questions they ask also give me information about the areas of importance for the client as well as their ability to recognize and respect common boundaries. Certainly, therapists who employ self-disclosure must do so in ways that are only in the service of the client and do not focus attention on the therapist.

Lastly, in working in a digital environment, communication via technology can be another way to build rapport. When all therapist–client interactions occur online or remotely, therapists' use of technology is all the more important. Yet, communication may be easier to misinterpret when conveyed via technology, especially text-based or phone communications, which lack the visual cues that might help confer meaning (Drum & Littleton, 2014). How we respond to clients through technology also matters. Therapists who do not respond or who are slow to respond to emails, client texts, or chat messages may risk eroding client trust. This issue merits pausing to consider your responsiveness to prospective clients and to existing clients. Many of us have experienced times (perhaps in this moment) when our inbox or voicemail is full of client inquiries or when a client has sent an email at the busiest point in our week, when we were up against a pressing deadline or had a sick child at home. Most of us have been there, especially those of us who are sole proprietors with no staff or assistant to help manage the tasks of the practice. Add a pandemic and racial uprisings, and many of us have likely been stretched thin, if not completely overwhelmed, for months. While we may have valid reasons for not responding or for being delayed in our response, this may be interpreted as our being unreliable, our having broken a promise, or mere unprofessionalism. It is important, too, that we attend to the tone of our messages. Often, we may err on the side of formality or professionalism, but for clients, this may translate into coldness or emotional distance instead of the warmth and support that they expect and need. This can not only erode the trust necessary for therapeutic rapport but also trigger clients and be more difficult for those who have issues of trust or feeling safe with loved ones or authority figures. These possibilities underscore the value and importance of being clear with clients about our availability and what they can expect in terms of our response times to emails, texts, and chats.

BOUNDARIES AND PROFESSIONALISM

The digital landscape can affect personal and professional boundaries. We know that the emotional and physical distance experienced through text-based technology can alter the ways people communicate, particularly in communicating with greater frequency and in more casual language than through face-to-face communication (Drum & Littleton, 2014). TMH therapists are most often advised to avoid casual styles of communicating with clients via text and email because these communications are still components of client records. As mentioned above, it is important to communicate in ways that maintain the professional relationship, but it is also important to take into consideration the times when we have to practice in suboptimal circumstances, such as while sheltering at home during a health pandemic. Many therapists may have experienced something similar to Sam, from the introduction chapter. Thus, we may have found ourselves disclosing more about our personal or home life than we typically provide under normal circumstances. For some therapists, this disclosure may have been foreign, causing them to question their professionalism and boundaries. For others, it may have felt refreshing and humanizing, more authentic even, to share their experiences. If managed in a professional way, self-disclosure can provide therapists with an opportunity to be more known and fully seen by clients. This may, in turn, deepen the therapeutic relationship. Consider this example of a recent interaction:

> **Me:** Let's go ahead and get started. In this moment, how are you? What are you bringing into the space today?
>
> **Nicole:** I'm tense and tired. I've been really stressed and overwhelmed with the kids being home and just juggling everything. I don't quite know how to handle all of this.
>
> **Me:** It's understandable that you are overwhelmed. This is a lot for everyone, especially parents. [*Loud laughter in next room from my daughter's virtual class.*]
>
> **Both of us:** [*Laughter.*]
>
> **Me:** Perfect timing, huh? I did not plan that! [*Laughter.*] I will put on my headphones so it is a little quieter.
>
> **Nicole:** Obviously, you get it. I know you do. This week has just been hard.

In this brief exchange, my client describes the stress of a situation that many parents, including myself, have been experiencing during the pandemic. As I begin to affirm and reflect her feelings, we are interrupted by the loud sounds of my daughter's virtual classroom. This unintentional intrusion into the virtual therapy space was a reminder, in real-time, for my client that I was with her in this shared experience. She was able to witness me juggling therapy work with her even as the sound of my young child entered the room. While I already had a good relationship with Nicole when this happened, this event helped her see me more fully, not just in the multiple roles that I embody but also in the way in which she recognized that even as I held space for her in the midst of an extraordinarily difficult time, we were in it together. Certainly, there was something distinct about the context of COVID-19, of sheltering at home, and of living through this time that allowed our therapeutic relationship to deepen.

CRISIS MANAGEMENT AND EMERGENCY PROTOCOLS

Managing crises may be the most feared aspect of TMH. Yet, TMH has been demonstrated to be as effective as traditional in-office therapy for managing crises (McCord et al., 2020). As mentioned in Chapter 1, calls to crisis hotlines have increased during the COVID-19 pandemic, which is another reminder that people are struggling. Safety planning and crisis management from afar can be more complex than when addressed in person. Perhaps one of the most difficult aspects of crisis and emergency management via teletherapy is being unable to be physically present with clients. For those of us who have worked crisis hotlines or related services, this may be a familiar challenge—the need to so closely attend to voice, tone, volume, and choice of words to provide comfort to a caller. Unlike crisis hotlines, therapists usually have the benefit of a previously existing relationship with the client.

Crisis planning in a teletherapy session requires being prepared and identifying resources prior to the crisis so that providers can effectively respond in the event of a crisis (Cooper et al., 2020; McCord et al., 2020). Initial screening of clients for teletherapy and appropriate TMH modalities is an important preliminary step to ensure that clients have the necessary support. Recall, that verification of client location should be conducted at the beginning of each session. Knowing the client's location allows us to consider in advance what emergency and support services are nearby. During an initial intake session, the therapist should make note of the nearest emergency personnel so that this information is rapidly and easily accessible should an emergency arise during a session. In addition, therapists should have a personal emergency contact in the client's record.

Safety concerns that arise during teletherapy sessions are typically the same as in-office crises (Luxton et al., 2016). Examples of crises include risk of harm to self or others and, less commonly, medical emergencies. As would be true of an in-office visit, if a client exhibits worsening suicidal ideation and the therapist has concerns about the client's safety, immediate clinical intervention is necessary. A primary consideration is first ensuring that the client experiences the felt support of the therapist. This may be easier to do with clients with whom we have an established relationship. For newer clients, explicitly verbalizing that, though the relationship is new, we, the therapist, are there with them in the crisis may be of particular significance. With clients who are cooperative and able to cocreate a safety plan and even contact a support person within the session, this process is easier. In cases in which a client may be denying the severity of the crisis or will not commit to enacting the safety plan, the intervention must be escalated. Specifically, the therapist may need to call the emergency contact or emergency personnel in order to ensure the safety of the client. Again, the therapist must know clients' precise location in order to direct emergency personnel to them. Consider the following example:

Melissa is a 27-year-old biracial (Korean and white American) woman. She presents with a history of significant depression and anxiety. She began experiencing her first depressive episode during college and eventually sought counseling at the university counseling center. Melissa has been in counseling off and on for the past several years, and she began taking antidepressants two years ago. Multiple members of Melissa's family struggle with severe depression. She reported that her older brother attempted suicide during a depressive episode a few years ago and that she has two aunts who have undiagnosed mental health issues. Melissa reports that because of their family history, her parents are very supportive of her and encourage all aspects of her mental health treatment.

Melissa reported in a session that she had been feeling pretty stable prior to COVID-19: She was dating someone, and things were going well in the relationship. For the past year and a half she had been teaching preschool children at an early education program that she loved. Early in the response to COVID-19, Melissa was laid off from her job because the school closed. Because of the shelter at home order, she also felt isolated and "stuck at home" with "toxic roommates." While her parents were able to help her financially, Melissa became increasingly anxious and depressed. She sought out virtual therapy for support. A month into treatment, Melissa's symptoms began worsening, and during a video session, she reported suicidal ideations that scared her.

Melissa's experience of worsening depression is one that was likely far too common during the pandemic. Let's consider how to best respond to Melissa during the video session. First, it is prudent to have screened and documented Melissa's history of depression and family history of suicide attempt during the initial intake session. Based on the information provided, Melissa reportedly had been stable for some time and not in crisis. Her symptom history and duration, coupled with her family history, suggest that Melissa would likely benefit from close clinical monitoring in which her symptoms were being tracked and any triggers identified. Assuming depression and anxiety are within the clinician's area of expertise, it would seem that Melissa is appropriate for teletherapy. Due to her history and that she is a new client, she would likely be best served through video sessions rather than asynchronous methods of support. In addition to the video sessions, the therapist might recommend the use of a mood- and symptom-monitoring phone app to track her symptoms and share this information with the therapist. This data could also be reviewed with Melissa during sessions to better interpret the data and understand her subjective experience.

During the session in which Melissa expresses suicidal ideations, it is important to begin assessing the severity of these symptoms. For example, the therapist should ask about the specific thoughts, the frequency of these thoughts, any plan she might have to act on these thoughts, and any means she might have for self-harm. The thoughts alarmed Melissa, which may indicate that she does not want to harm herself, but she may not feel in control of her actions. This would also be helpful to explore. In cases of suicidal ideation, it is important to cocreate a safety plan. The safety plan typically helps clients understand their triggers or warning signs that indicate that they need to reach out for additional help. This plan typically has multiple steps that gradually escalate along with the severity of the crisis. In this example, one would work with Melissa to identify specific triggers, not just the broader context of a pandemic and unemployment but the specific situation, thoughts, or feelings, that led up to the suicidal ideation. It is also helpful to discuss tangible, healthy ways of comforting oneself and managing these thoughts and emotions when they arise. For example, if the therapist has been working on mindfulness practices in sessions or if Melissa is a yoga enthusiast, these are healthy methods of coping to recommend she practice when she experiences triggers that might lead to suicidal ideation. For situations in which clients need greater support, discussing what options the client has, giving special consideration to limitations imposed by the pandemic, would be an essential aspect of safety planning. For example, is it possible for Melissa to go stay with her parents or a friend for some period? Many therapists have worksheets that they use in their planning sessions. Others may write down the information and give it to the client. In a TMH session, the plan and resources can be typed up and securely emailed or messaged to the client. Depending on the video platform being used, it might be possible to share the document at the end of the session or even use a whiteboard feature during the session to write the plan out. Lastly, it is important to remind the client of after-hours crisis management and support procedures. If you do not provide 24/7 availability, ensuring that the client has crisis hotline information in the safety plan, along with her own emergency contacts, is essential.

For clients who appear to be in immediate danger of harming themself yet are uncooperative in activating the safety plan or are unable to confirm that they are safe to be home, greater intervention is necessary. The client must be reminded of the therapist's ethical and legal obligation to keep the client safe and then discuss available options. There are multiple ways that therapists can communicate this, and this is never an easy conversation. For some therapists, having these types of difficult conversations over video may be uncomfortable or anxiety-provoking. For example, the therapist might say to Melissa:

> *Melissa, I am concerned about your safety and well-being. From what you have shared, you are not safe to be home right now. Since I care about you and I am ethically and legally required to ensure your safety, we need to get you more help and support. Our options are limited.*

Then, clearly articulate the available options for the client, including more intensive treatment while staying with a friend or family member or hospitalization. The therapist could have Melissa call a family member on speaker phone while continuing the video call. If involuntary hospitalization is unavoidable, emergency personnel must be deployed to the client's location. A therapist can communicate this to the client by stating that they will call paramedics on their phone while remaining in the video session with the client.

While safety planning and suicide intervention is complex, this domain remains largely the same when using VC. The primary difference is that the client is not physically within the therapist's office when the call is made. In some less common situations, a teletherapist may be concerned that a client might attempt to harm themself while emergency personnel are en route. Recall that clients who require greater levels of support and are seen in a remote environment are likely best served with VC forms of TMH.

Should a previously stable client, being seen via asynchronous forms of TMH, become less stable, there are ways to support the client and effectively intervene. A therapist who is communicating with a client only via text or email is unable to use behavioral observations to help build rapport and assess severity of symptoms, requiring an over-reliance on verbal communication, such as writing out explicitly supportive and empathetic statements. When an emergency contact person or supportive friend needs to be contacted during an asynchronous session in which the client is communicating only by text or chat with the therapist, the therapist may not be able to verify that the client has actually contacted the support person nor to participate in that conversation. In this situation, some therapists might deem it necessary to be on the call or to contact the support person on behalf of the client. Client location would remain necessary in case emergency personnel need to be alerted. Again, robust screening for appropriateness for TMH is necessary prior to beginning to work with a client. Moreover, maintaining contact with and support for a client in crisis is essential until an emergency contact or friend can be with them.

WORKING WITH CHILDREN AND ADOLESCENTS

When using TMH to work with children and adolescents, there are a number of specific considerations. An in-depth exploration of child-specific TMH is outside of the scope of this text, but some considerations merit inclusion. As mentioned in Chapter 1, recent pre-COVID-19 research showed that only 3% of therapists (as represented in the research) provided TMH to children and 12% provided TMH to adolescents (Glueckauf et al., 2018). This is noteworthy in that it demonstrates that a large portion—potentially the majority—of child therapists had never provided TMH before the pandemic. Yet, most adolescents have smartphones and are accustomed to communicating through technology (Vogels, 2019). TMH may actually be a preferred method of mental health care delivery for this demographic. It is unclear how the implementation of TMH with children and adolescents during the pandemic has affected child therapists' perceptions of TMH or if it is now or will be more widely accepted and implemented with child and adolescent populations. Therapists who work with children and parents may wish to further explore TMH for practice development and to better meet the needs of families.

Engaging in teletherapy with children requires some unique considerations. The physical space and environment for TMH with children is especially important because much of this work relies on observations, interactions, and engaging in play (Gloff et al., 2015; Nelson et al., 2017). For TMH with children, the home environment must be spacious enough to support assessments, which can require physical movement and activity, the family must be equipped with cameras capable of transmitting images sufficient for the therapist to make observations, and the space should be large enough for the therapist to see the client as well as the client's parents/caregivers. Possibly one of the greatest benefits of using TMH with children is that it offers the therapist the opportunity to observe interactions between child and parent/caregiver as well as other children or pets in the household. Another benefit of therapy in the home environment is that the safety and comfort of being at home may foster therapeutic rapport and allow children (and their caregivers) the emotional safety to open up more quickly (Geller, 2020). Other benefits include ease of scheduling, ease of coordination of family therapy, and reduced disruption to school attendance (Gloff et al., 2015; Stephan et al., 2016). When working with children remotely, however, it is important to remember that safety and privacy concerns remain. If there are concerns about abuse or a parent overhearing a sensitive conversation with an adolescent, for example, this must be managed with sensitivity and care. In this case, when the sessions occur in the household, the client may use headphones, employ a white noise app, or play music in the background to minimize the involvement of "overly involved parents," or the therapist and client can brainstorm other creative solutions.

Consent and assent are also important considerations for work with children and adolescents. Consent and teletherapy were discussed some in Chapter 2, but therapists working with minors must also remember that, with few exceptions (e.g., a minor who is in the military or an emancipated youth), minors are unable to legally consent to therapy. Yet, it is best practice that the youth play a developmentally appropriate role in being informed about and agreeing to treatment, also known as assent (Nelson et al., 2017). Involving the child in a shared decision-making process allows them to assent and empowers them to collaborate on their own health.

When working with children in teletherapy, best practice still includes play and game-based therapy, in addition to any useful parent-based training and family therapy (Nelson et al., 2017). Many practitioners now often refer to this therapy as "teleplay therapy," which refers to engaging in play therapy primarily through VC. Though the therapist is in a different location, there are several activities and games a therapist and child can play using VC. For example, many teleplay therapists work collaboratively with commonly used toys, such as play dough, building blocks, Legos, and art supplies, that they can build or create with at the same time. The therapist can read the child a book that is based on the child's presenting issues or on skills the child is working to build.

For adolescents, there are even more available options. Many therapists who work with adolescents integrate games. Many adolescents already engage in live, multiplayer virtual gaming, which makes this an optimal way to integrate gaming into therapy. Depending on the adolescent's presenting issues, asynchronous messaging and chat may also be viable and attractive TMH choices for some teens.

Training and support of the client's parents remains critical in this work and was even more necessary during the pandemic, when parents and children alike experienced inordinate amounts of stress and upheaval of daily routines and structure (Pierce et al., 2020). Because families were home 24/7 during the pandemic, there were many opportunities to observe parent–child interactions as well as the specific ways that children (and parents) were adjusting to being home and how they were being affected by the limited contact with friends or extended family members, etc. For children who have difficulty regulating emotions or for those whose home environments provide little structure, this was likely all the more difficult.

Mental health professionals have advocated for the expansion of TMH services for youth (Gloff et al., 2015). COVID-19 presented an (emergency) opportunity for many child therapists to try this out and led the way for increased training in this area. Many proponents of children's mental health advocate for school-based TMH, perhaps in addition to traditional models of delivery, to increase access to more comprehensive care (Stephan et al., 2016). School-based TMH presents concerns around privacy and less collaboration with family, which merit consideration. It is clear, however, that TMH appears to offer more expansive ways to meet the mental health needs of children and families (Nelson et al., 2017).

TERMINATION OF SERVICES

Therapist: I want to check in with you to see how you think you are progressing toward your therapy goals.
Client: I feel a lot better . . . of course, I'm not 100%, whatever

that means. But I don't feel as depressed. I have more energy, and I'm in a better space with my mom. I feel like I finally have boundaries.

Therapist: I am so glad that you are doing better and using what you have learned here in your relationships. It sounds to me like you have met the goals that we set for therapy. How would you feel about beginning to transition out of therapy?

Terminating therapy is perhaps one of the most difficult aspects of clinical work; we often avoid it. Preparation for termination of services begins from the beginning of the therapeutic relationship. Approximately 20% of clients leave treatment early (Swift & Greenberg, 2015), which is important to keep in mind because this means that we have the opportunity to plan our termination with a lot of our clients. Because goals are established and intentions set at the beginning of therapy, therapists should be continually assessing clients' progress toward these goals. When progress is not being made, it is also important to check in with clients about this. Specifically, failure to make progress merits reflection on clinical fit, client satisfaction, and the focus of the work the therapist–client are engaging in as well as *how* that work is ensuing. In terminating therapy via technology, TMH therapists would do well to be particularly attuned to language and nonverbal communication. Even clients who have accomplished their goals in psychotherapy commonly have mixed feelings—positive and difficult emotions—about life without therapy or without the therapist (Swift & Greenberg, 2015). In telehealth visits—especially by phone or chat, when visual cues are absent—therapists may be more likely to miss this kind of communication from their clients due to the subtleties of these expressions. Comprehensive research with therapists across theoretical orientations suggests that there are several common tasks or processes that are important in terminating therapy (Norcross et al., 2017):

- Prepare for termination
- Process feelings of both client and therapist
- Discuss client's future functioning and coping strategies
- Help client employ new skills beyond therapy

- Frame personal development as a life-long process
- Anticipate post-therapeutic growth and generalization
- Reflect on client goals and improvements
- Express pride in client's progress and mutual relationship

As mentioned, termination is something that is ideally planned; both clients and therapists are likely to have mixed feelings about termination, especially after working together for a long time. Use the time and space leading up to termination to identify and discuss what went well, what was gained during therapy, and the multiple ways the client will continue to apply what was learned to new and different situations as they continue to grow. Some clients benefit from first moving to less frequent sessions or from taking a break from therapy prior to official termination. Many clients benefit from hearing the therapist state explicitly that the client will be ok, that they will do well, or that we will miss them. In an age of increased acceptance of therapy, therapists must remain vigilant in keeping therapy intentional and not letting themselves fall into a pattern of codependency in which clients continue to see the therapist simply because they have always seen the therapist. In this way, therapists may inadvertently enable dependency and contribute to clients' lack of autonomy and progress and dysfunction. The tendency toward codependence may be even more pronounced when clients can easily access therapists by VC (Drum & Littleton, 2014). Lastly, when clients are terminating therapy because they have met their treatment goals, it is important to celebrate this as a positive accomplishment and a reflection of their growth—in these cases, termination of the therapeutic relationship is an indication that things are going well for the client. Clients should be reminded that therapy is a life-long resource that they can return to, should additional needs arise. For clients who are terminating for other reasons such, as clinical fit or inability to commit to the therapeutic process, it is standard practice to provide referrals and a follow up plan, even in remote practices (Norcross et al., 2017). One of the benefits of technology is that today's follow-up plans may now also include digital and virtual resources, such as helpful apps, relevant podcasts, or even games, to continue specific work outside of therapy.

CONCLUSION

As mentioned in Chapter 1, before the widespread use of TMH during the COVID-19 pandemic, there were prevailing misconceptions about TMH, and the default belief was that in-person treatment was safer, more effective, and ultimately superior to virtual options. The research suggests otherwise—telemental health appears to be a safe and effective option for a wide range of people. This does not mean that teletherapy is the same as in-person therapy or that it does not come with its own challenges. Indeed, there are multiple clinical considerations in TMH, yet the heart of therapy—the therapeutic relationship—remains the same. Therapists must be intentional about *how* they convey their therapeutic presence online because therapists' presence is a primary contributing factor to the therapeutic relationship. One of the gifts of teletherapy is that it presents an opportunity to be open to new and perhaps more intentional ways of engaging with clients. In the next chapters, we will discuss existing and emerging ways that therapists are engaging in psychotherapy that challenge the status quo to meet the needs of today's clients.

4

WELLNESS APPROACHES AND OUT-OF-OFFICE THERAPIES

Thus far, this text has focused on teletherapy and the changes in psychotherapy as we all increasingly rely on technology and inhabit more digital spaces. Another area of evolution in therapy has been the prioritization of wellness and increased integration of overall health and well-being. As mentioned in the Introduction, the wellness industry has exploded in the past decade. Therapists are increasingly locating the practice of psychotherapy as a healing science and art within both health and wellness spaces. This is also being reflected in how many therapists are integrating wellness into their personal and professional lives. One need only notice the increasingly common dual credentials of "psychotherapist and yoga teacher" to appreciate the linkage. Therapy now appears to be more wellness centered, and it is also more common to see therapy move beyond the confines of the therapy office to nature-based settings and home environments. In these ways, therapy is evolving into a practice that is not confined to place and is capable of reaching more people by being in the service of public wellness, not just the reduction of symptoms for the few who are lucky enough to access mental health. With the rise of wellness-centered perspectives, spiritual integration, and out-of-office approaches to therapy come new clinical and practice management considerations. In this chapter, we will delve deeper into what it means to have a holistic or wellness practice as well as into approaches for safely and effectively working outside of the office while continuing to serve our client's well-being.

HOLISTIC AND WELLNESS-BASED THERAPIES

Holistic psychotherapy is a broad, commonly used term that refers to an overarching whole-person philosophy or perspective that views the mind–body–spirit as interconnected (Zencare, 2020). Holistic psychotherapy can be viewed as distinct from traditional models of psychotherapy, which are rooted in Western allopathic medicine designed to diagnose and treat mental illness. Instead, holistic psychotherapy often includes complementary and alternative medicines and centers on the whole person, the person's strengths, and ways to move the person to optimal health, not just the absence of symptoms (Barnett & Shale, 2012). A state of wellness moves beyond the absence of disease and refers instead to an affirmative state with the presence of physical and mental well-being indicators, such as strength, happiness, optimism, and resilience (Jain & Jain, 2019). Research supports several benefits to mental wellness. Higher degrees of mental wellness result in better overall functioning, specifically better physical (e.g., sleeping, eating, exercise) and mental health (e.g., less depression and anxiety, higher resilience), better interpersonal relationships, and greater work productivity (Barnett & Shale, 2012; Jain & Jain, 2019).

References to holistic psychotherapy have become far more commonplace yet are seldom clearly defined. It is even more difficult to assess how therapists are incorporating holistic therapies into their work with clients. The ambiguous use of the term "holistic therapy" may be confusing to clients because they may have specific expectations for "wellness" approaches that may not be aligned with a therapist's "holistic therapy" services. This lack of a clear definition may be due to the fact that most training programs focus on the diagnosis and treatment of mental illness, not the promotion of health. Counseling programs usually focus on typical development and a strengths-based approach. Yet in general, training on how to implement a wellness-centered model of therapy is not standard in graduate counseling and psychology programs. Thus, many therapists who identify as holistic or wellness-centered may not adhere to a particular theory of wellness, which may result in less intentional, or even haphazard, integration and application of wellness into counseling. Even more worrisome, some therapists may begin to use wellness terminology or broad notions of spirituality for marketing purposes though they have little training or competence in these areas of care. Consider, the following situation:

Margaret has been a therapist for about 5 years but only recently became licensed because she had a number of personal barriers to acquiring the necessary supervised clinical hours. She recently decided to open a part-time private practice to supplement her income from working in community mental health. Margaret sublet an office in an affluent neighborhood but found that the area was saturated with therapists, many of whom had been practicing for much longer than she had. To differentiate herself and try to market her services to a more defined group, Margaret began to describe her services as "holistic therapy, with your health in mind." She sent emails and placed cards at several popular private workout facilities, at nutritionist and acupuncture offices, and at weight loss clinics. She began to receive new referrals from colleagues as well as clients directly seeking counseling related to health issues. Margaret felt confident in her ability to provide broad support but did not have any training in this area.

Clearly, there are some ethical issues with Margaret practicing outside her areas of competence and not having completed professional development to competently provide this type of therapy. However, Margaret is not alone. While therapists need not be a certified yoga instructor to integrate breathing into therapy, many of us may not have received continuing education or other types of professional development to help inform this model of care. There have been several early wellness models and there is a robust body of research to guide therapists in conceptualizing clients' presenting issues and overall needs from a wellness perspective and, more importantly, to help guide therapists in wellness-centered interventions to promote client health. Jain and Jain (2019) introduced their WILD 5 wellness program, in which they used the empirical research on psychological health and well-being to identify five mental wellness elements along with several interventions that therapists can use to promote health in their clients. While their model comprises a complete 30- or 90-day plan that can be worked with or without a therapist, having the support of a therapist may be most effective, especially for clients who have difficulty with change or with consistently engaging in healthful behaviors. Moreover, using the WILD 5 recommendations or implementing another wellness plan may be a streamlined way to integrate a wellness model into one's existing therapeutic approach. The WILD 5 model identifies five critical elements of wellness: exercise, nutrition, sleep hygiene, mindfulness, and social connectedness.

WILD 5 (Jain & Jain, 2019)

Exercise
- 30 minutes daily of moderate intensity exercise

Nutrition
- Incorporate the Mediterranean diet
- Log all meals, snacks, beverages

Sleep
- Engage in at least four of the six sleep hygiene practices:
- Avoid all electronic devices for 90 minutes before bedtime
- Avoid daytime napping
- Eliminate ambient light in the bedroom
- Enjoy a warm relaxing bath or shower prior to bedtime
- Establish and maintain a regular bedtime each night
- Avoid caffeinated drinks 10 hours before bedtime

Mindfulness
- Practice at least 10 minutes per day

Social Connectedness
- Meet or talk with at least two friends or family members per day

Let us briefly consider the components of the WILD 5 model. Most therapists are familiar with the robust body of research that clearly demonstrates the mental health benefits of exercise. Engaging in psychoeducation with clients about the positive benefits of exercise can be informative and can motivate them to exercise specifically as a mental and physical health benefit. Encourage clients to engage in moderate intensity exercise for at least 30 minutes daily because the additional support and accountability in therapy may increase the likelihood that a client will start or maintain the practice (Jain & Jain, 2019; Sharma et al., 2006; Weir, 2011). Nutrition also affects mental health, yet many therapists find that they avoid assessments or interventions focused on improving nutrition. Research has demonstrated a positive correlation between nutrition and positive mental health (Lassale et al., 2019). Specifically, a Mediterranean diet has been associated with higher amounts of happiness, resilience, and energy (Lassale et al., 2019; Jain & Jain, 2019) in addition to the physical health benefits. The authors of the WILD 5 model highly recommend that clients adhere to a Mediterranean diet and log all meals, snacks, and beverages. Some therapists may feel uncomfortable discussing nutrition or coaching clients in this area, perhaps because it is outside of their expertise. Certainly, therapists should be mindful to adhere to the ethical requirement that they not practice outside of their expertise nor provide medical advising. Having said that, therapists may find themselves eschewing the power and influence they have that could be used to promote good health in clients. Therapists may inadvertently hide behind ethical codes to avoid what they determine to be outside of the scope of therapy. Yet, even mere psychoeducation about the effects of nutrition on mental health might be just the additional information and support that a client needs to engage in healthier behavior. Providing clients with nutrition information, connection to health-centered apps, or referrals to nutritionists they know may not only improve client health but also foster collaborative and integrative care. Some clients may not want or need to see a nutritionist but may be open to thinking about or integrating nutrition into their overall therapy treatment plan. A therapist's avoidance of intentional assessment and ongoing discussion about nutrition might constitute a missed opportunity to promote wellness with clients. Given the role of nutrition in mental health, not addressing nutrition may reduce potential progress toward client goals. Moreover, today's therapists must be willing to consider the needs and expectations of a more health-conscious and wellness-centered client demographic to remain both relevant and helpful.

Sleep is also a component of wellness that is addressed in the WILD 5 model. Discussions of sleep hygiene have long been an important aspect of psychotherapy, especially in the treatment of depression and anxiety (Freeman et al., 2017). Given the marked increase of sleep disturbance since the beginning of the pandemic (Hurley, 2020), increasing our knowledge and intentional support in this area is even more imperative. Providing clients with the directives proffered in the WILD 5 model as well as monitoring and supporting progress with it may increase the client's integration of these daily practices. Again, application of appropriate technology—such as through the use of common phone and fitness watch features, apps, and even sleep journals—may help clients integrate healthy habits. Also included in this model is mindfulness, an area of psychology and psychotherapy whose use has exploded in recent years. Because of its widespread popularity, mindfulness will be discussed more in detail below. Lastly, the Jains name social connectedness as an essential element of wellness. An emphasis on social connectedness may be even more important during and after a time of protracted social distancing, during which many people experienced extended times with limited or no physical contact with loved ones, working from home, and marked increases in digital social interactions coupled with marked decreases in in-person interactions. The immediate effect of these social changes has been an acute increase in mental health symptoms; the long-term effects are still unfolding. Clearly, social connectedness is important for our physical health and mental well-being (Seppala, 2020). Social support and connectedness are associated with better health outcomes and, at a minimum, remind us that we are not alone. Thus, intentional inclusion of social connectedness and the therapist's prescription for specific amounts of social engagement may support clients to intentionally engage in this practice. Let's briefly consider the integration of this model in this brief case scenario:

Sharon is a 42-year-old Jewish woman who decided to seek counseling after years of failed relationships and what she described as "low-grade depression." Sharon was successful in her career, working as an attorney for a nonprofit, but felt that she had focused on her career to the detriment of everything else. She had friends but realized that they lacked depth or any real intimacy. They primarily got together for dinner or happy hour. With the onset of the pandemic and no separation between home and work, Sharon found herself working even more hours and lonelier than ever. During the pandemic, Sharon became clear that she wanted a partner and family and became committed to developing a healthier and more balanced life. She wasn't sure exactly what to do but set out to become mentally healthier, and she needed help to do so.

In this case, Sharon is clearly seeking wellness and optimal functioning, particularly in creating balance in her life. Sharon is a prime candidate for wellness integrated into her overall therapy plan. The structure of the WILD 5 model might be a good fit for someone who, like Sharon, is seeking clear and tangible direction around how to move forward in different aspects of her health and well-being. Integrating the WILD 5 program with supportive therapy may allow Sharon to better understand her prior avoidance of intimacy and how to reconnect with herself and with others. A structured plan to integrate these five elements of wellness may feel more tangible and less overwhelming for someone new to these practices. For example, if Sharon is accustomed to ordering delivery instead of cooking, having structured guidance around nutrition, diet, and cooking may help to make the switch to making meals at home feel more manageable. From a psychological perspective, understanding Sharon's relationship to food is also of interest. Having a therapist walk through the plan, helping to identify and interrupt negative patterns, can be helpful in fostering sustainable change. The social connection aspect of the model is particularly important, considering Sharon's lack of emotionally intimate relationships. We often fail to adequately locate social connection as a critical aspect of mental and physical wellness. Sharon may benefit from support, and even coaching, in this area.

Most of the wellness practices I've just discussed are part of common health information, yet it is important to remember that 1) some clients may not have access to this information, particularly as it relates to their mental wellness; 2) integration of this information into therapy may help increase health literacy for clients; and 3) therapists may benefit from the structure of this or other models to help them integrate wellness more intentionally into a holistic treatment plan. Lastly, it may be helpful to remind ourselves that while a wellness orientation is not new, indeed it is ancient, it serves as a radical departure from the ways in which many therapists have been trained. To this end, traditionally trained therapists may find themselves defaulting to diagnosis and symptom reduction in lieu of a model that seeks to move clients beyond the mere absence of symptoms. In so doing, we limit the potential of therapy to promote overall health and well-being and may inadvertently minimize or eschew the connection between mind and body.

Mindfulness

Mindfulness, as applied to secular psychology, refers to a conscious and nonjudgmental awareness of the moment (Germer et al., 2013). Mindfulness invites us to be aware of our thoughts in the moment without adhering to or judging a right or wrong way to think or believe. This awareness of one's thoughts, feelings, and experience of the now is in contrast to the habitual autopilot or mindlessness that characterizes many of our states of being. With origins in Buddhism and Hinduism, mindfulness is not new, despite its more recent popularity in the West and specifically within mental health. It was popularized in psychology through the work of Jon Kabat Zinn, the founder of the Mindfulness Based Stress Reduction program (also known as MBSR). Since that time, research on the physical and mental health benefits of mindfulness have abounded. Physically, mindfulness can boost our immune system, improve sleep quality, and even change the parts of the brain associated with attention, memory, and emotional regulation (Davidson et al., 2003). The mental health benefits are even more remarkable. Mindfulness can reduce stress and negative emotions and foster emotional well-being (Weinstein et al., 2009). Further, it can help improve focus, attention, and decision-making abilities. Particularly important is the improvement in the ways we see ourselves and in our ability to be more compassionate with others, including partners (Carson et al., 2004). Relatedly, Dan Siegel, known for fathering interpersonal neurobiology, coined the term *mindsight*, which refers to the combination of one's insight into their own interior world (thoughts and feelings) and one's perspective of or empathy for others (Siegel, 2010). A thorough explanation of the neurobiology of mindfulness is outside the scope of this book, yet, it warrants mentioning here that, beyond the benefits described above, mindfulness increases the expansive neural network in our brains called the *connectome* (Siegel, 2010). This is especially significant because the level of integration of the connectome has been found to be the best predictor of well-being (Siegel, 2017). Overall, the mental, physical, and interpersonal benefits of mindfulness are near countless, and mindfulness has been deemed to have value across groups and in multiple settings.

This compelling research suggests that we may be moving toward accepting some form of mindfulness integration as a best practice in psychotherapy. It would not be surprising if mindfulness became a required aspect of psychotherapist training and/or continuing education. While mindfulness based stress reduction and mindfulness based cognitive therapy have structured ways in which mindfulness is integrated and employed, there are multiple ways that mindfulness can be cultivated individually or integrated into any form of therapy. There are also specific practices, such as meditation, breathing exercises, and yoga, that therapists can prescribe for clients that can help cultivate mindfulness (Jain & Jain, 2019). Therapists may encourage clients to use easily accessible apps to help them get started with specific mindfulness practices. Yet, it is noteworthy that mindfulness meditation and mindfulness in therapy are not synonymous. Many of the mindfulness practices mentioned can be prescribed and practiced outside of therapy, yet therapy does not stop at awareness of thoughts. Rather, a primary benefit of bringing the benefits of mindfulness to therapy or incorporating mindfulness within therapy is to *use* that awareness and those insights in service of client goals. For example, through meditation or mindful journaling at home, a client might become more aware of specific beliefs about themselves or their life. Therapy does not stop at the awareness of these underlying beliefs and thoughts. This is where the work really begins, as therapists delve deeper to sit with, understand, disrupt, and transmute any negativity into something more positive and healing for the client. Mindfulness can also be a way to allow clients to become open and present to whatever thoughts and emotions emerge yet not become overwhelmed by it in the moment (Siegel,

2010). To this end, some therapists now teach mindfulness strategies that clients can employ to promote emotional regulation, reduce overall anxiety and/or to disrupt negative thinking during times of heightened anxiety.

The therapist's own personal mindfulness practice may shape how wellness-centered we are open to being with clients. Specifically, our awareness of the moment might better allow us to be present in the moment with clients and to use immediacy as a source of engagement and intervention with clients. For example:

> *"When you began talking about your dad, I could feel the sadness and tension rise. I noticed that your voice changes when you talk about him. I'm wondering if we can pause for a moment and sit together with this. Can you go back to that thought of your dad and just return to your breath and your body. What do you notice?"*

Research suggests that therapists who engage in mindfulness meditation may have a greater sense of well-being and lower burnout rates (Davis & Hayes, 2011). Moreover, many of these therapists report an expansive sense of compassion and empathy, which positively shapes their relationship and work with clients.

Body- and Movement-Based Therapies

Body-centered, or body-first, therapies are often considered a branch of the more well-known somatic psychotherapy. Foundational to somatic psychotherapy is the idea that there is a functional unity or sameness to body and mind (United States Association of Body Psychotherapy, n.d.). Somatic psychotherapy is identified as a holistic model of therapy in that it incorporates mind, body, spirit, and emotions in understanding health, dysfunction, and the healing process. Body-centered approaches value and center on the bidirectional and dynamic relationship that exists between the physical body and one's overall psychological well-being (United States Association of Body Psychotherapy, n.d.). Thus, somatic therapies invite therapist and client to identify and use the body's innate wisdom as information about how and where in the body a client might be holding unresolved pain. Somatic approaches have become increasingly popular, especially in the treatment of trauma. Somatic experiencing is described as a type of body-first therapy in which clients attune to the physical and sensorial bodily experience beneath their feelings to illuminate the ways a trauma survivor might be stuck in an activated crisis response (Brom et al., 2017; Levine & Crane-Godreau, 2015). Somatic experiencing therapy uses knowledge gained from how animals physically discharge trauma to help clients to physically release the tension they are holding and their unresolved trauma. Some somatic sessions may primarily include body work, whereas other sessions may rely more on talk therapy and verbalizing issues. Which method is used depends largely on the specific body-therapy modality being employed, the client's presenting issues, and the therapist's treatment plan (United States Association of Body Psychotherapy, n.d.).

Many therapists—especially those who identify as holistic therapists—are becoming increasingly aware of a need to integrate some amount of body consciousness in psychotherapy. While body-centered therapies are becoming increasingly common, there are ethical and legal considerations with these approaches. First, while many therapists who integrate a body-centered approach do not engage in touch with the client, some do. This presents concerns about appropriate boundaries with clients. This may also have complex effects on the clinical relationship, given the varied meaning and experience of touch by clients, which may be even more pronounced with clients with trauma histories. Even for body-centered therapists who incorporate yoga and movement into therapy, there are distinct considerations around risks. Ethics regarding this will be discussed more in Chapter 7.

Nature-Based and Outdoor Approaches

Even before the health-risks associated with practicing therapy within an enclosed office due to COVID-19, therapists were beginning to move therapy outdoors or to integrate nature into some aspects of psychotherapy. Many practitioners go on walks with clients or prescribe nature-based activities based on their own personal experiences or intuitive knowing rather than on formal knowledge of or training in ecotherapy. This makes sense, given the lack of inclusion of ecotherapy or other nature-based approaches in traditional training. Ecotherapy is grounded in ecopsychological theory and focuses on a client's relationship to nature (Hasbach, 2013). Ecotherapists contend that we are often disconnected from nature and its therapeutic benefits, especially given the rise in reliance on technology and urban lifestyles (Hasbach, 2013). Engaging in nature-based sessions or integrating nature into therapy are ways not only to connect clients to nature, but also to use nature as a therapeutic metaphor. In her explication of the benefits of outdoor therapy, Hasbach (2013) identifies heightened sensory awareness and attunement with nature; mindfulness of the moment; benefits of spontaneous interactions with and occurrences in nature; and becoming an additional witness to the client's narrative as benefits of ecotherapy. Nature becomes a therapeutic partner who also holds space for the client, their woundedness, and their healing (Hasbach, 2013). Since the beginning of the COVID-19 pandemic, there has been greater interest in and attention to outdoor activities, such as camping, hiking, and travel to national and state parks. Thus, there may be an even greater interest in nature-based therapy as the pandemic continues and even beyond.

Other benefits of nature-based therapy include the egalitarian power-sharing that organically occurs when meeting in a space that does not belong to either client or therapist. In walk-and-talk therapy, which can occur in any outdoor environment, it is theorized that the mind and body are integrating through the dual processes of engaging in the physical labor of walking and the cognitive and emotional labor of verbally processing client information (Gritzka et al., 2020). Some therapists argue that clients may be better able to be vulnerable and more open when walking side-by-side instead of being contained in the therapy office, pressured to sit across from and look directly at the therapist (DeAngelis, 2013).

Critics of this model problematize this more egalitarian approach as being fertile ground for boundary issues in therapy (Dockett, 2019). For example, some worry that a therapist might be too relaxed or distracted by nature and thus miss important clinical information. Certainly, ecotherapy may not be appropriate for all clients and presenting issues. Not all therapists will necessarily be inclined to engage in therapy in natural settings, and this venue may not always be practical. There are also ways to engage in ecotherapy that do not require leaving the office, such as by intentionally integrating nature-based lessons or metaphors or by greening the office

(Hasbach, 2013). Greening the office refers to intentionally bringing elements of nature, such as plants, water, shells, or rocks, into the office.

For therapists who do not identify as ecotherapists or who do not themselves spend a lot of time in nature, conducting sessions outdoors or integrating nature into sessions may feel daunting. There are theories and tools to guide therapists considering or reflecting on ways to integrate ecotherapy or engage in nature-based work. One of the most well-known theories is Reese and Myers' EcoWellness Model. This model includes seven domains of wellness. Unlike Jain and Jain's (2019) model, the ecowellness model centers nature as an important aspect of wellness. Rather than present this model in its entirety, it might be helpful to consider the three primary dimensions of EcoWellness and how they might be useful in conceptualizing client issues and well-being as well as potential ways to integrate nature-based practices into your work. The first dimension is *access to nature*, which refers to the client's environmental conditions and not only the extent to which they have access to nature, such as green space, but also the extent to which they are exposed to or surrounded by environmental toxins (Reese & Myers, 2012). Therapists can assess the access to nature dimension by asking clients about their neighborhoods, housing, and available green space (e.g., backyard, garden). This information provides helpful information on potential environmental stressors and how these contribute to, interact with, or compound the client's presenting issues. In addition, this information allows the therapist to better understand the natural resources around the client that may be integrated into counseling to promote wellness.

The second dimension is *environmental identity* (Reese & Myers, 2012). This dimension focuses on the extent to which someone is connected with or drawn to natural environments. Having a positive orientation toward nature is associated with positive well-being. The orientation can be assessed by asking clients how they feel about outdoor and/or nature-based activities, such as camping, hiking, gardening. The third dimension of EcoWellness is *transcendence*, which refers to experiences of positive self-transcendence, such as awe, heightened awareness of and connection to nature or a Higher Power, connection to others, and feelings of love and peace. Reese and Myers (2012) offer these questions to consider integrating in work with clients:

- How has being in nature affected your relationships with others in your life?
- How does time spent in nature affect your sense of community with others?
- How does being in nature affect your ability to connect with something bigger than yourself?

Consider the following case example:

> **Kat** is a 26-year-old white woman who presented to counseling primarily with relational and work-related stress. For about a year, Kat had been in a relationship that she described as "complicated." The relationship was very passionate, and they enjoyed spending time with friends and going to various social events. Yet, they both had insecurities, and her partner was often quick to become jealous, which resulted in frequent conflicts. Kat had also recently begun a new job that required longer hours, and she felt that her career was going nowhere. The relational conflict coupled with job stress left Kat feeling anxious and pessimistic, which were not her usual ways of being. Kat was spending less time visiting her family and friends back home, a few hours away, and consequently she felt disconnected from them as well. Kat sought counseling for what she believed was likely depression and anxiety. Certainly, Kat was right to seek out counseling as a supportive resource as she navigated the multiple stressors in her life.

Many therapists have clients like Kat who present with work and relational stress. We may not initially consider if or how a connection to or disconnection from nature may be a factor in the client's presenting issues or a potential resource in therapy. Recall that there are specific questions that can be added to intake paperwork or existing questions that can be revised to assess this aspect of wellness. For example, asking Kat about her family and background resulted in her sharing that while she was growing up, she lived in "the middle of nowhere." She stated that this was difficult for her socially but that daily she spent hours outdoors in a forest.

Because it was a coastal area, she also frequently spent time on the beach, swimming or just collecting seashells. While Kat loved living in the city now, she often missed the quiet of the forest, which she described as her "happy place." This background information is essential, not only from an ecotherapy framework but also for understanding the internal and external resources that Kat experiences as helpful. In my work with Kat, I integrated nature in a few ways. First, it was clear that nature was a space that allowed Kat to reset, to come back home to her body, and to reduce overall feelings of disconnection and anxiety. Kat and I discussed ways to better integrate nature into her life, which included trips home but also places she could go locally, such as the park, hills, and a nearby lake. While Kat was excited about this integration, she seldom made space for it; there were often barriers and reasons why or how life got in the way of it. So, we began to schedule nature-based sessions at a park with a pond. After two nature-based sessions, Kat began integrating nature on her own. During our sessions, we incorporated mindfulness practices such as awareness of breath and attunement to thoughts and bodily sensations as she sat in and with nature. We practiced breathing and grounding strategies, walked, and processed Kat's thoughts and feelings about her relationship and career path. We were also able to integrate nature-based metaphors into the counseling. For example, during times when Kat felt unsure about what she was feeling or wanting in her romantic partnership, she would often jokingly say, "what would the trees say?" She began to recognize that it was in nature that she felt centered and witnessed by the forest and hills in ways that allowed her to experience clarity and peace regarding her needs. In this way, Kat began to try to access that same clarity when she was not in nature: she began to create an internalized natural space for herself in other settings.

The benefits of nature-based therapy in this case were evident: Kat experienced less anxiety, felt greater clarity, and regained access to an important resource and coping mechanism. These shifts allowed her to feel better and move toward greater wellness. In addition, she connected to the skills she already possessed so that she could better navigate the relational and work-related stressors she had reported.

There are also challenges and risks associated with nature-based therapy that are important to note. First, prior to moving therapy outside of the office, there are multiple considerations. Namely, the client must consent to it and be made aware of the risks and potential threats to confidentiality. In Kat's case, the chosen location did not involve physically strenuous or potentially dangerous terrain. The ability of the client to walk, hike, or otherwise access the location must be considered. Clients (or therapists) with mobility issues may not be able to safely participate in some or all kinds of nature-based therapy. Thoughtful and intentional selection of location is key. It is prudent to discuss in advance how sensitive conversations or a client becoming emotional should be handled if others are nearby. Ultimately, the client should be reassured that the therapist has a plan and that the therapist will help navigate these challenges. Therapists should have clients sign an additional informed consent that outlines the potential benefits and risks, and the therapist should document any discussion and any concerns in the client's chart. Lastly, therapists will need to consider the amount of time required to travel to and from nature-based settings that are not proximal to the therapist's office. Reflecting on cost of these sessions and billing issues, such as third-party payor restrictions, are also necessary. If these costs or time are different for the client, this must also be made clear to the client before scheduling the session(s).

Nature-Based Therapy Informed Consent Checklist
- ☐ Define nature-based therapy and rationale
- ☐ Potential benefits and risks
    - Is client aware of physical requirements and risks?
    - Is client aware of potential threats to confidentiality?
- ☐ Outline crisis or emergency response plan when not in-office
- ☐ Costs and limits to third-party payment or reimbursement

Wellness and Spirituality

The rise in attention to wellness also coincides with shifts in how people think about religion and spirituality. We are witnessing a generation that largely conceptualizes and practices wellness at the intersection of spirituality. Millennial and Gen Z individuals have largely turned away from organized religion, although two-thirds of Millennials report believing in a Higher Power and many engage in daily prayer (Alper, 2015). For many, practicing wellness is a form of spiritualty. This makes sense when we consider that many wellness practices, such as yoga and meditation, have roots in ancient Asian and African spiritual traditions. New York Magazine (LaRocca, 2019) called Millennials the *Astrology Generation* because of their widespread embracing of astrology, tarot, crystal use, and myriad energy healing practices, such as Reiki. This underscores the theory that even as people turn away from organized religion, they continue to engage in broader wellness and spiritual practices as a way of being connected to the self, to others, and to a Higher Power. New ways of practicing spirituality can also be viewed as a form of technology. People are increasingly using specific tools—including digital tools, like apps and web spaces—to access their interior world, such as consciousness and intuition, as well as to connect to spiritual communities or a Higher Power (Fischer, 2020). While this trend toward using digital tools to access spirituality and spiritual communities has been researched primarily in Millennials and the Gen Z population, we see trends across other demographics. Thus, it is important for therapists to be attuned to the myriad ways in which clients today are searching for meaning and connection. Therapists who do not practice and are not open to the traditions accepted by their clients may inadvertently minimize or even condemn some of the clients' practices. If a therapist marginalizes a client's spiritual practices, the therapist may be perceived as out of touch or judgmental, which is likely to harm clients' openness and vulnerability that is necessary for effective therapy.

HOME-BASED THERAPIES

Home-based therapy, or therapy that takes place in a client's home, has a long history, particularly in social work and family therapy traditions (Boyd-Franklin & Bry, 2000; Zur, 2015). Historically, home-based therapy has been reserved for clients who were physically home-bound or had significant barriers, such as lack of childcare or transportation, to coming into the office (Boyd-Franklin & Bry, 2000). There is increased research, however, supporting the value of out-of-office and home-based approaches to therapy for clients beyond these demographics and across multiple presenting concerns (Zur, 2015). Working with clients within their home environment has distinct benefits. First, being in a client's home balances power dynamics merely by shifting the meeting location. The therapist coming into the client's space instead of the client being in the therapist's office may allow some clients to feel safer and may promote the development of therapeutic rapport. In the home, the therapist is also able to observe the client's living conditions, such as organization, cleanliness, and available resources. In addition, neighborhood and community issues can also be observed, such as safety, interpersonal dynamics, and available supports or stressors. Being able to personally witness the client's environment allows the therapist to better understand the dynamic relationship between the client and their environment in ways that are not possible when the client merely describes these things.

In the home environment, the therapist is also able to observe partner and family dynamics in real time (Boyd-Franklin & Bry, 2000). While some of these dynamics may manifest in the therapy office, they may occur organically and more spontaneously in the home environment. Working in the home environment may also allow for interventions that are possible only within the home. For example, if working with a parent and child on specific dynamics that present during the evening routine, being able to observe the evening routine and intervene in vivo is significantly different than listening to their description of the issues and discussing or even role playing what to do in the future. Being with clients in the moment and place of conflict allows the therapist to disrupt entrenched dynamics or patterns of behavior and allows the client to experience a different outcome. Moreover, the therapist and client can debrief and process what the change was like in the moment. This same shift may take substantially longer if relying only on in-office treatment, especially if the clients are resistant or have barriers to engaging in the difficult behavior at home.

While there are many benefits to working with clients in their home environments, it may not be appropriate for all clients nor be a fit for all therapists. Working in the home with clients who have issues with impulse control, violence, or aggressive behavior, clients who are actively engaging in substance abuse, or clients who experience abuse or domestic violence may present potential safety threats to either or both the therapist and the client. Careful screening is required to determine clinical appropriateness for home-based therapy. Some therapists who engage in home-based therapy may conduct an initial intake session in the office or by video prior to going into the client's home environment. This practice allows the therapist to conduct a comprehensive clinical interview and assess whether home therapy is suitable for the client. In clients with histories of aggressive behavior, having been in treatment or having had a long period of sobriety may reduce the therapist's concern about the client's suitability for home-based therapy. In addition to performing the clinical assessment, it is important that the therapist and client discuss boundaries and expectations prior to beginning home-based therapy. For example, clients should be made aware that therapy should occur at a kitchen table or living room area. Since the pandemic, many people may still prefer an outdoor area, if possible. Privacy and confidentiality should also be discussed, especially if other family members will be home during sessions.

Despite the benefits of home-based therapy for the therapeutic process, it may not be a good fit for all therapists. Take a moment to reflect on the following questions:

Pause | Reflect

- What comes to mind when you think of home-based therapy?
- Would you engage in home-based therapy? Why or why not?
- With which clients or types of clients would you consider engaging in home-based therapy?
- Consider the home and neighborhood environments. Are there particular types of homes, types of spaces, or specific neighborhoods in which you would be more comfortable conducting home therapy? Why? Consider what this is about for you and what your responses say about your sense of safety and comfort.
- Take a moment and think of one of your current clients. Select a client with whom you have worked for some time or with issues

that do not feel particularly challenging to you. Consider your relationship with that client, their presenting issues, and your interpersonal dynamics, including in the therapeutic relationship. Now imagine going into this client's home. What might that feel like? What different information would you have? How might therapy with that client be different if conducted in their home? Why do you think these differences would emerge?

• Now consider a current or previous client that was challenging in some way. Perhaps it was difficult for you to connect or access empathy with this client. Perhaps the client was guarded and defensive or triggered personal issues for you. Again, imagine going into this client's home. What comes to mind? What would be different?

Your responses to this reflection exercise will reveal a lot about your conceptions of home-based therapy as well as how comfortable you might be seeing clients in *their* space. Your ideas and experience of safety are connected to what feels familiar and to your social definitions of neighborhood and community safety. People are often more comfortable, and thus report feeling safer, in areas that are more familiar or where they blend in racially or economically (Cho & Ho, 2018). Would you feel uncomfortable or unsafe visiting a client in a lower-income neighborhood or a predominantly Black or Latinx community? Would you feel uncomfortable or unsafe visiting a client in a high-income neighborhood or a community of primarily white people? Are you triggered by thinking of conducting therapy in smaller spaces, such as a small apartment, or exceedingly large spaces? Does the thought of going into the home of someone who is very privileged or very underprivileged trigger you? Your discomfort with in-home therapy may arise from fear, shame, or implicit biases to which you need to attend as part of ongoing personal development.

This reflection exercise may have allowed you to more carefully consider your clients and how your relationship or work together might shift if you met in their home environment. Some of us may immediately identify ways in which the therapeutic relationship might deepen or how we might be able to enact specific interventions in a different way in the home environment. Others may immediately think of the environmental barriers to successful in-home therapy, such as distractions (e.g., others in the household or pets) or issues around privacy or our own comfort engaging with or challenging clients in the same way at their kitchen table.

Honestly, some of us therapists engage in our best work within the confines of the therapy office and may find it difficult to be flexible and adaptive in the face of the distractions that occur in someone's home. Others may have difficulty fostering depth of engagement outside of the office. It is important to note that some therapists may feel less comfortable and less confident about their skills in this area because most of them weren't trained to think of clients' homes as appropriate or valued spaces for therapy. We may automatically relegate home therapy to social workers and deem that in-home therapy is not "real" therapy. Yet as mentioned, for some clients, the home environment might be the location where the most effective work can occur. Home can become a sacred location for change. For other clients, the home environment may subvert therapy efforts due to the lack of safety, the lack of freedom of possibilities, and the presence of abuse. Some therapists may not want to practice only within clients' homes but would be open to integrating home-based work into their practice model. As with nature-based sessions, home-based therapy may be offered on a case-by-case basis or as is clinically necessary for clients. Some clients may receive therapy only in the home, whereas other clients may be seen only within the office. This flexibility and the adaptive nature of session location may be appealing to many clients, which may be a way to establish a niche practice or stand out among other local practitioners.

ETHICS AND OUT-OF-OFFICE THERAPY

There are distinct ethics and practice management considerations for therapists who include out-of-office therapy, such as nature-based settings or client homes, as one of their services. From a strictly risk-management perspective, many therapists are advised against offering out-of-office services. Yet, times have changed, and perspectives of what therapy looks like and where it occurs are evolving. Ethical issues will be discussed in more detail in Chapter 7. However, it is worth noting here that when the service is clinically indicated, remains professional, and the rationale is justified, therapists may feel comfortable proceeding intentionally, seeking consultation when necessary, and consistently documenting client suitability for this form of therapy. The decision to engage in out-of-office treatment requires the therapist be able to think through potential pitfalls, challenges, and ethical concerns, such as limits to privacy. Maintaining clear communication with the client about their comfort and any concerns the client may have is also essential. Ethics evolve with the field, so as the field moves forward, there may be changes in the ethical guidelines around this work. Therapists who integrate specific wellness practices and who engage in out-of-office therapy should also ensure that liability insurance extends to these practices.

There are also benefits to practicing in-home therapy in terms of practice management. Like teletherapy, engaging in home-based therapy may reduce overhead costs because the therapist would not need a physical location. On the other hand, some of the *necessary* costs may be less obvious, for example, the costs of using a car, including its maintenance, gas, parking, or tolls, must be considered. Estimating the amount of time spent in traffic is also important to quantify because this contributes to time (and money) lost. While therapists could theoretically use public transportation and ride sharing, this option may be less available or less reliable in some cities. In addition, therapists must consider storage of files, documents, or any other confidential client information. While many therapists may have moved to online or digital systems of managing and storing client information, therapists who still maintain physical files must consider where and how to ethically and securely store these files. Scheduling, drive time, and billing are also considerations. Strategic planning of clients with regard to time of day and geographic proximity may help mitigate issues of time and distance between clients. Relatedly, if clients live in areas where there are specific safety concerns for the therapist, being intentional about when appointments are scheduled may help foster a sense of safety. Lastly, therapists should respect boundaries and cultural considerations when practicing in home-based settings. It is common for people to offer guests a drink or something to eat. When practicing in a therapist's office, the therapist is rarely on the receiving end of such an offer. Some therapists may feel uncomfortable accepting drinks or food from a client, but it may be considered rude to not do so when one is a guest in someone's home. For therapists and clients alike, home-based therapy may feel less formal, especially after spending increased amounts of time in someone's home. This comfort and familiarity can be used to deepen the therapeutic relationship and work in service of the client's counseling goals and the promotion of wellness. It is important that this comfort not shift boundaries in ways that are counterproductive to counseling or that invite the potential for harm to the client or the therapeutic relationship.

CONCLUSION

Wellness and out-of-office approaches to therapy hold great promise. These approaches appear to be aligned with the direction of many people across age groups who are becoming more health conscious and/or those who practice wellness at the intersection of spirituality. Such an approach to therapy may be appealing, especially to Millennial and Gen X individuals. The research on wellness practices, especially mindfulness, is substantial and may be moving toward an established best practice in therapy. This may result in required training for new and continuing therapists. Given the ethical and clinical concerns about in-office therapy, the advent of nature-based therapy is timely and may hold a new appeal to therapists and clients who may have not previously considered it. In light of the global concern about contracting COVID-19 and the increased attention to overall health during, and likely following, the pandemic, an increased attention to health and wellness in therapy remains essential. When locating therapy within wellness spaces, however, it is important to also be aware of the criticism of the wellness industry as being predominantly white while profiting from cultural appropriation of other groups. Therapists must ensure that as we move from one industry, criticized for its reductionism and failure to employ a holistic understanding of human experiences, we don't trade that for different yet equally troubling and problematic issues.

5

CONCIERGE THERAPY

Retainers. Membership Fees. Subscription-based pricing. VIP therapy. Fewer clients and more money. Is this the future of psychotherapy? Thus far in this text, we have been discussing ways that psychotherapy has been evolving to make it *more* accessible. Yet, another way that psychotherapy may be expanding is through greater interest in and use of concierge therapy. Prior to COVID-19, there had been a marked interest in personalized therapeutic services. The concierge model of therapy has increased in popularity in recent years and offers multiple benefits for both therapists and clients. Through membership fees, greater access to the therapist, faster response times, flexibility in scheduling, location, and duration of services, concierge therapists seek to provide a more individualized client experience than traditional therapy. Concierge therapists may be able to see fewer clients, thereby reducing their overall caseloads and increase revenue outside of managed care systems. This allows for increased attention to individual clients and greater focus on and the integration of many of the wellness and holistic models of psychological well-being discussed in Chapter 4.

Definitions and models of concierge therapy can vary. In general, one can think of it as having a psychologist or other mental health professional on retainer. This unique therapeutic relationship provides clients and therapists with the flexibility to cocreate a plan that meets their therapy and overall life goals. Sessions may be held in clients' homes, clients' or therapists' offices, or other locations for increased flexibility, privacy, and personalized care. A combination of services may be offered, which can include counseling, psychoeducation, coaching or motivational practices, or integration of wellness services, such as mindfulness and meditation, to create calm and order in life. With the added flexibility afforded by concierge services, consultations or check-ins can be done as needed using telehealth modalities, such as phone, text, email, or video. Before the pandemic, more practicing therapists were adding concierge therapy to their provided services. While the need for mental health providers across sectors is likely to remain high given the mental health crisis that continues to unfold, it is unclear how the economic repercussions of the pandemic will affect the market for concierge therapy. In addition, elite models of medicine came under extreme scrutiny during the height of the pandemic, when there has been a necessary prioritization of public health. Even as there is advocacy for increased access to quality mental health and for offering a model of care that is appealing to a wider range of consumers, there are therapists (and clients) who likely will remain interested in concierge therapy. Yet, there remains a dearth of literature providing direction and guidelines for concierge practitioners. In this chapter, I will introduce concierge therapy and discuss helpful considerations in this complex practice.

BACKGROUND

In the late 1990s in Seattle, a group of frustrated primary care physicians sought to innovate primary health care by offering patients an elite healthcare experience in which they received faster, more personalized care (Weise, 2014). Initially, they referred to this as "highly attentive medicine" (Weise, 2014, n.p.). Access to this service required high monthly retainers or recurring membership fees in addition to the standard fees for service. Concierge medicine was popular with physicians who were tired of the bureaucracy of medicine, of low reimbursement rates, and of the widening gap between specialists and primary care physicians (Clark et al., 2010). Affluent patients who were paying high insurance premiums but received limited contact with their physician desired increased time with their provider and found this elite model of healthcare appealing. You have seen advertisements or joined concierge health and wellness centers. They often appeal to wellness-oriented consumers due to their spa-like settings. While still in its infancy, concierge healthcare has grown in popularity, including expanding to mental health care. Since expanding to mental health care, there has been much interest and variation in services provided. Like early physicians drawn to concierge medicine, many mental health providers express similar frustrations with low insurance reimbursement rates and overall constraints in the parameters of clinical treatment within managed care (Babayan, 2015). Most therapists who work with insurance carriers can relate to this sentiment. Many therapists may have intentionally transitioned to a fee-for-practice model because of these issues. Thus, it makes sense that concierge therapy may appeal to therapists seeking greater freedom and flexibility in the care they provide.

Though concierge medicine has begun to extend to the mental health field, there has not been a consensus about a primary method of practicing concierge therapy. Thus, this area is ripe with opportunity as there are currently multiple ways to practice. Some therapists no longer require membership fees, and some even accept insurance. Others seek to offer clients a premier experience through greater flexibility in scheduling, location of services, longer sessions, or little-to-no wait for an appointment. Many concierge practices integrate wellness services and leverage technology to provide a range of services or 24/7 access to a therapist (Lynch, 2012). Some therapists offer only concierge therapy while others have integrated limited concierge service into their overall practice.

Concierge therapy has historically been associated with more affluent populations yet may be more accessible than when it was first introduced in the medical community. Like telehealth and virtual therapies, the growth of concierge practices appears to be related to shifts in healthcare and the ways that young adults especially value choice and personalized services even in healthcare. Because many individuals are now responsible for increased individual contributions to their health care costs (e.g., health insurance premiums, higher deductibles, etc.), many consumers may be more open to paying out of pocket to have access to the type of care they desire. In addition, recent research estimates that approximately 30%–60% of private practices are fee-for-service and have moved away from insurance (Babayan, 2015). Thus, offering concierge therapy may be aligned with the current business models of many practitioners.

There is no research on clients who seek out concierge therapy nor evidence of its effectiveness over traditional therapy models. Even with its potential benefits, concierge therapy may not be a good fit for everyone. Indeed, there are distinct ethical, legal, and clinical concerns. Therapists must conduct a thorough clinical screening and assessment to ensure that a client's needs can best be met using a concierge model of care. Issues such as privacy and confidentiality, especially when engaging in out-of-office treatment, can frequently emerge, as discussed in Chapter 4. Clinicians must also assess whether this model works for them personally and whether it is aligned with their philosophy of care and the types of clients and issues they see in their clinical practice. Concierge therapy is complex and therapists need resources to navigate these complexities. Astute clinicians in private practice must consider multiple ways to diversify their practice to best meet the needs of a wide range of mental health consumers while thriving in the business of private practice. Concierge services is one therapeutic modality to do this. Let's consider the multiple models for practicing concierge therapy.

MODELS OF CONCIERGE THERAPY

Concierge practices appear to differ primarily across two dimensions: 1) concierge only practices versus those that integrate concierge therapy into a traditional practice; and 2) practices that require monthly or annual membership fees or retainers versus those that do not. Let us discuss these differences and potential benefits to the practitioner and the client.

First, in a concierge-only practice there are multiple benefits for both therapists and clients. A concierge therapist can see fewer clients overall and focus on meeting the needs of the few clients. Because the therapist in a concierge-only practice sees only a small number of clients, the range of benefits the therapist can offer may be more expansive than therapists in other practices. For example, a concierge therapist may offer clients 24/7 availability by text, appointment availability within 24 hours, out-of-office sessions, wellness coaching, or other telehealth options. For full-time therapists offering only concierge services, collecting a retainer or monthly membership fees may be (financially) necessary in order to maintain the small caseload. Those clinicians who are practicing part-time or who have a lower overhead may not require the financial security of monthly fees or a retainer in addition to fees-for-service. Typically, insurance is not accepted for concierge services, but some therapists are beginning to accept insurance for in-office or covered telehealth visits. In these situations, clients would pay for the concierge monthly or retainer fees and insurance would be billed for covered services.

Clinicians interested in transitioning to concierge therapy for some clients can begin by adding a small number of those clients into one's traditional practice. For example, for a full-time clinician who typically works 25–30 clinical hours per week, it is possible to reduce the overall number of clients and have 10%–15% of the practice devoted to concierge clients. However, there may be limits to the benefits one can offer within a model like this. When integrating concierge clients into a traditional practice, the therapist may not have the time, resources, or the scheduling flexibility to offer services such as immediate appointments or clearing their schedule to travel to a concierge client. For example, if a therapist has 3 concierge clients but still sees 20 traditional, nonconcierge clients, providing concierge services may require cancelling or rescheduling a non-concierge client in order to accommodate the last-minute request of a concierge client. With greater acceptance and widespread use of telehealth, some potential scheduling barriers can be reduced. The therapist might not be able to schedule an immediate in-person appointment, but a telehealth session might be a more readily available option. One benefit of an integrated model for therapists, who may be conflicted about or uncomfortable with the perceived elitism of concierge therapy, is the opportunity to have a few concierge clients who pay higher fees for additional services which offsets costs or otherwise allows the therapist to offer a sliding scale, a reduced fee, or to see pro bono clients. Regardless of which model of concierge therapy is chosen, strategic business planning is necessary to ensure that therapists understand the cost and profit implications of the fee structure and caseload they choose. See Table 5.1, which outlines ways a full concierge practice may align with or differ from a practice that integrates select concierge clients. Note that these are only examples, and therapists have the autonomy to craft a model that works for them, their clients, and their business needs. With these models of integration in mind, let's turn to how to determine if concierge therapy is right for you as a therapist.

Example Models of Concierge Practice

Full Concierge Practice	Concierge Integration
Only concierge clients	Traditional practice with select concierge clients
Retainer/membership fees	Higher fee/subscription-based pricing
24/7 availability	Therapist states availability
Quick appointments or same day availability	Faster availability (e.g., same week scheduling)
In or out-of-office, home-based sessions, telehealth, synchronous, and asynchronous	Office or video
Insurance may not be accepted; some services may not be reimbursable	Insurance possibly accepted for covered services or superbill provided for reimbursement

DETERMINING IF CONCIERGE THERAPY IS RIGHT FOR YOU

There are many factors to consider to determine if concierge therapy is right for you as a clinician. Burnout and compassion fatigue are major issues of concern for therapists; many of us may be experiencing these now, after months of a pandemic and crisis care. Concierge therapy may cause some clinicians to feel more passion for or commitment to their work because they are able to focus on particular clients of interest. This may contribute to reduced burnout and less compassion fatigue. Yet, the concierge therapy model is not a good fit for all therapists. Factors such as personality and one's ability to work with clients who have increased needs or expectations of a therapist can be personally difficult and clinically challenging. Therapists must also consider what it is like to work outside of the therapy office, particularly in a client's home or office, as mentioned in Chapter 4. Therapists are trained in traditional models of care and are often most comfortable being in the driver's seat, where they determine time and length of sessions and where they feel in greater control of the session. Thus, concierge therapy that occurs outside of the office may challenge many therapist's notion of power and even their effectiveness. Other therapists may struggle with setting high enough fees, perhaps due to the devaluing of the profession or their own challenges with assigning a high monetary value to their time and expertise. Clinicians who come into the field to work with economically impoverished populations may question if private practice and, specifically, concierge therapy is aligned with their values, especially at a time when more people may need access to mental health.

Therapists must also consider whether the populations with whom they ordinarily work or the issues they typically address in sessions are appropriate for a concierge model. Also, it is important for a clinician to consider their motivation for venturing into concierge therapy because this information may shape their approach to and experience of concierge therapy. There are multiple factors to consider in this deliberation. Take a moment to pause and think about what brought you into the field and why you stay in the profession.

Pause | Reflect

- Why did you choose the field of psychotherapy? Go beyond the desire to "help people," and consider what in you was drawn to this type of heart work.
- If you have been in the field for a while, why have you stayed? What sustains you?
- Take a moment to reflect on your clinical work and your practice. What type of clients do you find to be the most difficult clinically? Are there particular personalities, age groups, or diagnostic or clinical issues that trigger you or that you avoid?
- Lastly, describe your ideal private practice. What would it look like? How many clients would you see? Would you focus on a particular set of issues or a particular client population? Would you offer different services or expand your services? Have any of your feelings about these topics changed as a result of the pandemic?

Take a moment to review your responses to these questions. What do you notice about your ideal practice compared with your current practice? Consider how many clients or how much of your work you consider to be "difficult." Is there a relationship between how much of your current work is with difficult clients and what you want for the future of your practice? How much has your vision of your practice (or your life) evolved as a result of the pandemic? Consider which aspects of your work are rewarding, which are frustrating, and what you want to focus on in your practice as you continue to read. Your responses here may help you determine if concierge therapy is a fit for you. As noted, there are many factors to consider in discerning whether concierge therapy is a good fit for each therapist. No research has been conducted on the reasons therapists in traditional practice transition to concierge therapy. Yet, two of the primary driving forces that might motivate a therapist to consider concierge therapy are frustration and fatigue. Frustration might stem from high caseloads, feeling bound to insurance mandates, a lack of autonomy to offer services that are outside of the scope of what insurance will cover, or just feeling burned out. Most of us have experienced one or more of those feelings at some point—perhaps in this very moment. Some of us may be especially vulnerable to burnout during a pandemic with no clear end in sight. Concierge therapy allows therapists to at once reduce their caseloads and increase their clinical autonomy. By choosing to work with a select group of clients who seek out personalized care, therapists can offer more attention to each client as well as determine what type of treatment might best meet each client's clinical needs. This likely sounds exciting and you might think many therapists would be running to sign up for it. Yet, concierge therapy may not address all of these issues; it is a departure from traditional therapy and comes with its own challenges.

Training

One of the biggest barriers facing therapists who are considering concierge therapy is that we may not feel that we are sufficiently trained to conduct concierge therapy. As mentioned in previous chapters, most traditional counseling and psychology programs prepare students to provide one-on-one therapy, and sometimes couples or family therapy, within the therapist's office for a standard 50-minute session. Therapists are trained to assess, diagnose, and devise a treatment plan. Much of the clinical research, and even continuing education, is also based on this model. Deviation from this model may bring one's competence into question, which can be unsettling. Some of you may have heard of concierge therapy but perhaps, as with other emerging models of therapy, in very limited or uninformed ways. Reading this text, engaging in continuing education, and consulting with other concierge therapists can help increase knowledge, skills, and competence, which are also ethically required.

Personality

There are also therapist and client personality factors that must be considered in determining if concierge therapy is a fit. Consider for a moment the following questions:

Pause | Reflect

- What types of personalities are difficult for you personally and professionally?
- What is difficult about these personality styles?
- What does it trigger for you?
- What personality characteristics do you think typify clients who seek out concierge therapy? Why?
- Would your reactions to these personality styles be a problem in clinical relationships?

If you are engaging in honest reflection, this exercise likely immediately prompted thoughts or even specific people—including clients—to come to mind. And many people have an image in their mind of what a *typical concierge client* might be like: their background, perhaps even their presenting issues. Pause for a moment and consider where you get these images and ideas. Is this rooted in the data of who seeks out concierge medicine or therapy or on your own personal experience? Many therapists have assumptions and biases based on what we may have passively consumed and inadvertently internalized from media or others' accounts. This is important to think critically about and interrogate because it shapes our perceptions of and openness to concierge therapy. In addition, it may unduly color our expectations of concierge clients.

Clients who seek out the concierge level of care have not been well studied. Some concierge practitioners describe their clients as highly motivated individuals who are accustomed to having choice in their healthcare and a voice in their treatment (Lynch, 2012). Many clients may have researched different types of therapies and treatment approaches and have seen other therapists in the past. Some may have had negative or frustrating experiences with previous therapy and may believe that concierge therapy will afford them an opportunity to have their needs better met. Others may be individuals who wield a lot of power in their personal and professional spheres and are used to being in the driver's seat, perhaps even dictating what happens in many areas of their life. These are qualities that are often associated with professional success and that are often rewarded. Within the clinical relationship, this might mean a client who has a difficult time trusting the therapist to take care of them as they navigate the exploration of vulnerable emotions. For other clients, this might manifest as clinical resistance. If you are a therapist who typically struggles when working with a client who is fully empowered or who navigates the world from a position of privilege and entitlement, then concierge therapy may be a challenge until you grow more adept at how to empathically and effectively engage with people who express those qualities. If you are a therapist who tends to pathologize clients or personally get triggered by clients who come into therapy having already defined their issues for themselves or who seek to make clear the limited time commitment they can make to therapy, this may also be an area for further exploration before you pursue this type of therapy. Many therapists are trained in a model of therapy that presumes that the client will be a more passive recipient of the therapist's expertise or guidance. We may inadvertently pathologize clients as being "resistant to treatment" if they do not engage therapy in the socially prescribed way.

Many therapists may feel unsettled or frustrated with these types of clients. Think back to your responses to the reflection questions. Did you name as difficult any personality characteristics such as controlling, entitled, or noncompliant? Take a moment and consider how it might feel to work with more clients you experience as having these qualities and what that might trigger and how this might affect how you show up in these clinical relationships.

Other therapist personality traits may also need consideration, such as personal flexibility. Clients who seek out concierge therapy desire flexibility in therapy. In other words, they are paying additional fees for the therapist to accommodate them. They may have demanding careers with hectic work hours. Many people struggle to juggle the demands of work, family life, and commutes. In order to squeeze in mental health care, some people may benefit from a therapist with scheduling flexibility. For some clients, this might mean later evening appointments, while for others it might mean meeting less frequently for sessions of longer duration. Still others might need location flexibility. Many therapists may be opposed to offering this flexibility. Take a moment to consider how it might feel to offer a client a 9 p.m. appointment for an in-office session. Does something feel inherently "wrong," "unsafe," or unprofessional about meeting with a client at that time? Does this incite any feelings of concern? Does your personal life, such as a need to be home with young children, preclude you from offering these times? Imagine a client sending you a text message that they would like to meet tomorrow, but you already have your day planned. How do you imagine a last-minute request for a noncrisis session would feel? Does that shift your perspective of the client or the treatment you would provide? If you are someone for whom last minute changes in schedule are personally difficult, then offering sessions with short notice as a benefit of concierge therapy might not be prudent. If your boundaries around personal time and/or family responsibilities preclude you from being available outside of traditional business hours, such as nights and weekends, it is important to honor this. Nights and weekends may not be an aspect of concierge therapy that you offer. Or, this may be an option you offer virtually but not in person. It is important to be explicit about this boundary at the beginning of treatment. In addition, it is always prudent to be clear up front about the protocol for after-hours needs and emergencies.

Theoretical Orientation

Theoretical orientation may also have a role in determining if concierge therapy is a good fit for you as a therapist. Therapists who are analytically oriented and value the relative anonymity of the therapist, more rigid boundaries, and an emotionally distant client–therapist relationship are unlikely to be a good fit for concierge therapy. Many analysts view any deviation from the blank slate norm and traditional in-office treatment as being a boundary crossing that is likely to negatively affect transference and the clinical process (Zur, 2007). Because concierge therapy is built upon the personalization of client services, this approach appears to be counter to the stance of psychoanalytic theory. Analysts who are interested in transitioning to concierge therapy may benefit from additional or refresher training in other theoretical models, such as existential, systems, and feminist theories, that are better aligned with concierge therapy. Existential, systems, and feminist theories are arguably better suited for application in concierge therapy for numerous reasons. These theories posit an egalitarian therapist–client relationship and challenge the traditional position of therapist as expert of a client's life. In addition, these theories allow space for different therapeutic modalities and the integration of cultural and systemic factors influencing individual psychological health. While these theories were not, of course, inherently developed for concierge practice they allow space for and encourage therapist flexibility to conceptualize and move away from a prescriptive one-size-fits-all therapeutic process to meet client needs.

In sum, there are multiple factors to consider in determining if concierge therapy is a good fit. Therapist flexibility, training, and theoretical orientation are all important to consider in working with higher need or higher expectation therapeutic relationships. Reduced caseload and increased revenue are benefits, but they may come at a personal cost if this model is uncomfortable, triggering, or impedes the way you show up in the clinical relationship.

IS CONCIERGE THERAPY RIGHT FOR MY CLIENTS?

Just as concierge therapy may not be a good fit for some therapists, it is also important to think critically about its suitability for particular clients. Generally speaking, many clients who are a good fit for private practice may be a good fit for concierge therapy. Yet, this may not always be the case. Consider Kim, for example. Kim is a young adult client who seeks therapy for depression and anxiety issues. She has been in counseling before and would like to use her employer-paid health insurance benefits to cover as much of counseling as possible. Kim is a prime candidate for private practice-based therapy. Indeed, many private practice clinicians would jump at the opportunity to work with a client like Kim. Contrast Kim with Monica, who also struggles with depression and anxiety and has been in counseling before but has not been successful in committing to the process. She works an atypical work schedule, is able to pay out of pocket (she does want to seek reimbursement from her insurance provider), and would like to combine in-office sessions with nature-based and teletherapy sessions. There are a few differences between these clients' profiles that differentiate them relative to concierge therapy. First, Monica presents with concerns that are treatable in a private practice setting, and she would need schedule and setting flexibility to commit to therapy in order to experience therapeutic gains. While more information is needed to ensure that Monica is appropriate for teletherapy and any other out-of-office therapies, scheduling and setting flexibility as well as having agency in treatment preference might be key factors for Monica to commit to the therapeutic process.

Therapists must think critically about the presenting issues and diagnostic conditions that may not be appropriate for concierge therapy. Like any other treatment modality, concierge care must be based on best scientific evidence and sound clinical judgment. Beginning concierge therapists are encouraged to initially consider questions such as:

- Is this a client with whom I want to be engaged in an intensive concierge relationship?
- Are this client's presenting issues appropriate for or can they be effectively addressed using a concierge model?

From a clinical perspective, considering diagnosis and symptom severity is imperative when determining fit for concierge therapy. In general, clients who have low to moderate levels of impairment are deemed most appropriate for outpatient, private practice settings. Thus, screening and assessment to determine diagnosis and level of functioning are essential. A concierge therapist with a wellness-centered and strengths-based perspective, would also want to know what the client's internal and external resources are so that you can best support them in their optimal functioning and overall state of well-being.

Screening and Assessment for Concierge Therapy

Screening and assessing clients for their appropriateness for concierge therapy may be the most important aspect of concierge therapy. The first level of assessment includes whether the client is appropriate, given their specific clinical needs and the therapist's areas of expertise. This can be done through an initial phone screening or in-person consultation. For therapists who have a concierge-only practice, it is prudent to ensure that potential clients are aware, from the initial phone conversation or email, that you are a concierge therapist. This may be an opportunity to provide a brief overview of concierge therapy along with the key benefits of concierge therapy and any limitations. Providing this information at the initial phone screening may save the therapist and prospective client time if this type of therapy will not meet the client's needs. For example, a therapist might state the following in an initial consult:

> *Thank you for your interest in my services. I am a concierge therapist, which means that I provide personalized therapy services to a small, select group of intentionally chosen clients who are best suited for this flexible therapy modality. Instead of insurance mandated clinical approaches and session limits, we cocreate a therapy and wellness plan with the scheduling flexibility to meet your needs. Monthly fees are required and can cover traditional in-office therapy focused on your primary issues, video-based sessions, and even home or nature-based sessions, when that is appropriate. The plan can also include wellness and executive coaching, if that is part of a client's needs. Let's talk*

about whether this model might be a fit for you and what this kind of therapy requires.

Broadly speaking, the assessment that is conducted after the initial intake and early sessions is similar to evaluating and determining a recommended treatment. In general, it is most common that therapists assess: 1) history of presenting symptoms; 2) client motivation and readiness for change; and 3) level of functional impairment. From a more strengths-based and wellness-centered perspective, therapists should also consider assessing: 4)) the client's strengths, internal resources, and external resources; 5) areas for personal growth; and 6) adjunctive or complementary needs (i.e., spiritual integration, nutritional counseling, movement and exercise).

In evaluating whether someone is a good fit for concierge therapy specifically, therapists should attend to the important factors for successful outpatient therapy, including psychological and emotional stability and available social support. Assessing emotional stability typically includes assessment of previous and current suicidal ideation and homicidal ideation, the presence of psychotic symptoms, and the presence of disabling psychological symptoms that impair a client's overall quality of life and/or ability to function. The use of objective measures may provide additional support for the clinical interview and for clinical judgment.

Further assessment may be required to evaluate whether a client is appropriate for the particular services included in concierge therapy, such as out-of-office therapy and teletherapy. It may be helpful for a therapist to think of this additional level of assessment as useful for guiding treatment planning. Refer back to the guiding questions provided in Chapter 3 as a resource for evaluating inclusion and potential exclusion for specific types of TMH. Consider, for example, a client with a history of suicidal ideation and hospitalization within the past six months who currently reports emotional stability. Some therapists who offer crisis support may be comfortable taking on this client. However, given the importance of being able to assess nonverbal indicators of mental health, the therapist and client would likely be best served by in-person or video sessions as the primary treatment modality. In addition, safety planning and engagement of additional supports, if necessary, are traditionally better employed in person, although this has changed with the pandemic and widespread use of teletherapy. In general, clients who are not currently emotionally stable are best served by more intensive models of care that include crisis availability and collaboration with other health professionals.

Clients Appropriate for Concierge Care

Clients likely to do well in concierge therapy are often those who are flexible, want greater voice in their healthcare decision-making, and have an articulated desire for a more individualized treatment plan (Lynch, 2012). Depending on the cost structure that the therapist establishes, early assessment of and discussion about the financial investment of concierge therapy is prudent. Because accommodating treatment preferences is associated with positive therapeutic outcomes (Swift et al., 2018), having an open discussion with a client about the ways the therapist may be able to accommodate their preferences and what specific ways this can be done—potentially differently—through concierge therapy may increase interest and engagement in a concierge relationship. The more explicit the therapist is about how they plan to incorporate the client's needs and preferences into treatment planning, the more positive and empowered the client is likely to feel about the course of therapy and, potentially, their hopes that concierge therapy will be a helpful resource (Swift et al., 2018).

Clients for Whom Concierge Care Is Inappropriate

Determining which clients are not appropriate for concierge therapy is not black and white. There are, however, some important considerations that help guide clinicians in this determination.

Consider the following questions for which an affirmative answer may indicate that concierge therapy is contraindicated:

- Would increased therapist availability foster emotional dependence?
- Would concierge therapy inadvertently undermine client autonomy?

- Is this client able to respect professional boundaries?

Relative to specific clinical issues and diagnoses, the following issues *could* disqualify a client for concierge therapy candidacy and thus necessitate additional assessment:

- Active suicidal ideations with need for hospitalization or very recent stabilization
- Personality or characterological issues that may be reinforced through constant therapist access
- Clients with emotional instability or severely decompensated or actively violent

Many clinicians should automatically rule out clients with more severe symptomatology, such as actively suicidal clients, severe bipolar disorder, and disabling depression, or some psychotic disorders, such as schizoaffective disorder. This recommendation is generally based on clinician availability, additional necessary resources, and/or even the increased clinical responsibility and potential risk that comes from working with recently stabilized clients with suicidal histories. Considering the level of care and support someone might need when they are suicidal, however, concierge therapy might allow the therapist the time and resources to provide the necessary therapeutic support that is not possible within the constraints of a traditional 50-minute session once per week treatment plan.

Beyond suicidality, it is prudent to consider multiple factors in working with and supporting clients and families with severe distress or mental health issues. First, as noted throughout this text, therapists are required to work within their areas of expertise. Recall that designing a concierge practice is, in part, an opportunity to immerse oneself in more intensive therapeutic work with the clients and populations about whom one is most passionate. Therapists who are competent in and enjoy working with this client population may have a unique opportunity to establish a niche practice and work with higher need clients in a private practice setting. Within the traditional therapy framework, therapists are commonly concerned about working with clients who have more severe symptoms due to the constraints this style of therapy places on treatment, including limited number or frequency of sessions. Concierge therapy may eliminate many of these barriers, and thus these concerns.

Concierge therapy with high-needs clients presents therapists with the opportunity for greater flexibility in devising an intensive treatment plan. For some clients, more intensive treatment than what is typically available in a traditional out-patient private privactice may be more effective in meeting their clinical needs. Concierge therapists who work in an integrated health setting and/or who collaborate with psychiatrists, outpatient group programs, or other care providers, can orchestrate more clinical time and attention for clients who need it. Importantly, therapists who do not offer after hours or crisis availability are advised not to accept actively suicidal or emotionally unstable clients nor clients who may have issues with safety.

Some of the very clients drawn to concierge therapy may be those who struggle with codependence. Some clients may be appropriate for concierge therapy, but the clinician may determine that the client would be best served by being seen within the structured setting of the office. Therapists engaging in a concierge practice are encouraged to make these clinical judgments and/or make alterations to the treatment setting or modality as the client's situation or functioning changes. As is customary, documentation of any changes and their rationale is necessary. This should also be discussed with and agreed to by the client.

LEGAL AND ETHICAL ISSUES IN CONCIERGE THERAPY

While legal and ethical issues are discussed at length in Chapter 7, there are distinct ethical obligations for therapists who are interested in a concierge practice. Namely, there are specific concerns that emerge in concierge practices around boundaries, fees, and working with high-profile clients.

Boundaries

First, the flexibility and increased access to one's therapist inherent in concierge therapy may make the therapeutic relationship more vulnerable to boundary violations. Concierge therapists assume greater responsibility for maintaining the frame of therapy regardless of how much a client is paying, where meetings occur, or for what specific reasons a client seeks help. This can be done in multiple ways, including communicating, verbally and through written policies, what is appropriate in terms of communication between sessions, what is included in the retainer (if one is required), and what the defined treatment or wellness plan is. Defining and communicating this framework at the beginning of therapy gives the therapist something to refer back to if a client deviates from the established norms and agreements. In addition, if clients are frequently communicating with the therapist between sessions, it may be helpful to openly discuss why this is happening from a practical and clinical perspective and to remind the client of the policies.

Fees

Another ethical and legal area of concern in concierge practice is with fee setting. As mentioned previously, widespread suffering is now common due to the COVID-19 pandemic and the effects of racism; there is an increased need for access to mental health. Many therapists may struggle with the idea of exclusivity during a time when current and prospective clients may have lost jobs and may be experiencing economic hardship. Public perspectives of mental health care are often different than those regarding medicine or other professional services, including the public's expectations around cost, although this has begun to shift after witnessing the far-reaching mental health effects of the COVID-19 health pandemic. Even before the current economic climate, some may have believed that it is morally wrong for therapists to charge a high hourly rate or require a retainer. Some therapists may have internalized these messages because of their financial upbringing, social class, or politics. Clinicians are often uncomfortable and even unskilled at the business aspects of private practice. This may result in internal struggles when setting fees, which may feel like the commodification of our expertise, time, and services. Many practitioners may have entered the helping and healing arts field, including social services, with a sense of social responsibility that may stand in contrast to a capitalist model of financial gain. Thus, being in the business of private practice, especially concierge therapy, may present a moral dilemma for some therapists. Many of the questions and internal tension that arise due to this moral dilemma appear to be more of a reflection of a mental health field and healthcare system that devalue mental health. Devaluing mental health contributes to the narrow pathways that mental health professionals have to earn—even marginally—comparable salaries to similarly educated medical counterparts.

The therapists' own comfort in understanding and discussing financial issues is important on many levels. The establishment of the professional clinical relationship with a client is done, in part, by the payment of a fee. Also, professional fees allow therapists to make a living, provide services to others, and advance the profession. Ethically, therapists are required to make clients aware of their fees as early as feasible in the clinical relationship (APA, 2017a). Even when practicing concierge therapy, fees should be clear and consistent.

If a therapist is uncomfortable discussing financial matters, including their professional fees, clients might infer that the therapist may be uncomfortable discussing the client's financial stressors, which may also become a clinical issue. Some therapists may be, or may become, unduly influenced to continue unnecessary clinical treatment with clients who pay high fees. In these cases, the continuation of therapy is, arguably, more about the therapist's financial gain than the client's well-being. This is particularly important, considering that many therapists may have had more frequent financial conversations with clients during the economic crisis that accompanied the pandemic. Some therapists may have lost clients due to financial issues and thus may have relied on fewer clients for their financial solvency.

Therapists who are part of insurance panels have the additional consideration of insurance mandates. Many third-party payers require providers to have set fees that apply to all clients, regardless of insurance status. This is an important consideration for therapists who wish to see concierge clients and also continue to serve on insurance panels. In addition, if a client may not be able to sustain the cost associated with concierge therapy, it is imperative that therapists discuss this with clients as early as possible (see Standard 6.04 in APA, 2017a). Consequently, concierge therapists must be clear about their hourly fees, any membership fees, specific recurring fees, and what services are included in these fees. Again, fees should not be a surprise—even for concierge clients. To clarify services and fees, it is recommended that concierge therapists have a separate consent form that delineates specific concierge services and their associated one-time and/or recurring fees.

High-profile clients

Clients with a high public profile are often good candidates for concierge therapy. High profile clients may include entertainment industry professionals, professional athletes, elected representatives and campaigning politicians, socialites, and well-known business industry professionals. These clients (or others connected to them) have distinct privacy concerns related to popular interest in their life and may present unique clinical and ethical concerns for therapists. Some high-profile clients may, understandably, have concerns about even beginning therapy for fear of threats to confidentiality. Many high-profile individuals are subject to extreme violations of privacy and, especially at this time when people can be awarded large sums of money for revealing personal information about high-profile people, it is understandable that they have concerns about trust and breaches of confidentiality. This has resulted in nondisclosure agreements (NDA) being commonplace in many personal and professional relationships with people living in the public eye (Lobel, 2018). President Trump even publicly joked about the proliferation of NDA's for people of wealth. Though the therapy relationship is already confidential and protected by law, some clients may need additional reassurance or have additional personal requirements before they are willing to work with a therapist. In these cases, it is important for the concierge therapist to consult with the client about any additional requirements they might have, such as signing of an NDA or specific guidelines around note taking. For example, if you are asked to sign an NDA, you need to have it reviewed by a lawyer who specializes in healthcare. In addition, it may be helpful to discuss with the client (or their business manager) the ways in which therapy is already a privileged relationship and is legally protected—we are already legally bound to confidentiality, with important exceptions.

High-profile clients may also have distinct needs in terms of session time or location. For example, some clients may not be able to come to a therapist's office location without attracting the attention of others or being

noticed in a waiting room. It is also possible others seeking to view or pho-
tograph a high-profile client may unintentionally draw attention to other
clients who may be in a waiting area or exiting a therapist's office. Clients
with this degree of public recognition may benefit from accommodations to
ensure their privacy and to protect the privacy of other clients.

Maintaining confidentiality may also be a challenge for concierge therapists practicing out-of-office or working with clients who have assistants,
managers, accountants, or other third parties who are involved in some
aspect of the clinical relationship. Ethically, therapists must discuss confidentiality and boundaries with the client's staff or team members and
secure an authorization to release information if the client wants the therapist to be able to communicate with or coordinate with any of these individuals. For example, if a client uses a business manager to handle financial
issues and a personal assistant to manage scheduling, separate authorization forms would be necessary for each of those individuals that is limited
to the scope of the respective communications. If you are practicing concierge therapy and more complex issues arise, consult with a lawyer experienced in concierge healthcare.

Clients who do not have a high public profile but are related to, employed
by, or otherwise associated with a high-profile individual may also have privacy concerns. Some of these individuals may be legally bound by an NDA.
They may have concerns about revealing information that is clinically relevant to their personal therapy yet may breach a standing NDA. These clients
may request that names and details related to the high-profile individual be
omitted from clinical notes to legally protect the client. These are all valid
concerns that people living in the public eye (or their loved ones) may have.
Yet, any requests that violate therapists' ethical and legal obligations cannot
be upheld. For example, therapists are ethically and legally required to take
clinical notes. This is in the best interest of the client as well as the therapist.
It is important to remember that as a guiding rule, if something is essential
to the client's underlying issues, diagnosis, and treatment, then generally, it
should be included in clinical notes (APA, 2007). Yet, the decision of what
to include or the amount of detail is left to the therapist's discretion. These
situations are complex and extend beyond what most therapists have to consider in daily practice. It is also important to provide psychoeducation to

clients (and/or their management and staff) about the protections that surround therapy. Clearly, trust-building and rapport are paramount to work with this population.

The situations just described involving boundaries, fee issues, and the complexities of working with high profile clients are issues for which to be prepared in concierge practice. Therapists who are interested in practicing concierge therapy would benefit from additional training and support in how to handle complex situations with clients who cross boundaries.

Consider how you would handle or respond to the following scenarios with concierge clients:

- A client (or their personal assistant) repeatedly schedules and cancels appointments
- You have a wealthy or entertainment industry professional who wants you to travel with them on vacation in order to continue treatment, and so that you can have a getaway
- A client sends a lavish housewarming gift to your home address that you never provided them
- A client offers you a "tip" or a "bonus" for a job well done in recent sessions
- You run into a client while out shopping and they want to "run something by you"

How a therapist might handle these situations with traditional therapy clients might differ from how we handle them with concierge clients. Concierge clients pay a higher premium to have greater access to their therapist and may need guidance on appropriate limits and boundaries with the therapist. Therapists who might struggle with how to set the boundary in the moment should seek out professional development in this area. Consider the following case with Brian and the way in which these issues can arise.

Brian is a campaign manager for an elected representative who sought counseling for anxiety and concerns about a series of failed romantic relationships. Initially, Brian was able to come into the therapy office; however, shortly after beginning treatment, he was involved in a highly publicized and contested legal issue in the news. Because of his involvement in these issues and the amount of publicity he was receiving, Brian became concerned about meeting in my therapy office. After discussing meeting location options and their clinical implications, we agreed that we would meet at his office or use a secure, HIPAA compliant telehealth video system. Additionally, Brian was concerned that if the media or his political rivals learned that he was in therapy, the content of sessions might somehow be accessed. Brian also expressed concerns about the well-being and legal protection of the therapist. He offered the assistance of his legal team "should that become necessary."

There are a number of potential clinical and ethical issues that emerge in this snapshot of the clinical work with Brian. Specifically, there are considerations around out-of-office treatment, threats to confidentiality and privacy, and access to external information about the client through the media. Consider this example and how you might feel if one of your existing clients was suddenly thrust into the media and subject to a wide range of polarizing political scrutiny. Typically, it is frowned upon for therapists to look up personal or professional information about clients, such as by viewing their social media pages. In this situation, however, this kind of information may be difficult to avoid because it is in the public sphere. Clearly, this is a complex issue to navigate. Given my strong clinical relationship with this client, combined with a theoretical orientation that values more open and transparent processing, I chose to bring this complexity into the room and talk to Brian about what he preferred in terms of my exposure to and consumption of news coverage. Brian noted that it would make things easier for him if I knew some of what he was dealing with in the media. He reportedly felt that this would give me a better understanding of specific anxiety triggers and ways to best manage the flurry of press. To this end, there were times that he forwarded articles or news coverage in hopes that I could review these before our next scheduled meeting.

There are also a number of issues in this kind of case that alter the power dynamic in the therapeutic relationship. First, it is important to underscore that, in this example, the client worked closely with an elected representative and was involved in highly politicized issues. In addition, meeting with a client in *their* office may cause the therapist to feel like the tables are turned. Some therapists may find themselves consciously or unconsciously intimidated by working with a "high-power client." Others may be intimidated and/or very concerned about working with a client who was involved with a public issue that could potentially become a legal issue for the client. It is not uncommon for therapists to avoid clients who are involved with legal matters or lawsuits. Yet, terminating therapy with a client who becomes involved with a legal matter may also be considered client abandonment. It is paramount that therapists be aware of their own triggers and responses to these issues. Therapists with clients who are dealing with highly publicized issues or contentious legal matters would benefit from consultation with respected colleagues. Brian's case demonstrates some of the complexity that can be involved in working with high-profile individuals. While this case is certainly not representative of all high-profile cases, given Brian was involved in a contentious public issue, it provides a glimpse into some of the additional factors that may need to be considered.

The following brief checklist might be helpful for therapists beginning concierge therapy.

Beginning Concierge Therapy Checklist

☐ Provide clients clear description of concierge therapy including required fees and included services

☐ Clarify any services that are not provided or not included in required fees

☐ Obtain informed consent specific to concierge therapy

☐ Obtain authorization to release information and communicate with any third parties (e.g., personal assistants, business managers, accountants)

☐ Provide feedback in real time about boundaries and limits

☐ Engage in continued professional development on issues related to concierge practice

CONCLUSION

Concierge therapy presents opportunities for therapists and clients to personalize therapy in ways not previously available in mental health care. Through concierge therapy, therapists can integrate teletherapy, out-of-office and home-based sessions, and wellness or executive coaching, instead of or in addition to traditional in-office therapy, to meet their clients' needs. Therapists interested in concierge therapy can develop fully concierge practices in which they work with a limited number of clients who pay higher fees or a retainer. Other therapists may want to integrate a few concierge clients into a traditional practice to complement their current services. It is important to honor the concerns of therapists who struggle with the perceived elitism or potential access issues of concierge care. Therapists who are interested in a concierge practice with less affluent populations are encouraged to design a business plan that allows them to engage in the work they want to do with communities of interest while maintaining a financially solvent business. Yet, there are real concerns about health disparities and inequitable access to mental health care. It is critical that the systemic issues that created and that maintain an inequitable, tiered healthcare—including mental health care—system in the United States be viewed within a larger sociopolitical context. Individual therapists certainly have choice and agency in the type of work in which they engage as well as in the settings in which they work and the populations they serve. Individual therapists' choices do not change an inequitable system or the overall devaluing of the mental health field that leads to dramatically disparate rates of compensation compared to their medical colleagues. Part of the next movement of psychotherapy appears to be expanding pathways of both serving others and being well-compensated.

6

RACE AND POWER
IN TODAY'S THERAPY

During the first week of June 2020, I noticed a sharp increase in the number of emails and voicemails I was receiving—they seemed to pour in—all from self-identified Black/African American people seeking therapy. It was the week following the murder of George Floyd Jr. by Minneapolis police officers. People all over the United States and around the world began to publicly and collectively decry anti-Black racism and police violence against Black people. Even amid a global pandemic, the abject racism foundational to American culture and society has again come exploding to the surface. Even as people protested in the streets and put their bodies on the line, my phone rang and the emails kept pouring in. One voicemail from a young woman sounded more like a plea:

> "Hi, my name is Jess. I've been looking . . . trying to find a Black therapist for a while. I just . . . I . . . there is just too much going on, and I don't know . . . (sigh) . . . I would really like to try therapy. It's really hard right now. I hope you are available and can see me . . ."

Jess's experience is not uncommon. The fields of psychology and psychotherapy do not reflect the diversity of this country. Therapists today are predominantly white and female-identified (APA, 2016). This is even more pronounced in private practice. Moreover, white therapists in private practice most often see white, cis-heterosexual, middle-class clients.

There have long been cries for the field of psychology, and psychotherapy by extension, to not only diversify but also to decenter whiteness and decolonize the science and practice (Grzanka et al., 2019). As businesses, universities, and organizations scrambled to separate themselves from racism and respond to the Movement for Black Lives, our inboxes and social media timelines were full of statements in support of Black people and Black lives. Even national psychology and counseling organizations issued similar statements, reminding its members of their professional responsibility to advocate for social justice (ACA, 2020; APA, 2020). In the ACA's (2020) bold statement, they proclaim:

> *Our stance is: Black Lives Matter. We have a moral and professional*
> *obligation to deconstruct institutions which have historically been*
> *designed to benefit white America. These systems must be dismantled*
> *in order to level the playing field for Black communities. Allyship*
> *is not enough. We strive to create liberated spaces in the fight*
> *against white supremacy and the dehumanization of Black people.*
> *(ACA, 2020, para. 4)*

Questions remain as to what this means for everyone in the field, the majority of whom identify as white, and how this translates to specific therapist positionalities and behaviors in the therapeutic encounter with clients across racialized and other social identities. The time during which it was acceptable—even preferred—for mental health and wellness practices to be steeped in whiteness and other hegemonic cultural norms has expired. People across racial groups are no longer here for therapy with or to work with therapists who embody—intentionally or by default—these outdated ideals. We must recognize that the therapeutic endeavor—including the therapy room—is a racialized space that is not free from the racial trauma endured elsewhere. Even therapists who are trained in multicultural psychology and who consider themselves to be "culturally competent" may be inadvertently practicing in ways that replicate or perpetuate that which they are seeking to redress (Grzanka et al., 2019).

There is much work to be done in this area if we therapists are to live up to the ideals of our profession and promote public wellness. Today's psychotherapy must be intentionally antiracist and social justice oriented and must use an intersectional approach to understanding clients' multiple identities and the multiple oppressive systems that impede their psychological well-being. Let's discuss ways that therapists across identities can begin to engage in this hard work and shift their approach—within the office and digital spaces—to one that is not just performative or rhetorical, in which we update language on a website or social media to include today's terminology, but that is a full embodiment of an antiracist and social justice praxis that fosters the safe space and refuge today's clients need.

BACKGROUND

Criticism of the racism and white centeredness of the field of psychology is not a new issue. Dr. Martin Luther King Jr. addressed attendees of the American Psychological Association convention in 1967 as fellow "concerned friends of good will" and implored its members to critically reflect on the APA's role intervening in a society "poisoned to its soul by racism" (King, Jr., 1968, pp. 1–2). In an eerily familiar description, Dr. King further stated, "The white majority, unprepared and unwilling to accept radical structural change, is resisting and producing chaos while complaining that if there were no chaos orderly change would come (King, Jr., 1968, p. 2)." The Association of Black Psychologists (ABPsi) was established in 1968, soon after King addressed the APA, when a group of Black psychologists could no longer tolerate the APA's failure to acknowledge its racism. They demanded the APA be more racially inclusive and promote an antiracist praxis and a more culturally expansive understanding of human experience. In the years since the founding of the ABPsi, and later other ethnic psychological associations (e.g., Latinx Psychological Association, Asian American Psychological Association), there has been advocacy for greater inclusion of People of Color, queer and trans people, and the issues most germane within these communities. Counseling psychologists, in particular, exerted a strong voice in advocating for multicultural psychology. Multicultural psychology was a major step toward greater inclusion in the field of psychology, and this step made visible the ways that a hegemonic universal psychology may not render itself applicable to all people (Grzanka, 2019; Miller et al., 2018; Vera & Speight, 2003). Though multicultural psychology was initially thought to be more inclusive than mainstream psychology, which was known for its erasure and pathologizing of People of Color and the issues of most concern to these communities, multiculturalism continued to perpetrate harm on racially minoritized individuals by comparing their cultural groups to an established—white—norm. This resulted in reductionistic models of large cultural groups, most often portraying them as culturally homogenous.

Recent criticisms of multicultural psychology and cultural competence models point to the emphasis on the more socially palatable notion of "culture" over an explicit naming of race, power, and structural systems of oppression (Grzanka et al., 2019). This illustrates that not enough has changed in terms of the face of psychotherapy or the type of therapy being propagated. Even within multicultural psychology, the emphasis is most often still on individual and intrapsychic locating problems and the responsibility for *coping* within the individual. In recent years, there has been more emphasis on social justice-oriented counseling, that is, movement beyond an individualistic understanding of psychological health to a more expansive understanding of the systemic factors that affect individual well-being (Gorski & Goodman, 2015; Vera & Speight, 2003; Watts, 2004).

There has recently been a movement away from training white therapists to "competently" work with "other" racial groups and toward a greater emphasis on the need of understanding white racial socialization and whiteness as a social system that impacts us all (Grzanka et al., 2019; Miller et al., 2018). To this end, there has been advocacy for a structural competency in which counseling is informed by a consciousness and critical understanding of systems of oppression and structural level inequities that particularly affect the health and well-being of People of Color. As many African American or Black, Native/Indigenous, Latinx, and Asian American therapists (and many clients) have attested for decades, there is now more widespread agreement and advocacy for an emancipatory and liberation-oriented therapy (Comas-Días, 2020; French et al., 2020; Haddock-Lazala, 2020). The COVID-19 related racism against Asian Americans as well as the recent uprisings against white supremacy and state sanctioned violence against Black bodies may have created the social pressure for therapy and psychotherapists to do more—not just for Black and Brown clients but also for, perhaps especially for, white clients.

Liberation and race-conscious approaches to therapy are aligned with the expectations of clients today. Clients are more accustomed to having access to information about prospective therapists' views, as may be found on social media, through media appearances, in marketing materials, and even the topic(s) of the therapist's research. Clients, especially young adult clients, expect transparency about and integration of the sociopolitical context in which they live. This makes sense given the present political moment. Even therapists who profess to practice from a more systemic or critical orientation may fall short of integrating such a perspective within their clinical practice. Let's discuss ways to start this work, for those who are beginning the journey, and how to deepen this work, for those seeking ways to more explicitly engage in an antiracist, intersectional, and liberation approach to counseling.

THE PERSONHOOD AND POLITICS OF THE THERAPIST: IT STARTS WITH US

Most therapists were required to take a graduate course on diversity or multicultural counseling. I taught and designed the curriculum for these courses for multiple years. In these courses, students learn that to work with diverse groups of clients across social identities, they must first turn the mirror toward themselves. Students are often implored to do their own work first by reflecting on their social identities, their access to power and privilege, and ways that they are oppressed by and beneficiaries of oppressive systems. These courses are difficult for students across identities, but they are always most difficult for white students who have had the privilege of never having needed to reflect on race and racism. This was even more difficult when the process was being led by a Black-identified professor. The work of my racially minoritized students was difficult yet different: for some of them, their life-long experiences were affirmed through the racial identity and cultural theories that were taught in the class. Racially minoritized students also frequently had difficulty bearing witness to some of the white students' denials of racism and other forms of oppression, defensiveness, and gaslighting. My queer students (especially those who were Black and Latinx) would often have similar difficulties. I often wonder, years later, about the students who were most defensive, those who reluctantly engaged in the work, and the students who provided negative course evaluations in which they remarked on my "agenda" or, even better, my "anger." While the gendered racism and the coded language that appeared in my evaluations was difficult to stomach, I came to expect them. I wonder about what the students who wrote them are like now and if they ever *really* engaged in the work. I wonder about their clients and who they see. Are they subtly inflicting harm upon their Latinx clients by not fully seeing them or by engaging in microaggressions? Are they allowing white clients to avoid seeing themselves and their participation in racism? Some therapists may think that they took the one course, and now they are done; they are "culturally competent." As therapists, we know that the work of self-examination is a life-long endeavor. But some of us may not have reflected on these questions since that class or since our last uncomfortable cross-racial experience. The current racial climate has provided an opportunity to bring to the foreground issues of race and power, heteronormativity, toxic masculinity, ableism, and religious hegemony and for us to reconsider these issues ourselves. This may also require a process of unlearning. Let's take a moment to pause and reflect and identify areas for personal growth and exploration.

Pause | Reflect

- How has the current racial uprising and racial justice movement affected how you think about race?
- How do you address race and racism in therapy? Has this changed since the most recent racial uprisings?
- Do you address issues of race, culture, sexual and gender identities, social class, and differing abilities with all clients? How?
- Which areas of identity do you feel most comfortable discussing? Why?
- What do you think this indirectly or directly communicates to clients?
- Do you move beyond identification of identities and discuss systems of oppression?

Now, take another moment to reflect on your responses. Notice your responses and any patterns that emerge. We all have areas of identity with which we feel most comfortable or well-equipped to discuss but do you avoid the other areas? Most of us have been forced to think more critically about race, and specifically anti-Blackness, as a result of the uprisings and increased visibility of white nationalism. How does this affect your therapy work with clients? Many therapists—especially white therapists—may benefit from practical guidance on how to do this. Next, we discuss intersectional and liberatory approaches to counseling to guide therapists' integration of issues of oppression in therapy.

INTERSECTIONAL AND LIBERATORY COUNSELING APPROACHES

A thorough explication of liberation-centered approaches to counseling is outside of the scope of this book, yet many current social justice and liberatory focused models of therapy build upon early work in this area, thus a brief discussion to promote this rich tradition is warranted. Liberation psychology, rooted in the early work of Frantz Fanon in the 1960s and Ignacio Martín-Baró in the 1980s, is a critical and decolonial approach that centers the lived truths and knowledge of the oppressed (Fanon, 1963; Freire, 2000; Martín-Baró, 1994). Liberation approaches contest the hegemony of a universal psychology that does not reflect the wisdom, traditions, and realities of the people it purports to serve. Liberation therapies are not new, yet they remain timely, especially in light of the current racial climate and mass political uprisings in the United States and around the world. Liberation therapies are founded on an openness to the emancipatory potential of therapeutic encounters in which the multiplicity of perspectives and experiences is honored. Liberation therapy is collectivist and justice oriented and considers the larger sociopolitical context in which the individual human experience occurs (Haddock-Lazala, 2020). It follows, then, that liberatory therapeutic responses support not only individual but also collective intervention (French et al., 2020). Liberation therapists invite clients to delve deeper to uncover the ways in which they may have internalized harmful narratives about the individual and collective self and clients' positions in the world. Such an approach does not necessitate theoretical exclusivity; rather, a liberation approach can be used within an integrative and holistic model of healing and wellness (Comas-Días, 2020).

Liberation psychology lends itself well to an intersectional understanding of clients and the multiple forces that limit the full expression of our humanity. Intersectionality, borne out of the Black feminist tradition, is a critical structural framework for understanding multidimensional identities and the multiple intersecting social systems that work together to marginalize and oppress people based on these identities (Collins, 2000; Crenshaw, 1989). From a liberatory perspective, the multiplicity and complexity of identities results in more opportunities for identity-based and oppression-related trauma. The experience of oppression is, by definition, one of violence, harm, and trauma (Fanon, 1963). Instead of pathologizing the victim-survivors by diagnosing and focusing treatment on coping or adjusting to the violence of daily oppression and subjugation, we must consider ways to support clients to resist oppression, in service of their mental health, and to transmute anger, distress, and trauma into personal transformation. The importance and therapeutic value of identifying and naming racialized stress and trauma and other identity-based trauma is paramount, especially today. It is essential that therapists engage in a strengths-based and trauma-informed approach that reflects a nuanced understanding of complex trauma, the ways in which social and cultural groups can share trauma (e.g., cultural trauma, gendered and sexually based trauma), and how these traumas can extend across generations (intergenerational trauma). Liberation psychology emphasizes the process of recovering historical or ancestral memory that may also help heal trauma, especially related to racialized trauma, and encourage post-traumatic growth (Bryant-Davis & O'Campo, 2005; Kirkinis et al., 2018). For example, a therapist might ask a client how their parents and grandparents dealt with and survived racism. Viewing current day struggles as an extension of intergenerational struggles allows clients to connect to the intergenerational strength and resilience that is also their inheritance.

Understanding the positionality of the liberation therapist is also key. Liberation therapists engage in role flexibility, connect from a position of equal power in the relationship, and value openness and transparency in the interest of fostering authentic connection between therapist and client. To this end, liberation practitioners are encouraged to connect with clients through *radical humility* and *radical empathy* (Comas-Días, 2020). In the engagement of radical humility, the therapist relates and connects to the client from a space of mutual humanity, as opposed to maintaining a position of "expert." From a mutual humanity perspective, therapists can employ sensorial ways of knowing and can embody the client's distress through radical empathy (Haddock-Lazala, 2020). Again, this appears to be in alignment with the expectations of today's clients for an authentic and more transparent relationship with the therapist. For therapists who are interested in better understanding and/or in engaging in liberation therapy with clients, the following constructs, grounded in liberation theory and research (Comas-Días, 2020; Friere, 2000; Haddock-Lazala, 2020), can be employed in multiple ways as clinical interventions within sessions.

Liberation Psychology Constructs and Interventions

- **Concientización**, or consciousness-raising, refers to engagement in a process of critically raising awareness of individual issues within the context of oppressive societal structures and using that information to engage in liberatory action.
- **Acompañamiento**, or accompaniment, is a process in which therapists stand with or alongside clients in solidarity and bear witness to their testimony and healing.
- **Dialoguing** is a process in which therapist and client engage in a practice to promote consciousness-raising through asking questions such as: *For whom? In favor of whom? To what end?*
- **Justice-oriented psychospirituality** refers to the integration of culturally embedded spiritual beliefs and practices that support client meaning making, promote a positive sense of self and connectedness with other living things, and enhances a justice orientation.
- **Testimonio** refers to the telling of one's story or exposing of an embodied truth. Clients recount their experiences of oppression, trauma, and marginalization.

Let's consider the following case and reflect on common therapist's responses as well as the ways that therapists can engage with a client from a liberatory perspective.

Janice, a young African American woman, works as an office manager for a large property management company. She sought counseling for what she described as a painful amount of anxiety. The company where Janice works is predominantly white and male. Janice described it as basically a "bro* convention," referring to the way the men act and relate to everyone in the workplace. The company expects everyone to work long hours and be readily available. During the pandemic, she had been expected to be available on Slack 24/7 and would be reprimanded if there was a delay in her response. As Janice's anxiety increased, she noticed that it was impairing her productivity at work and her relationship with her partner.

There are multiple issues of concern in Janice's case. More information about the workplace is necessary to understand the range of harm and specific triggers, yet it is clinically paramount to therapeutic rapport and the development of any type of authentic therapeutic relationship to explicitly affirm that this is a difficult, and likely harmful, environment for her as an African American woman. Consider the following potential exchange:

Janice: Ugghhh. This situation with my boss has become unbearable. No matter what I do, it seems like I am angry or mean or something. He told me that I should smile more! He even put it in writing on my evaluation. I have to deal with this racist shit every day, and I'm not sure what to do.

Therapist: This sounds frustrating, like it is becoming unmanageable. I wonder if your boss is picking up on your frustration and perhaps that is what he meant?

---

* The term "bro" is used to connote bro culture, which is associated with toxic masculinity and hypermasculinity, subtle and overt endorsements of aggression and violence, and which is imbued with racism, sexism, and homophobia (Berdahl et al., 2018).

Many therapists—especially non-Black therapists—working with Janice might shy away from explicit affirmation of a racist or otherwise toxic environment. Consider why that might be, and if it is true for you, what that might be about for you. If you are someone who would intentionally avoid such an explicit statement or someone for whom such an explicit statement would be difficult, take a moment to reflect on this avoidance. Now, return to Janice and consider what it is like to be a young African American woman working during this particular social and political moment in a predominantly white male environment—one she describes as a "bro convention." What might she want and need from a therapist? What might she want and need from a Black therapist (assuming she was able to see one of the few Black therapists available)? What might she want or need from a non-Black therapist of Color? It is most probable that she would have easiest access to a white therapist. What might she need or hope for from a white therapist? How does the gender identity of the therapist shape what Janice might want or need? One of the most important aspects of therapy is being seen and having our pain witnessed. In this scenario, the client described her experience and names it as racism. She also states clearly that this is something she experiences daily and that her boss is wielding power in particular ways, including writing it in an evaluation. The therapist's response in this example not only fails to acknowledge the magnitude of Janice's emotion (frustrating instead of acknowledging unbearable) but, more importantly, it denies her experience of racism by questioning it, thus implying that the client is *wrong* in her interpretation and naming of her *own* experience of racism. Therapists question and we invite—even challenge—clients to consider multiple perspectives within any given situation. How and when we do so matters. The failure to name and give voice to the pain and harm of this situation is not only a missed opportunity to connect and build therapeutic rapport, it also puts the therapist at risk of being complicit in the common act of minimizing the effects of racist, misogynistic, and otherwise harmful experiences and environments. Worse yet, Janice may have then experienced therapy as an extension of the racialized harm she experienced in the workplace. Put simply: this kind of response would likely result in therapy no longer being a safe or affirming environment.

A common approach in the treatment of anxiety would be to instantly begin discussing triggers and ways to cope with or manage the anxiety. That is what most of us are trained to do. While Janice would likely benefit from the integration of mindfulness, it is important that we first affirm the harmful external realities that include, but are not limited to, working in an emotionally (and potentially physically) unsafe environment during a social and political period of pronounced concern for Black people. When we immediately jump to "coping," we indirectly communicate that it is the client's responsibility to *adjust to* or *cope with* living or working in harmful, potentially traumatizing environments. To truly witness a client's pain and experience, we must see and affirm them by speaking aloud that what they are experiencing is *real*. Many therapists who struggle to name and affirm racist, sexist, and transphobic environments do not have the same reluctance or difficulty in naming and affirming other abusive relationships or toxic family dynamics. Some therapists may be able to relate to relational and familial environments, but naming a racist workplace (or societal conditions) feels different to them in some way. Therapists must ask themselves why and consider the potential impact on their clients. Racism operates in many insidious ways. Too often, People of Color have their experiences of racism—especially more subtle forms of racism and microaggressions—minimized or dismissed. When therapists move first to teach coping strategies, they locate themselves, and therapy, in alignment with these same oppressive traditions. In so doing, therapists inflict additional harm. This is particularly poignant: the very person and safe space that Janice went to for help may be harmful if her therapist is unable to say the uncomfortable things and sit with difficult truths. Affirming the client and racism, and the nuanced ways in which racism works in the world and in their lives, is central to the development of an authentic, healing relationship. The failure to develop an authentic relationship and strong therapeutic rapport leads to premature termination. Worse, some clients may learn that therapy is not a space of healing, and in fact, it can be just as traumatizing, if not more so, than the racism they experience in other spaces. Consider the following more affirming and liberatory response to Janice:

Janice: I received a message on Slack today from a colleague that just threw my entire day off. The guy's tone was rude, he acted as if he was my supervisor when he is not, and basically insulted my work ethic.

Therapist: Wow, Janice. That sounds really disrespectful and hard to deal with even over Slack. I know the environment at work, especially all of the microaggressions, has been wearing on you.

Janice: Yes, I used to want to explode. Now, with all of the layoffs, I just don't want any problems. I don't want to lose my job. So, I get in my head and end up overthinking everything and anxious all day. Then my partner got pissed because I was irritable and snapped at him.

Therapist: It sounds like you went from questioning the guys at work to turning that inward on yourself and your partner and even questioning your job security. Who benefits when you do that?

Janice: That [*expletive*] who sent me the message.

Therapist: Who or what else benefits when you turn those emotions toward yourself?

Janice: [*pause*] They all do . . . [*pause*] . . . this is how it works. We begin to feel powerless and try to save our [*expletive*] job, so we stay in our place.

Therapist: You mentioned feeling powerless. Let's talk about your power.

In this exchange, the therapist affirmed and made visible the experience of racism and microaggressions the client experienced. Engaging in the process of *dialoguing*, the therapist used the question, "Who benefits when you do that?" to engage or increase the client's critical consciousness. With the awareness of how common racialized and power dynamics play out in individual exchanges (even over apps), the client and therapist can delve deeper to discuss and access power. This response to Janice is occurring *prior to* or instead of a discussion about coping with "her" anxiety. From a liberatory and intersectional perspective, fostering critical consciousness around what and why she is experiencing anxiety may help Janice engage in a practice of resistance that leaves her feeling more empowered with greater access to a wider range of ways to navigate these situations. It is worth mentioning that there are also risks in working from a strengths-based and resilience-promoting approach. There is often an individualized focus on the resilience of racialized people, and especially of Black women, such as Janice, but it is important to also locate this resilience as part of a communal and intergenerational legacy of resistance and resilience. Moreover, therapists must ensure that they do not unwittingly minimize the vulnerability and harm that people have endured in our acknowledging of their strength and resilience. This is particularly important in working with Black and Brown women, whose strengths are often celebrated (even romanticized) and weaponized against them. We must ensure that, in witnessing a client's testimony, we hear and see the full range of strength, resilience, harm, and trauma, not just the parts that feel good for us to witness.

Let us turn to another aspect of identity and another method of engaging in liberatory counseling.

LGBTQ+ AFFIRMATIVE AND ANTIHETERONORMATIVE THERAPY

An intersectional and liberatory approach to counseling means that, even with race consciousness, we are also attending to sexual and gender identities as well as the structural systems that marginalize any identities outside of the heterosexual or gendered norm (Adames et al., 2018; Trevor Project, 2020). For some therapists,[*] exploring sexual identity may be more comfortable than exploring race and racism. Others may have grown comfortable with race yet not the intersections of race and sexual or gender identity. Let's engage in some critical reflection by considering the following questions:

---

[*] I want to start this section by acknowledging that I write this as a cis-het Black woman who is afforded the benefits of heteronormativity. While I inhabit many queer spaces and have been entrusted to walk alongside many Black and Brown queer-identified clients, I do not have the lived experience, especially the distinct manifestations of heterosexism, homophobia, and transphobia, with which the LGBTQ+ community lives. My intention is to foreground voices and scholarship from within the LGBTQ+ community instead of relying on my own or other outsider perspectives. Readers are encouraged to privilege the voices and scholarship from within the community.

Pause | Reflect

- Do you consider yourself and your office to be "safe spaces"? How do you center, affirm, and support LGBTQ+ and nonconforming gender and sexual identities?
- Do your practice paperwork and intake procedures and language you use reflect sexual and gender fluidity and client agency in identification?
- In what ways do you explore the intersections of sexual orientation and gender identity with other dimensions of identity?
- In what ways do you support, perpetuate, or otherwise benefit from heteronormativity?

The history of pathologizing nonheterosexual, trans, and nonconforming gender identities within mental health is long (Grzanka & Miles, 2016). A full account of this history is outside the range of the present exercise, but it is noteworthy to mention that: 1) it was not until 1973 that homosexuality was removed from the DSM-II; 2) gender identity disorder was only revised and renamed gender dysphoria in the most recent DSM-V in 2013; and 3) same sex marriage has only been legal since 2015. These all represent major strides in LGBTQ+ rights yet are very recent in the history of this country and of the mental health field. While important, these achievements do not fully portray the more complex reality of LGBTQ+ individuals and their families. Therapists must be keenly aware of the strides that have been made but also of the rise in violence against this population, of identity-based stressors and discrimination, of heterogeneity and issues within the LGBTQ+ community, and of the LGBTQ+ community's unique mental health needs. Let's briefly deconstruct these issues and consider the significant cultural and generational shifts that have occurred around LGBTQ+ acceptance.

With increased visibility, understanding, legal rights, and acceptance of LGBTQ+ people has come a rise in a generation that increasingly self-identifies as part of the LGBTQ+ community. According to a recent GLAAD study (2017), Millennials are the most sexually fluid generation to date, with approximately 20% identifying as something other than strictly heterosexual. Perhaps more revealing is that 12% identify as gender nonconforming or trans (GLAAD, 2017). This data reflects a significant shift in public culture in which young adults and youth have space to identify in different ways, including the use of more expansive terminology than previous generations. Remarkably, this same generation is less likely to report knowing someone who is gay or lesbian, primarily because of the evolution of possibilities, language diversity, and less rigid identification with a binary gay/lesbian versus straight identification. Increasingly, young adults conceptualize and talk about these aspects of their identities outside of an essentialist binary perspective. Gen Z and Millennials are also more likely to accept and be allies of the LGBTQ+ community. Notably, older generations have also reported increases in LGBTQ+ acceptance, and the majority of people surveyed in the United States now report being either supportive or an ally (GLAAD, 2017). It is important that therapists reflect on how attuned they are to these significant cultural shifts and how identity and language are reflected in the therapy they provide.

Despite wider acceptance and reported allyship, members of the LGBTQ+ community still experience hate crimes and gender-based violence and are more likely to have experienced verbal and emotional abuse (National Alliance for Mental Illness, n.d.). Over the past few years, hate crimes against LGBTQ+ community members have continued to rise. Recent reports indicate that 2020 has been the deadliest year on record for trans people, with the majority of fatalities being Black and Latinx transwomen (Human Rights Campaign, 2020; National Center for Transgender Equality, 2020). Though queer people have needed to be resilient, it makes sense that they are extraordinarily vulnerable to psychological distress with higher rates of depression, anxiety, and substance abuse (Meyer, 2015). These rates are even higher for trans people. Trans people exist on the margins, even within queer and supposedly safe spaces. Marginalization is even more pronounced for Black- and Brown-identified trans people. Given the chronic stress of discrimination and polyvictimization, it is not surprising that trans people represent one of the populations at highest risk for psychological distress, which can manifest as trauma, depression, anxiety, and higher rates of suicidality compared to cisgender people (National Center for Transgender Equality, 2020).

The LGBTQ+ community has high rates of mental health service utilization yet frequently reports negative experiences with therapists, many of whom have little competence in their areas of need. This is troubling given the higher rates of psychological distress and exposure to violence and trauma in this population. The focus of this section is working directly with LGBTQ+ individuals in therapy, but because of the high rates of trauma and violence perpetuated against this community, we should also consider who the perpetrators are of such harm. Therapists must consider that also within our offices are people who are homophobic and transphobic, and we must challenge ourselves around the ways we attend to and intervene when we hear heteronormativity in sessions with non-LGBTQ+ individuals. Considering the need for safe space for LGBTQ+ people, this necessarily means that our justice- or activist-oriented therapy and work cannot be relegated to clients who identify as LGBTQ+. We must be intentional about fostering anti-heteronormativity wherever it is present. Let's now turn to clinical approaches to working with LGBTQ+ individuals.

As previously mentioned, changes in diagnoses are recent evolutions in the way the mental health field views sexual orientation and the range of gender identities and expression. With the multicultural wave of counseling came increased attention to and advocacy for inclusion of LGBTQ+ individuals and the issues of concern within these communities. This often mirrored what inclusion looked like for many specific racial groups, such as one chapter on the topic in a book focused on broad issues. More recently, the field of psychology has advocated for affirmative therapy. LGBTQ+- or gay-affirmative therapy intentionally espouses a positive and affirming view of LGBTQ+ individuals and their families and acknowledges the multiple ways that existing within a larger context of heterosexism and ever-present homophobia and transphobia impacts their lives (Smith, 2015). Smith (2015) advocates for movement away from affirmative counseling in favor of an anti-heteronormative counseling model, in which therapists dismantle the heterosexual hegemony that pervades therapeutic spaces by identifying and naming heterosexual and cisgender privilege. As noted above, this is something therapists can also provide to clients outside the LGBTQ+ community. Taking an anti-heteronormative perspective also results in the expansion of one's thinking about work regarding LBGTQ+ issues beyond working with queer-identified people. Smith argues that while affirmative therapy provides a space in which the client's sexual and gender identities are validated, it fails to acknowledge the social systems that necessitate such affirmation. The very affirmation we provide may inadvertently perpetuate the practice of centering a heterosexual norm. Smith also contends that therapists should assume that all people have internalized heteronormativity that must be acknowledged and disrupted (Smith, 2015). Thus, returning to the reflection questions at the beginning of this section, it is important to be willing to sit with (and regularly return to) the question about the ways that we each perpetuate or benefit from heteronormativity.

> **Anisa** and **Kris** present for couples counseling due to a protracted period of relational conflict and poor communication. Anisa is a 36-year-old Southeast Asian cis-woman who works as a yoga and meditation teacher. She describes herself as femme and sexually fluid, attracted to people across the gender identity spectrum. Kris is a 46-year-old Black Caribbean nonbinary person who states that they (preferred pronoun) are attracted to femme presenting women. Kris works in leadership at an arts-based education non-profit organization. Anisa and Kris report that they met online a few years ago and connected instantly across multiple important areas of life. The relationship became serious quickly, and they moved in together after dating for a few months, in part because Anisa had a bad roommate situation and needed to suddenly move out. They both describe their relationship as loving and supportive overall, but when they are triggered or disagree about things, it can escalate into a major argument with yelling and harmful things said to one another. Both Anisa and Kris have trauma histories that get triggered in the relationship. Anisa reports that she has engaged in a lot of individual work around the sexual trauma she experienced in college and feels comfortable talking to Kris about her needs when triggered. Kris spent part of their childhood in the foster system, experienced physical abuse, and has been disconnected from most of their family for the past 30 years. Kris reported having tried

individual counseling one time in their mid-thirties and described
it as a "disaster" because the therapist knew nothing about Black
people and "didn't know what to do with someone who looked like
me [Kris]." Anisa and Kris both agree that how they express anger
and hurt is unhealthy. They want to learn how to better show up for
one another when they are emotionally triggered instead of allowing situations to escalate.

Anisa and Kris are a couple who have a lot of love and connectedness
in their relationship. Their relationship is complex, given both of their histories of trauma as well as their differences, such as race, age, and gender
identities. Their difference in previous therapy work may also be important in terms of where each of them is in their trauma healing. From an
intersectional, affirmative, and anti-heteronormative approach to therapy
with Anisa and Kris, it is important to honor all of their identities and the
complexities of these identities, including the strengths and challenges
they present. For example, Anisa is from an Indonesian family that is non-
observant Muslim but traditional in many ways. Her cultural heritage is
particularly salient for her and even informed her choice to work as a yoga
and meditation teacher. She reports seeing this as the work of her ances-
tors. Yet, her sexual fluidity was not well-accepted in her family, and her
choice to partner with someone who is Black also revealed "deeply rooted
anti-Blackness" within the family. This has forced Anisa to come to terms
with aspects of her culture (and family) that are difficult. Given the traumas experienced, Anisa and Kris are attuned to the ways that trauma can
manifest in their relationship. It is also important to make space for the
chronic stress and traumas that often go unnamed or are minimized, such
as the daily experiences of racism, sexism, and heterosexism. Consider the
following exchange:

Therapist: We are witnessing a lot of anti-Black racism and attention to police violence against Black people. How has this
affected you all?
Kris: It's hard, especially with things already being rough with the

pandemic. But we've been dealing with this for years. In some ways, it's the same thing.

Anisa (speaking to both Kris and the therapist): I worry about Kris and how people read them. Kris is often read as masculine or genderqueer and I worry about the police. And, I think Kris does too. Kris doesn't say it, but I see the difference. You have been anxious and tense and not sleeping well. I think you may want to minimize it, but it's affecting you.

Therapist: Anisa, I hear your concern for Kris' safety. This is also a newer personal experience for you, being with a Black partner. And, Kris, it sounds like Anisa is sensing that your body is holding this racial stress.

Kris: I'm Anisa's first Black partner. It's different for her even though she has always dealt with color stuff. She's a yoga teacher, she is always talking about what is happening in my body. The reality is that I am probably anxious and tense . . . but isn't that the norm? I'm Black and queer and grew up with shitty people around me. I have spent my life on guard. That's called survival.

Therapist: This is certainly how a lot of us manage racism and all the isms around us. Kris, take a moment and check in with your body and what your body is experiencing even as we discuss this. Can you give voice to your internal experience?

There are multiple aspects of identity that are attended to in this brief exchange. The intersection of race and gender expression becomes evident in the discussion of how people might automatically categorize Kris. In addition, we hear the racialized differences in how they experience and hold the present moment. We can see that Kris normalizes anxiety as a way of being and surviving their specific identities in a racist and heterosexist world. Thus, as is apparent from this dialogue with Kris and Anisa, it is important, from an intersectional approach, to be able to hold the multiple identities and power structures that are at play in someone's life and that are manifesting throughout the therapy process. Moreover, embodying race-consciousness and awareness of social systems necessitates an understanding of race and racism within queer spaces as well.

For therapists seeking guidance and support to develop in these areas, the APA published the *Guidelines for Psychological Practice with Transgender and Gender Nonconforming Persons*, which provides helpful direction. In addition, the Queer Affirmative Caucus of the American Association of Marriage and Family Therapists has set forward helpful recommendations and concrete steps that therapists can take in addition to employing intersectional, affirmative, and anti-heteronormative therapy. Specifically, they suggest that affirmative therapists, or those seeking to become an affirmative therapist, should: engage in an ongoing practice of self-reflection in which they examine their beliefs, identities, and privileges; ensure that their practice has an affirmative environment, that affirming language is used in intake paperwork, and that preferred names and pronouns are used; provide affirmative therapy to all clients, irrespective of identity; and challenge heterosexual and cisgender client biases when these are present. The Queer Affirmative Caucus of the American Association of Marriage and Family Therapists also contends that being an affirmative therapist does not occur just in the therapy space, rather they challenge affirmative therapists to live an affirmative life in which they become aware of and advocate for LBGTQ+ social justice issues. The information provided here is also provided in checklist form in Appendix B for therapists to use when updating their practice materials. Readers should recall and be cautioned that updating practice materials and using the checklist alone are insufficient. Rather, the therapist's updated materials should reflect their shift in understanding and their approach to and commitment to provide inclusive therapy.

WHITENESS AND ANTIRACISM IN THERAPY

I have intentionally positioned whiteness and clinical work with white clients late in this chapter in an effort to avoid perpetuating the centering of whiteness. We are at a moment in this country when there is necessarily an increased attention on whiteness, on its insidious and dominant yet somehow fragile nature, and on the ways in which it permeates even therapeutic space (DiAngelo, 2018; Grzanka et al., 2019). Even with the rise of multicultural counseling, the focus was primarily on how white therapists can work competently with *diverse* (read: not white) clients (Grzanka et al., 2019). It has been more than 35 years since Helms (1984) introduced white racial identity theory, yet the mental health field has only recently begun taking steps to advance its articulation of the impact and clinical manifestations of white socialization and ways that the white clinicians, who comprise the majority of the field, can make whiteness visible and increase positive racial consciousness with white clients (Grzanka et al., 2019; Malott et al., 2019). The most recent racial uprisings and recent public attention to and openness to learning about whiteness, white fragility, and antiracism has resulted in soaring increases in book sales on these topics. Forbes (McEvoy, 2020) reported that sales of Robin DiAngelo's well-known text *White Fragility: Why It's So Hard for White People to Talk About Racism* increased by 2264% during the first two months following the murder of George Floyd Jr. Similarly, Ibram X. Kendi's *Stamped From the Beginning* increased sales by a shocking 6895% during the same period. Clearly, there is a surge in interest in these topics. Many of us experienced a client initiating a conversation about race for the first time. Others—both clients and therapists—may have been conspicuously silent about these issues. White therapists working with white clients may have struggled with whether or how to navigate these difficult conversations, especially if a client speaks in ways that suggest covert racist ideology. It is the avoidance of confronting client's subtle yet racially coded language that thus goes uncontested and unexamined by, often, well-intentioned therapists that merits further exploration here.

The mental health field is known for being politically liberal, progressive even. We therapists are helpers, healers, and often self-identify as "do-gooders." Yet, this moment is about honesty and reckoning. If we are honest in our critical reflection, many white people—including therapists—have been largely able to avoid any real interest or engagement with issues of racial justice and have been allowed to exist in a state of indifference, at best, including in therapy. Some of the first, and perhaps most important, questions white therapists must ask of themselves include:

- Why now?
- Why did I not care before now?
- Why did it/they (insert issue or group of people) not matter before now?

Before you retreat to the emotional safety and ego-protecting space of denial, these questions are not intended to publicly condemn or denigrate. Rather, these private questions are an invitation for you to acknowledge that there is nothing new about the present moment, even if we as individuals *perceive* a newness. The fact that we are just now seeing something does not mean it was not happening before. What does it say about therapy and about us as self-identified healers, progressives, and do-gooders if we are only now attending to the continued public killings of Black people? If we are to engage in honest critical reflection, we must necessarily start from a space of honesty and transparency, if only with ourselves. If we begin our reflection with a denial about our point of departure, we are skipping necessary steps in our personal and professional development and thus may be doomed to repeat patterns or to fall victim to defensiveness. Just as we would challenge our clients about their defense mechanisms and the ways they lie to themselves, so, too, must we challenge ourselves as therapists.

Even white therapists who self-identify as antiracist rarely, if ever, address racism in therapy with white clients (Stone, 2013). White therapists aspiring to engage in antiracist praxis must be willing to engage in their own (ongoing) work, particularly in how to interrupt this avoidance. We cannot purport to engage in antiracist therapy if we are unable to engage in the necessary hard self-examination, specifically around issues of race and racism. Second, we must commit to moving beyond the comfort of silence and avoidance. We must consider that in our avoidance of directly discussing racialized issues, we become coconspirators and enablers of white fragility. Sue (2015) described an antiracist white identity as requiring "personal and collective action to confront and end racism" including advocating for social justice in the policies, practices, and programs of our society" (p. 189). For antiracist therapists, this means acknowledging that racism is not compatible with wellness. Thus we must locate racist ideology and the distorted thinking that encapsulates it as part of a client's overall mental health assessment in the same way that we would intervene if a client demonstrated delusional thinking and detachment from reality in any other area of life (Thompson & Neville, 1999). While overt racist ideology provides clarity for assessment purposes, more often we encounter subtle forms of racist thinking. This is important to note, as it may be easier to minimize or avoid challenging the more subtle manifestations of racism.

Antiracist therapists also interrupt their own and their clients' superficial engagement with issues of race. This is not possible unless we therapists peel back the layers of what it means to be an ally. Some white people, especially those in early stages of their racial consciousness, assuage their guilt by outwardly appearing to be engaged in meaningful antiracist work. Put simply, these superficial behaviors are about being seen by self and others as a good or different kind of white person (e.g., the "woke" white person). Similarly, proximity to oppression and the oppressed (e.g., a Black friend or Latinx partner) is used as a metric for one's own racial redemption. As Natasha Stovall describes, white people often seek to differentiate which type of white person they are: "Farm to table white or Cracker Barrel white? . . . Electric car white or pickup truck white? Digital white or analog white?" (Stovall, 2019). While such analogies engender familiar yet stereotyped images, they risk endorsing the idea that being a liberal or socially conscious white person means that one is not racist. An intersectional approach to therapy with white clients also means fostering the client's understanding of themselves as a complex person with multiple identities, including a healthy racial identity. Indeed, race is a salient factor to promote psychological health in white clients, particularly in being able to associate positive aspects of whiteness instead of only associating it with oppression (Stone, 2013). And, from an antiracist perspective of therapy, discussions of race should also not be limited to combating racist statements in therapy, rather a race-consciousness should be interwoven throughout therapy (Stone, 2013).

Making whiteness visible in therapy is a difficult task, especially for white therapists, given the silence and avoidance that surrounds it. Certainly, many people are more aware of the challenges and potential emotionally reactive responses to discussions about race as a result of white fragility (DiAngelo, 2018). Many therapists fear that acknowledging racism in the room may threaten therapeutic rapport due to the psychic discomfort many white people experience in talking about race. This concern may be heightened for new clinical relationships in which therapeutic rapport is not well established (Drustrup, 2019; Sharf et al., 2010). Yet, to allow clients to espouse unchallenged racist ideologies (or any other prejudice) may indirectly convey to a client that the therapist condones or is in tacit agreement with such beliefs. As systems therapists contend, for deep, sustainable change to occur, including client's racialized views of themself and others, disequilibrium is necessary (Thompson & Neville, 1999). This will create discomfort and may be unsettling and may result in strong emotional release, some of which could be directed toward the therapist. As therapists, we are trained in how to support clients through their emotions, even if they are displaced onto us. If we find that we avoid this kind of emotional processing when it is related to racism, we must deal with our own discomfort before we can be comfortable and confident supporting a client in this area. Let's discuss the white racial affect that can emerge in discussions of race and racism as well as practical clinical strategies to navigate these situations.

White Racial Affect

White racial affect has been an important area of exploration of antiracism (Grzanka et al., 2019; Grzanka et al., 2020). Authors delineate white apathy, white fear, and white melancholia as emotions of racism (Grzanka et al., 2019; Grzanka et al., 2020). Many of us therapists may be familiar with the apathy or outright disinterest that many whites may exhibit toward issues of race. We may see this in loved ones or clients; we may struggle with this ourselves. Often, whites see race as an issue for People of Color (DiAngelo, 2018). White racialized fear is most often directed toward African American/Black and Latinx men and is a commonly documented emotional space for white people (Grzanka et al., 2019). Similarly, anxiety or fear of examining one's own racist ideologies or being viewed as racist by others is another aspect of white emotional affect that warrants clinical attention (Drustrup, 2019). Related to white fear is white melancholia, which is described as a collective feeling of loss or grief about white people's loss (or perceived shift) of racial power. This was widely witnessed during the 2016 and 2020 presidential elections in the United States. This is an important area of intervention for clinicians as researchers have noted that white melancholia can evolve into white rage, especially among white men (Grzanka et al., 2019). Take for example, the following clinical exchange:

Client: I had a conversation with a friend that didn't go well. I haven't been able to get it off of my mind.

Therapist: It sounds like this really affected you. Tell me more about what happened.

Client: Well, I have a friend from work who is Black. We have been close and everything. She is dating a new guy, and I am really happy for them. So, we were talking about how well things were going, and I just made a comment about how beautiful their mixed babies would be. I could tell that she got really upset.

Therapist: How did she respond?

Client: She said that what I said wasn't cool, and then she just changed the subject. I just didn't think she was sensitive like that.

Therapist: It sounds like you think that your comment was okay and that she was being sensitive.

Client: Well, I don't think that what I said was a big deal.

Therapist: I'm noticing that even as you describe this situation, you seem to be defending yourself. Can you talk about what you are defending?

Client: I mean her reaction made me feel like I'm some bad person. Like I'm some super racist or whatever. She knows that I'm not, so I don't know why she responded like that.

Therapist: Having someone hear something in a different way than you intend is hard. Are you open to the possibility that even if you didn't intend to offend her that was still the result?

Client: Clearly she got offended, but I don't think that should be my fault.

Therapist: It sounds like you are more invested in not being seen as offensive or racially insensitive than you are about having offended or hurt a friend.

Client: [*silence . . . eyes becoming wet*]

Therapist: I see that this is hard for you, even now as we discuss this. Can you talk to me about how you are feeling? Because it seems that this is a real opportunity for growth . . . if you are open to it.

In this client–therapist exchange, the client clearly becomes defensive and perhaps a little angry at the friend for having been offended and even verbalizes her offense: she triggered the client's fear of being seen as racist. The therapist affirms that having something you have said be received in an unintended way is hard while also challenging the client to consider the difference between intention and impact (DiAngelo, 2018). The therapist then brings the client back to the relationship with the friend and the opportunity for growth. The therapist also invites the client to become aware in real time of what they are experiencing in their body. Making visible to the client what was offensive is also important and can be done once the client is aware of their defensiveness and has more spaciousness for it.

White guilt is another often elicited emotion, and it is likely the most commonly discussed white emotion (Grzanka et al., 2019). The presence of white guilt and empathy can potentially indicate one's openness to changing one's racist thinking and behaviors, if only to assuage the guilt. Recognition of this emotional state is important for antiracist therapists because it is an opportunity to foster white racial empathy. White racial empathy refers to a clear understanding of and ability to feel the emotional pain of racially marginalized people, and this kind of empathy is likely a necessary prerequisite for white people becoming antiracist and also may act as a pathway to advance social justice through counseling (Grzanka et al., 2019; Stone, 2013). However, cultivating racial empathy can be a difficult task. It becomes even more difficult for those who lack personally meaningful relationships with people who are racially different from them and those who live in predominantly white areas (DiAngelo, 2018). Recent research suggests that an openness to diversity is associated with greater degrees of white empathy (Chao et al., 2015). There are specific clinical tools that are beneficial for therapists to integrate in this work, including the Psychosocial Costs of Racism to whites (Spanierman & Heppner, 2004); White Racial Identity Scale (Miller, 2017); and the Antiracist Checklist (DiAngelo, 2015).

In addition to the emotions of racism, researchers have identified the emotions associated with antiracism. Emotional markers of white antiracism include moral outrage, compassion, joy, and hope (Grzanka et al., 2019). Clinicians must note, however, that moral outrage at the realities of racial injustice without self-examination is incomplete. Clients must be willing to at once witness and understand racial and other injustices while holding what that means for them as more privileged and, potentially, as beneficiaries of oppressive systems. And, as Sue (2015) noted, an antiracist (white) identity is action-oriented and involves a commitment to dismantling racism. Let's discuss strategies that therapists can use to assist them in this difficult clinical work. There are many models for moving clients through racial identity statuses. For this discussion, I offer some helpful strategies that integrate the work of multiple scholars (Drustrup, 2019; Stone, 2013; Sue, 2015; Thompson & Neville, 1999) and that may be beneficial to incorporating these issues into the overall course of therapy. Below are some steps that you may find beneficial in guiding this work.

Therapist Comfort and Race Consciousness

A therapist's comfort with asking questions that may be uncomfortable for the client can go a long way toward putting the client at ease. It may help to introduce some questions with a preface or statement such as:

> *Let's talk a little bit about your background and identity. Some of these questions may be new or ones you may not have thought of in a long time or ever. That's ok, the intention is for us, together, to get to know different parts of your identity and the factors that shape who you are.*

Clients cannot move forward in understanding their racial identity without being exposed to racial stimuli, which likely includes some difficult conversations and potentially uncomfortable situations. For some clients, therapy may be the first or only space in which these types of conversations occur. Some scholars recommend slowly addressing issues of race with white clients to increase the likelihood of openness and to minimize the risk that the client will develop one of the negative forms of white racial affect.

Make the Invisible Visible in Therapy

People are often unaware of faulty thinking and distorted beliefs, as in the clinical example presented above. Think critically about, assess, and consider whether it is best to address the statement, faulty thinking, or belief within the session in which it came up or to return to the issue during another session (Stone, 2013). Sensitivity to timing of discussions can help prevent or reduce defensiveness in favor of client openness.

Affirm and Educate

When we identify and hear racist ideology or we hear or experience micro-aggressions in sessions, it is important that we unearth and affirm the emotions (often fear-based) that belie the harmful statement or behavior. This may be difficult for some therapists, yet those feelings are real and help us and the client to understand their fragility (DiAngelo, 2018). Just as therapists know how to challenge and confront clients with other issues (e.g., dishonesty or deception in sessions or with others) matters, so too does how we challenge racist ideology and microaggressions matter, both in tone and content of the message. The client must trust and feel safe with us in order to sit in the discomfort. Once a client is able to see or understand the offense, the therapist has an opportunity to provide some psychoeducation about the offensive statement, harm inflicted, etc.

Connect to Client and Social Issues

Often, racial ideology is related to other issues in a client's life or may manifest in ways that are related to other client concerns (Stone, 2013). For example, in the clinical exchange presented above, the client became defensive and blamed the friend for viewing them in a negative light. It is probable that this client becomes defensive and has difficulty in holding themself accountable in other situations or relationships. Being able to connect work on race to other client issues and locate it within a larger social context may be useful to the client and be a way of advancing social justice.

While the course of therapy for clients who come in with other concerns may not be focused solely on these issues, I encourage therapists to make the linkages when they arise in treatment. In addition, the therapist should encourage the client to continue to grow in their racial literacy and to move beyond their segregated comfort zones (Drustrup, 2019). Notably, clients may need guidance in how to appropriately and respectfully navigate new cultural spaces and ways of being.

Lastly, white therapists engaging in this work would benefit from support and community with other antiracist therapists (DiAngelo, 2018; Stone, 2013). This is difficult work that likely triggers personal issues in both client and therapist. Having other therapists with whom we can give and receive support can help provide perspective and sustenance.

ADDITIONAL AREAS

It is not possible to discuss within the contours of this chapter or text all aspects of identity and the multiple ways in which these identities intersect and are embodied. I want to point out some of the areas that are not discussed in detail yet are important. While social location, positionality, and power are discussed, particularly in reflecting on similarities and differences between therapist and client, it is important to consider social class as an important determinant of health—including mental health—that intersects with other identities, such as race and gender, in important ways. These identities are being felt in more pronounced ways for some clients due to the economic crisis caused by the pandemic. Therapists are encouraged to think about and reflect on key differences in these areas, particularly during the present political climate. For example, being a white man living in poverty is different from, and may result in very different needs than, being an undocumented Asian woman living in poverty. Moreover, social class may also be a predictor and/or determinant of who has access to mental health care, particularly within the private sector.

Second, issues of disability also have not been discussed. Disability is still understood to serve as "both a marker for difference and a rationale for differing" and thus, disability continues to serve as an identity (for some) and way in which people are oppressed (Presley, 2019). Readers should note, however, that perspectives on disability and able-bodiedness are evolving. From a critical and decolonial disability studies lens, there is movement away from disability as a social identity; and clinicians would benefit from critically examining the social norms that relegate particular mental and physical attributes as impairments (Schalf, 2017) and the social conditions that impede access to full participation in society. With the recent scrutiny of the police, more attention has been given to violent and fatal police responses to people with mental vulnerabilities, particularly Black men with persistent mental illness (Westervelt, 2020). During a time in which people are demanding increased accountability and the transformation (if not abolishment) of the police, how disability is perceived is an area of concern, particularly given the role of the police in responding to mental health crises in many cities. It would behoove clinicians to consider questions such as: *What conditions in this client's life are impairing their functioning? In what areas does this client not have full access to participate in family or community life?*

Lastly, gender is not explicitly discussed as an independent identity construct. I have prompted readers to think critically about the ways that gender intersects with other identities as well as trans and gender nonconforming identities. Therapists are often trained and personally comfortable in discussions of gender, especially when expressed in accordance with normative expectations. It is also important, considering the sustained #MeToo movement, that we continue to attend to gendered vulnerabilities and traumas. In addition, therapists working with male-identified clients have an opportunity to engage in consciousness-raising around masculine identity and male privilege. Consider ways to engage larger questions such as: *In what ways do you use male privilege? How aware are you of how much space you take up in the presence of women or femme-identified people? How has the way you take up masculinity shaped how you relate to yourself and to others? In what ways do you perpetuate or disrupt patriarchy?* Such questions may be helpful as ways to critically engage with a client around masculinity and particularly in connecting it with presenting issues such as depression, anxiety, and relational issues. It is important to note that each therapist is charged with the task of thinking about the complexities of identity, the ways that these intersect, and the multiple structures that shape these identities in ways seen and unseen.

CONCLUSION

There is, admittedly, a lot covered in this chapter. This is for good reason: there is a lot happening in the world and to its citizens, and those in our field are all attempting to respond . . . slowly. Our field is approaching its evolution similarly to the client who waited for a long time to start counseling and is now finding it hard to know where to start. The client who even admits that everyone had been pushing them to go to counseling, but they refused. The client who finally came in, nonetheless, and is starting. There have been voices of scholars and practitioners in our field who were engaging in the work and paving the way. They have left a trail of breadcrumbs, if only we will follow it.

The field of therapy must move beyond the idea that we are well-meaning. We must disrupt the idea that having good intentions is ever enough. We must center not just culture but also an understanding of the power and structures that uphold differential, hierarchical inequities that impede psychological health and well-being. In moving away from paradigmatically narrow and superficial understandings of diversity, we must consider issues of social class, ableism, and religious hegemony within minoritized communities, such as the LGBTQ+ community. We have to move beyond an emphasis on coping to an emphasis on: 1) identifying and locating racial stressors as larger systemic issues within a global context of white supremacy; and 2) acknowledging environmental conditions can impede wellness and that toxic environments should be resisted, not coped with. Therapists must forgo the comfortable temptations and trappings of "weak" intersectional analyses (Grzanski et al., 2019) and applications that assuage our discomfort while massaging our ego for having "brought race into the room." We must be willing to move toward a "strong" intersectional approach that transcends mere identity analyses to one that considers and deeply engages with structural issues. On this, the ACA (2020) states:

> All ACA members must be willing to challenge these systems, but also confront one's own biases, stereotypes, and racial worldview. Moving forward, our actions will be based on input from our members and the voices of others. We are committed to change. (para. 5)

7

LEGAL AND ETHICAL ISSUES

Thus far, I have discussed the ways in which therapy is evolving in response to a global health pandemic and the mental health crisis that followed, to greater acknowledgement of racial injustice, and to the changing landscape of healthcare in a world of increased consumer voice. Yet, professional ethics have not coevolved. Ethical and legal mandates guide those in the psychotherapy profession and hold practitioners accountable to set rules, even as the field grows and evolves. With changes to how we see clients come new ethical and legal considerations and concerns. When working within a digital environment or outside of the confines of the traditional therapy office, clinicians must be keenly aware of threats to established best practice and ethical standards. Therapists must consider factors such as virtual threats to security in the practice of telehealth, any threats to privacy and confidentiality within nature-based or video sessions, and threats to the maintenance of appropriate boundaries with concierge clients. Psychotherapy appears to be more flexible, transparent, and at times politicized, which may bring complexities and ethical vulnerabilities for which therapists should be prepared. In this chapter, we will identify relevant legal issues, including federal laws such as HIPAA. In addition, we will discuss state-specific and recently evolving laws, such as those involving licensure, that may affect telemental health, concierge therapy, and wellness practices. We will pause and reflect on clinical examples to demonstrate the ethical complexities of practicing now.

BACKGROUND

For many years, there has been advocacy for the centering of a social justice ethic within counseling and counseling psychology and a movement away from what has been viewed as a prioritization of the welfare of the profession over the concern for the public good and social morality (Prilleltensky & Walsh-Bowers, 1993; Serrano-Garcia, 1994). Previous versions of psychotherapy promoted therapist neutrality, yet from a social justice perspective, neutrality and silence also make a political statement. Prilleltensky (2012) makes clear the interconnectedness of wellness, liberation, and oppression, which are intractably political and psychological. Many in the field argue that an antiracism and social justice orientation is an ethical and moral imperative for therapists. The urgency of this stance is felt even more with the present racial justice movement and rise of white nationalism. As noted in the previous chapter, the ACA, in its ethical code and recent bold public statements, insists that counselors take up an antiracist orientation and work toward equity and fair treatment of all groups toward the dismantling of racist systems of oppression (ACA, 2020). The APA does not make as clear a declaration in its ethical code. The APA ethics code (APA, 2017a) appears to set a less ambitious bar in its statement that psychologists should engage in introspection of internal biases; it does not go further to delineate a specific path forward. But the most recent APA multicultural guidelines (APA, 2017b), the *APA Guidelines on Race and Ethnicity in Psychology* (APA, APA Task Force on Race and Ethnicity Guidelines in Psychology, 2019) as well as *Guidelines for Psychological Practice With Transgender and Gender Nonconforming People* (APA, 2015) provide much more guidance and specific direction for clinical practice. Yet, it is significant that these are guidelines and not ethical mandates for the field.

With greater calls for mental health practitioners to engage in social justice praxis, this absence of a mandate prompts questions. Specifically, researchers in the field have challenged therapists to consider socially just ethics, that is, to critically evaluate whether our professional ethics and principles are socially just. In addition, these researchers acknowledge that some therapists actively engage in social justice work that promotes psychological well-being and adheres to professional ethics codes (Toporek et al., 2012). These are two different positionalities that consider social justice and ethics and prompt important considerations for social justice-oriented therapists including reflection on the extent to which our field contributes to or impedes social justice.

With changes in therapy modalities and new and different ways of being with clients, we therapists must remain attuned to processes of ethical decision-making to guide us through new terrain. Engaging in ethical decision-making is related to the reflective practice necessary for therapists' personal and professional development. Rigid reliance on ethical rules and prioritization of risk management over client care is indicative of early stages of therapist development and also relates to where we are, personally, in thinking through the complexity and nuances of real-world therapy with complex people. A reflective therapist, then, is one who can acknowledge that complex and nuanced ethical reasoning is necessary to engage in the types of therapy expected in today's psychotherapy.

Throughout this text, I have discussed the ways modern psychotherapy approaches places the client into a position of greater power than in previous versions of psychotherapy. Clients seek out therapists because of their training and expertise, but clients are no longer expected to be merely passive recipients of the therapist's expertise. Today's clients expect their voice to be valued. In models of care in which the therapist engages in more self-disclosure, the client has greater personal access to the therapist, and the sessions are located in more intimate settings, such as a client's home or online, people may falsely assume that the therapists are not guided by the same standards and principles and that they may have fewer boundaries with their clients. Such popular notions are misleading because they give clients (or prospective clients) inaccurate expectations. Therapists, too, may be ill-informed about out-of-office, concierge, and integrative wellness therapies and thus may also hold misperceptions. While these perceptions may be common, there are numerous ethical and legal considerations when following more flexible models of care.

RISK MANAGEMENT AND LEGAL ISSUES

I recently attended a continuing education webinar in which the presenter stated unequivocally that "there is no place for politics in therapy." The presenter went further to state that it is "unethical" to broach politics and that "clients are not there for that." Predictably, the presenter was hit with a barrage of questions and comments from attendees. The presenter's comments are not only inaccurate but also reflect a bias in the field based on its early roots in psychoanalysis (Zur, 2015). The field of therapy and the ethics that guide it have largely been shaped by psychoanalysis; there remains an emphasis on anonymous, emotionally detached therapists as the consummate goal. Because of this bias, there is often a conflation of good therapy that is ethical and legal with therapy that is risk-free (Zur, 2007). Therapists, like other health and wellness professionals, must be aware of risks and make the most justifiable clinical decisions possible. In doing so, however, it is important not to confuse risk management with ethics. When we are guided primarily by a risk management perspective, we may inadvertently compromise client care (Zur, 2007). In the next section, we will discuss some of the ethics and legal issues that may increase risk for therapists as well as clients and ways to navigate these situations.

Licensure Issues

Let us begin by considering licensure and related regulatory issues as well as HIPAA since these are two of the primary legal areas of concern. Licensed mental health professionals are bound by and must adhere to licensing regulations in the practice of therapy across any therapeutic modality, including teletherapy. In the United States, regulations around the practice of mental health are complex and at times confusing due to the different types of licenses across states and jurisdictional differences. It is important to remember that while HIPAA is a federal health privacy law with which all healthcare providers are expected to comply, each state is a separate jurisdiction with its own regulations and requirements for counseling and mental health professionals, and that state requirements and regulations apply to the authorization to practice in person or through teletherapy. Generally, the rule of practice is that "licensure follows the client," meaning that therapists must be licensed to practice in the location of the client (McCord et al, 2020). For example, if the therapist is licensed only in California, she may only see clients who reside in California. She may not see clients located in other states.

Even before COVID-19, some states had their own waivers that permitted therapists licensed in other states to temporarily work with clients in those states. Also, some states had already enacted PSYPACT—the Psychology Interjurisdictional Compact—which is an agreement that allows mental health providers in PSYPACT states who meet certain criteria to temporarily work with clients in other PSYPACT states (Clay, 2020). During the crisis of COVID-19, however, a number of new measures were enacted to ensure continuity of care and expand access to mental health. First, several states issued their own new or additional temporary licensing waivers. The requirements differ by state. Second, the Centers for Medicare and Medicaid recognized PSYPACT, which means that therapists who work with clients who have Medicare or Medicaid and live in the states that have enacted PSYPACT legislation can be reimbursed for qualifying therapy services. These steps were seen as a major step toward reducing systematic regulatory barriers to mental health care.

Currently, 14 states have enacted PSYPACT and the PSYPACT legislation is pending in 10 other states. You should find out whether you are licensed in a PSYPACT member state (or one with pending legislation), since if you are, you may potentially expand your available client population across multiple states. It is also important to note that even if your state has enacted PSYPACT, there are necessary requirements to meet before you start your multistate practice. Recent graduates and unlicensed practitioners must first complete the requirements for licensure including passing the Examination for Professional Practice (EPPP) and any other state-specific requirements for licensure in a PSYPACT member state. Licensed psychologists need to submit an application with supporting documentation in order to obtain an Authority to Practice Interjurisdictional Telepsychology (APIT). For therapists who want to temporarily practice in-person therapy in other PSYPACT states ("temporarily" meaning for 30 days per calendar year), you have to obtain an interjurisdictional practice certificate from the ASPPB. Also, while the PSYPACT temporary authorization allows therapists to expand their client base, therapists must think critically about taking on clients who may reside in another jurisdiction under a temporary authorization.

We must consider what happens if we (or our clients) do not reside in a PSYPACT member state? Do we have the ability to continue working with the client? Consider the following scenario:

Elizabeth has a small private practice that she has maintained for the past several years. She enjoys the freedom of private practice and the clients that she sees but she has had a difficult time consistently maintaining her client load. She maintains part-time employment at a local college to have consistent supplemental income and health benefits. With the COVID pandemic, Elizabeth lost a number of her clients who were no longer able to afford therapy. She was also furloughed from her part-time college position. Elizabeth felt grateful that under her state's temporary practice waiver, she was able to practice remotely and began promoting her teletherapy work. She began accepting new clients from other geographic areas given her understanding of the emergency authorizations to provide access to mental health care. Because of this increase in her practice, Elizabeth was able to stay afloat financially during the pandemic. She also felt good about supporting clients during this difficult health and economic crisis.

Many therapists may be able to relate to one or more aspects of Elizabeth's experience. Through teletherapy, Elizabeth was able to continue to work, expand her practice, and meet prospective client's mental health needs during a pandemic. Her decision to see clients from other geographic areas, however, presents a number of ethical questions. Specifically, Elizabeth needs to know not only which jurisdictions are covered under any temporary state (non-PSYPACT) authorization to practice, but what the requirements are to practice within each of those remote jurisdictions. For example, if Elizabeth is licensed to practice in Texas and she has accepted clients from Florida under a Florida temporary waiver, she needs to know

Florida's psychotherapy licensing requirements, as well as whether there could be disciplinary consequences in Texas for practicing out of state. She also needs to know what happens after a temporary authorization for interjurisdictional practice expires and inform her clients in advance that she can only work with them for the discrete time period while the authorization is in place. She also needs to monitor the authorization to ensure that she is aware of when it will expire. Elizabeth needs to think about what will happen if the authorization expires during a critical time in her clinical work with a particular patient, and to know what the relevant state licensure rules allow. Elizabeth must handle these legal and ethical issues with care within the clinical relationship with clients. Short-term clients may be most appropriate to be seen under a temporary authorization given the time limitations. Clients with histories of abandonment and insecure attachment are not appropriate to be seen under this context as these clients benefit from more stability than temporary authorizations to practice permit.

These are complex legal and ethical considerations that affect our clinical work with clients as well as the development and management of our private practice. The temporary authorization of interjurisdictional practice (in some places) both by individual states and collectively through PSYPACT marked a major, albeit temporary, step forward in the ongoing efforts to promote access to mental health care. Yet, temporarily working with clients across state lines may open doors and opportunities for a short time that may be difficult to easily close. The decision to work with someone for short term care must be done thoughtfully and with intentionality. Therapists must be transparent with clients from other states that the work is temporary for an unknown period (or for a specific limited period under the applicable state law) and have a transition plan developed with the client for when that authorization expires.

Privacy, Confidentiality, and Security

Confidentiality remains a primary legal task as well as ethical consideration for therapists. Regardless of therapeutic modality, HIPAA requires that clinicians, as health care providers, "maintain reasonable and appropriate administrative, technical, and physical safeguards" to protect our client's electronic private health information (https://www.hhs.gov/hipaa/for-professionals/privacy/laws-regulations/index.html). As noted earlier, while the law does not specify the particular processes that clinicians must use, it requires that we consider the technical, software, and human resources to maintain security of client health information. In Chapter 2, we discussed the necessity of using encrypted systems for storage and transmission of client information in the practice of telemental health. As discussed, this obligation also includes holding any business associates to the same requirements. Even therapists who are not engaging in video sessions use business associates, such as medical billing services or IT services when we need computer assistance. Because the people who provide those services all have access to our clients' "protected health information," we are required to have them sign a Business Associate Agreement (BAA) to safeguard and hold confidential any private health information to which they have access. See https://www.hhs.gov/hipaa/for-professionals/covered -entities/sample-business-associate-agreement-provisions/index.html. Ultimately, TMH therapists must "maintain continuous, reasonable, and appropriate security protections" and should document what measures we have taken (https://www.hhs.gov/hipaa/for-professionals/privacy/laws -regulations/index.html).

There are additional threats to privacy and confidentiality that may arise in therapeutic work outside of the office. For example, when meeting with clients in their home, there may be others present who could overhear session content. Similarly, when meeting with clients in nature-based sessions, such as a park, other people may walk by or be in close proximity. These challenges are all commonplace in out-of-office therapy. There are several ways a therapist can help to mitigate these potential issues. First, therapists working with clients outside of the office should employ a specific informed consent that acknowledges the potential threats to privacy. This additional consent makes clear the known and unknown risks, which should be discussed with clients prior to engaging in any out-of-office treatment. Ultimately, informed consent is an issue of power that is fundamental to the intent of the ethical principle of autonomy (APA, 2017a), that is, to empower the client to have voice in and consciously choose their own treatment, and documentation of this process may also help manage therapist risk.

ETHICAL CONSIDERATIONS

Ethics and Social Justice-Oriented Counseling

Viewing psychotherapy as a social justice enterprise is likely new for many therapists. With the integration of social justice issues, such as many of those discussed earlier in this text, may come some hesitance or trepidation in some therapists. Toporek et al. (2012) suggest that when engaging in justice-based practices, it is important to remember that: 1) the personal is political; ignoring the psychopolitical realities of clients reflects a fragmented understanding of the multisystemic factors contributing to client health and may render the therapy unethical; and 2) we must attend to the internal and external forces that oppress clients.

In identifying ethical considerations in social justice-oriented counseling, Toporek et al. (2012) offer three primary considerations:

1. **Language and voice.** Therapists should ask: *who or what is being silenced? In what ways is that being reproduced or perpetuated in therapy?* We must examine the theories we use and ways we implement them as sources of potential harm.
2. **Power.** Social justice-oriented therapists should work to integrate methods that reduce power differentials, such as egalitarian approaches, when they are culturally aligned for clients.
3. **Values.** Political neutrality is a myth that can harm clients.

These ethical perspectives disavow the notion that there is safety in neutrality and in not engaging in social justice work. On the contrary, in silence there is the potential to perpetuate oppression and cause harm. Certainly, our ethical mandate is to do no harm (APA Code 3.04; APA, 2017a). As with any form of therapy, *how* we engage in the work matters. Establishing therapeutic rapport and forming an authentic (with boundaries) relationship with clients helps to safeguard against, or to create openness to repair, times when the therapist may misunderstand or wrongly perceive a client. Further, as stated in Chapter 6, the intention of any form of social justice-oriented counseling is to facilitate a client's health and well-being, so any approach used should be evaluated against that metric. The additional benefit of social justice-oriented approaches is that the benefits of the work also extend to the greater good. Practitioners should look to resources such as the most recent APA multicultural guidelines (APA, 2017b), the *APA Guidelines on Race and Ethnicity in Psychology* (APA, APA Task Force on Race and Ethnicity Guidelines in Psychology, 2019), the *Guidelines for Psychological Practice with Transgender and Gender Nonconforming People* (APA, 2015). In addition, the ethical guidelines put forward by organizations such as the Association of Black Psychologists (ABPsi, 2019) are valuable resources to guide therapists.

Ethics and Wellness

In Chapter 4, I discussed the ways in which therapy has become more wellness oriented by incorporating more holistic and body-inclusive methods of care as well as out-of-office therapies. There are some specific ethical considerations in wellness models of therapy: we therapists are required to practice within our areas of competence; and therapists who are interested in expanding their practice offerings to include yoga or nutrition counseling, for example, need to ensure that they are trained and/or have the proper credentials to do so. For therapists who are trained or credentialed in another area and want to integrate that into the therapy they provide, there are a few considerations: First, regulation of complementary and alternative therapies varies. Many states do not have specific licensure or regulations for many complementary therapies. To this end, states may not directly prohibit therapists from combining these approaches with counseling, but therapists may still be held liable for the ineffectiveness, dissatisfaction, or harm caused by a complementary therapy (Natwick, 2018). Moreover, therapists must consider whether their then-current liability and malpractice policies will cover them for claims made by clients treated by means of such therapies, and if they won't, what coverage is available if they want to engage in those complementary therapies. Some therapists may choose to not integrate a complementary or alternative therapy within counseling and have a separate practice, potentially with separate clients, for the complementary approach. In practices that have little or inconsistent empirical support but that a therapist wants to incorporate in some way (e.g. Reiki, aromatherapy), therapists must be especially thoughtful and proceed with caution and consultation (Natwick, 2018). As mentioned in Chapter 4, a specific informed consent (and potentially a waiver of liability, which, ideally, should be drafted or at least reviewed by a healthcare attorney) is required. This consent should ensure that the client is provided information about the approach, including what the complementary approach entails and the potential benefits and risks associated with its use, in easily understood language. This would include any additional fees, which is particularly important for clients who rely on insurance or other third-party payors. Lastly, boundary issues may arise, particularly in engaging in approaches with body-inclusive work that relies on touch or physical proximity to a client. Therapists wishing to employ somatic approaches should thoroughly discuss these issues with clients before proceeding, and should then proceed with caution. Therapists must think critically about the distinct needs of clients with trauma histories and boundary issues.

Boundaries

Clear and consistent professional boundaries are paramount to the clinical relationship and are necessary to protect the therapist and the client. Teletherapy as well as emerging approaches to therapy, such as out-of-office and concierge models of therapy, may make the therapeutic relationship more vulnerable to boundary issues. In addition, practicing liberation therapy, or other forms of therapy that promote a transparent and authentic therapist–client relationship, challenges the traditional blank-slate, emotionally detached boundaries. While ethical guidelines are explicit in some areas, they are less clear in others. Often cited examples of blurry boundaries are around acceptance of gifts, socialization and dual relationships with clients, therapist self-disclosure, and physical contact with clients. Some theorists argue that boundary crossings may lead to exploitation of or harming of clients if therapists are not cautious (Drum & Littleton, 2014). Yet, boundaries may be crossed if done carefully and as part of an intentional treatment plan that is in the best clinical interests of the client. Zur (2007, 2015) offers the following examples of clinically beneficial boundary crossings: appropriate use of therapist self-disclosure to establish authentic connection and foster therapeutic rapport; going for a walk with a client; home-visits with clients who are ill or would benefit from environmental assessment and intervention; or attending a culturally significant event with a client. For example, disclosing to a client that the therapist is a mother, is a member of a particular community (e.g., queer community), or has a child with special needs may go a long way in establishing rapport and credibility with a client.

Given the clinical necessity of boundaries, it is important to know how to differentiate between a boundary *crossing* and a boundary *violation* as well as how to discern if there has been an ethical transgression. Zur (2015) notes that in a boundary *violation*, the therapist engages in an abuse of power that is, ultimately, for the therapist's own benefit. Boundary violations inflict harm onto the client and the clinical relationship. For example, engaging in a sexual relationship with a client is a clear boundary violation that is unethical (and illegal in some states). On the other hand, the clinically beneficial boundary *crossings* described in the previous paragraph do not involve an abuse of power nor do they exploit the client in any way; moreover, they are likely to deepen the therapeutic relationship and to advance treatment goals.

Flexibility: Testing the Boundaries

One of the primary arguments against flexibility in therapy is concern around boundaries (Drum & Littleton, 2014). Even in working remotely, there are certainly ways in which boundary issues arise. Drum and Littleton (2014) identify two factors that contribute to potential boundary issues in teletherapy: 1) because all communication relies upon technology, therapist and client engage with one another in more frequent and more casual ways; and 2) we associate safety with the distance, and therefore do not think as critically about boundaries. Drum and Littleton (2014) name specific boundary issues that can arise in teletherapy such as therapy occurring at nontraditional hours, excessive out of session contact, lack of adherence to time boundaries, sending messages outside of business hours, and conducting video sessions in public settings (e.g., at a coffeehouse). The authors note that these factors may not be therapy violations but may result in the client misinterpreting the meaning of the therapist's behavior and/or the behavior or misinterpretation thereof may negatively affect the course of therapy. Drum and Littleton (2014) recommend, in part that therapists:

- schedule teletherapy sessions during business hours
- provide timely feedback to clients but set boundaries to avoid excessive out-of-session contact
- ensure a consistent and private meeting location
- model appropriate boundaries for clients (e.g., not working while sick or on vacation)

The potential boundary issues presented by Drum and Littleton (2014) are important for teletherapists to keep in mind. It is also important that therapists think critically about the therapeutic benefits of flexibility, heterogeneity of therapist style, and approaches to therapy. There is often a fear that if sessions occur outside of the office, are scheduled at nontraditional times, or offer more transparency, boundaries will automatically be transgressed and client care (and potentially safety) will be compromised. While these concerns are understandable, they appear to be grounded in the idea that location and schedule, not the professionalism and appropriate therapeutic relationship with the therapist, hold the boundaries for clients. Regardless of where a session is held, for what amount of time, or at what time of day, therapists are responsible for maintaining appropriate boundaries and framing of therapy. If therapy is being conducted in a way that deviates from the traditional 50-minute hour, in-office or by video, this should be done with intentionality and with a client-centered focus. Informed consent and ongoing clear communication about the therapeutic relationship ensure that clients know what to expect from therapists. These elements become even more important when practicing nontraditional forms of therapy. Moreover, it will be increasingly important to think critically about and set boundaries around the type of work that is clinically appropriate for each client and continue to use ethical and clinical best practices as the standard, even with flexible and emerging models of care.

Dual and Multiple Relationships

Dual and multiple relationships are also important ethical considerations. Dual relationships include situations in which a client also holds another role relative to the therapist, for example, as a student, supervisee, friend, or family member (Zur, 2007). There are many dual relationships, such as serving as a therapist to a current student, that are exploitative and harmful to clients and that present clear ways in which clinical judgment may be influenced or the therapeutic relationship may be negatively affected by the multiple relationships. It is important to note, however, that some forms of dual relationships are commonplace in certain communities. It is not uncommon in rural communities and specific cultural groups for clients to seek out a therapist who has a known identification with or involvement within a particular community. For example, prospective clients may wish to see a therapist who is a member of the deaf community because their membership in that community and their fluency in ASL would benefit the prospective client. Similarly, a prospective client may be comforted in knowing that their therapist lives within a historic African American community or belongs to and volunteers within the LGBTQ+ community. To this end, ethical guidelines have evolved in recent years to be more inclusive. In the most recent edition of the *Ethical principles of psychologists and code of conduct*, the APA explicitly notes that "multiple relationships that would not reasonably be expected to cause impairment or risk exploitation or harm are not unethical" (APA, 2017a, section 3.05). Zur (2015) further contends that a therapist's known community membership is foundational for developing trust and earning credibility within these communities and spaces. In these instances, it is more prudent to identify the existing or potential multiple relationships and discuss ways to navigate any complexities.

Consider for example, the case in which Eileen learns about a therapist's services when they meet at an event at their children's school. The school is a private school, affiliated with a local synagogue, that is well-known in the local Jewish community. Their children are not in the same grade and have not met. Eileen states, when she later contacts the therapist, that she has been looking for a therapist who understands her cultural and religious background as well as some of the stressors facing working mothers in their school community. In this case, Eileen and the therapist are part of the same school and faith community. They are likely to run into one another at school or school-related events. If they both participate in religious activities at the affiliated synagogue, this may present other opportunities for out-of-office encounters. Eileen reached out to the therapist because these areas of convergence were comforting for her, and this comfort is likely to help establish rapport upon which the therapist could base her treatment. It would be prudent for the therapist to first consider their own comfort with working with clients in the same school and faith community. For some therapists, this might be very comfortable and provide an opportunity to work with and address the distinct needs of their community. For others, time with family and faith community is personal, and the potential for regularly running into clients might be uncomfortable or feel like a violation of the therapist's need for personal space. For therapists who would be comfortable working with a client within their community, it would be prudent and consistent with professional ethical guidelines to discuss confidentiality and the limits of confidentiality in the event that they see one another outside the office. The therapist may want to ask Eileen how she would like to handle a situation such as if they are both at school pickup. Would Eileen want to handle anything different if one or both of them were with family members? Having this discussion in advance is not only clinically and ethically prudent, it is also potentially comforting or even liberating for the client, in that the client then knows they are empowered to determine how the therapist will handle the situation. Further, the client understands or has reassurance about the seriousness of confidentiality, even within shared communities.

Social Media

Social media has presented new and evolving ways to promote wellness, mental health, and therapy services. In Chapter 1, I discussed the proliferation of Instagram therapy and how some therapists have moved beyond the provision of information to what might be interpreted as professional advice and even live virtual sessions, which is not in accordance with the ethical guidelines for therapists' conduct. While some therapists are clear with their followers and with the public that what they provide on social media does not constitute therapy or a professional relationship, this may be confusing for some consumers. Some therapists are including live virtual groups or one-on-one coaching sessions as part of exclusive membership communities for followers. Certainly, any live sessions in which someone's personal challenges are discussed and in which a therapist provides support or guidance in any way may appear to be therapy. And if it is not therapy, this practice may also elicit questions around whether the therapist is engaging in a potentially exploitative relationship in order to promote their therapy skills and services. Engaging in live sessions and providing individual public advice in ways that could be construed as therapy to promote services are troubling in that they prioritize the therapist's interests over the needs of the individuals seeking the therapist's services. It is important to differentiate these situations from therapists who livestream discussions, lectures, panels, and interviews focused on important mental health and wellness topics. The spaces that the latter individuals and organizations create have the potential to be both informative and healing through the information they provide and community they create. Because of this potential for positive impact, social media has been argued to be one vehicle through which therapists may raise critical consciousness and advocate for social justice (Al'Uqdah et al., 2019).

Regardless of your personal social media presence, there are a few clear directives within the ever-changing world of social media. Ethical guidelines dictate that therapists should not "friend" clients on social media nor interact with them on social media. This issue may become more complicated if a therapist uses a social media manager who manages their social media profile, including approving social media connections. Due to confidentiality, the social media manager may not have access to a current or previous client list and therefore may have no basis for denying a friend request. Social media management and boundaries may be even more of a concern for therapists with large social media followings and/or those actively engaged with their social media followers. Consider, for example, therapists who have thousands of followers across multiple social media platforms. It is unlikely that all the followers are personally known to the therapist, and therefore it is possible that a follower may later seek therapy from the therapist or, conversely, that a current client may later connect with the therapist on social media. Consider the following case:

Jason had been in private practice for several years when he began presenting at more conferences and community events. He began writing articles for popular sites that were well-received by his clients and others. His social media following began to grow, and he soon had thousands of followers. Jason would often stream live discussions with other therapists focused on mental health and social justice issues. These live-stream discussions were highly attended and often resulted in more new followers. Many followers and others posted comments and wanted to interact around the content of the discussions. Jason noticed that a current client began attending most of these streaming discussions and posting comments. In addition, the client began posting comments on most of Jason's posts and tagging him on some of their posts. Upon exploration, Jason noticed that this client had been following him online for some time before they began working together. While Jason had never interacted with the person online or acknowledged that this person was a client, he was uncomfortable with the number of comments the person posted and that the person was tagging him in their posts.

This example highlights the complicated nature of social media and boundaries with existing clients and the public. Jason used social media in ways that many therapists appropriately use social media to promote mental health and their services. With thousands of followers, Jason could not personally know all of his clients, and, moreover, it is not unreasonable to think that potential clients would become interested in his services as a result of getting to "know" him through social media. The concern, however, is that this is a client who is attempting to interact with Jason more frequently through social media. This incites questions such as: *Does Jason discuss the limits and/or boundaries around social media with clients? Is this documented in his initial paperwork? Once Jason notices that the client is frequently commenting on his posts or tagging him in their posts, how does he handle this? Does Jason respond in any way? How would it feel for the client if Jason blocked this person on social media? It is reasonable to expect that many people would feel rejected and, depending on the client's presenting issues, this could potentially trigger other issues. Is this a client who, from a space of rejection and emotional reactivity, might begin posting negative reviews or comments about Jason?* Certainly, a conversation with the client in which Jason seeks understanding and clarifies (with care and sensitivity) the boundaries on social media is warranted. Jason would likely benefit from consultation with a colleague or mental health attorney for additional guidance and support.

Training and Education in Emerging Areas of Practice

Therapists who are interested in practicing in emerging areas must consider the educational and training requirements. Most of the ethical codes have specifications for therapists who seek to offer services beyond their area of expertise as well as those guiding therapists in the ethical engagement in emerging areas of practice. Specifically, the APA *Ethical principles of psychologists and code of conduct* (APA, 2017a, Section 2.01) requires that psychologists interested in engaging in a new service must "undertake relevant education, training, supervised experience, consultation, or study" (p. 5). For emerging areas of practice, therapists are called upon to take "reasonable steps to ensure the competence of their work . . . and to protect clients from harm" (p. 5). Reasonable steps may begin with using this text as an introduction to some emerging practices. They may also include consulting with peers who are engaging in the practice of interest, seeking supervision, or attending continuing education events focused on the emerging area. Ultimately, it is important to recognize that the profession is rapidly evolving; it is our responsibility to remain abreast of these developments, to continually assess our professional and technical knowledge and skills, and to maintain competence. Moreover, keeping up-to-date reduces risk and liability for the therapist and ensures that clients are receiving the best possible care.

The effectiveness of our work is also, arguably, an ethical issue. This may be of even greater salience with emerging treatment approaches. With the push toward a near sole-reliance on evidence-based treatment, many questions and concerns arise. First, there are many therapies and approaches to treatment that don't easily lend themselves to quantitative evaluation. While this does not mean that these therapies are ineffective, lack of easy evaluation essentially renders an approach unusable in this time of managed care and third-party payors. Second, there are questions regarding methods of evaluation, which may not provide clarity on effectiveness for specific racialized and other marginalized groups or ways in which an intervention integrates or advances social justice goals (Toporek et al., 2012). Ethical Code 2.01 states: "In those emerging areas in which generally recognized standards for preparatory training do not yet exist, psychologists nevertheless take reasonable steps to ensure the competence of their work and to protect clients/patients, students, supervisees, research participants, organizational clients, and others from harm" (APA, 2017a, p.5).

Gerber (2007) offers specific questions therapists can ask that can hold us accountable to reflection on, and evaluation of, the therapy we are providing:

1. If an intervention is helpful to an individual, does this come at the expense of others, specifically their family or community?
2. To what extent do our well-intentioned interventions support oppressive structures and inequities?

CONCLUSION

Ethical decision making can be a complex process involving multiple factors and considerations particularly in practicing in emerging areas. Risk management remains an area of concern; therapists should rely upon their clinical judgment and consult with experienced colleagues in areas that are emerging and do not yet have a strong empirical foundation. Therapists should ensure that their liability and malpractice insurance covers teletherapy, and any wellness practices, or out-of-office therapy. Licensure and jurisdictional issues remain contested and continue to evolve. Therapists who are interested in practicing across state lines should remain abreast of their own state's practices, including temporary waivers, if applicable, and monitor and advocate for PsyPact.

Therapists are bound to provide ethical care, to maintain confidentiality, and to maintain appropriate therapy boundaries, regardless of the therapeutic setting. Therapists should plan for and inform clients about any threats to confidentiality when they practice online or outside the office.

Social media engagement is presenting new and different opportunities for therapists to increase their visibility as well as to promote mental health services. With that comes new ethical challenges and grey areas to navigate. If we are practicing from a clearly articulated ethic and politic of social justice, this presents new complexities for us as we ethically reason through the clinical care we provide inside and outside of the therapy office. If we are to advance social justice, including racial justice during these times, it requires that we hold our professional ethics alongside what is most just and therapeutic for our clients and communities.

8

GETTING THROUGH IT ALL: SHARED TRAUMA, BURNOUT, AND SELF-CARE

Arguably, the role of mental health practitioners has never been more important. Therapists have served as essential workers during the COVID-19 pandemic, on the emotional frontline for months with no clear end in sight. Many of us, as mental health practitioners, may also work in hospitals or clinics, where we have been physically on the frontlines as well. We are personally and professionally responsible for providing support and holding space for what likely feels like countless people. With the heightened levels of stress associated with multiple teletherapy sessions, racialized trauma, and election stress on top of the continuing pandemic, therapists also feel the stress of it all.

> **Client:** I don't know how you do it. I couldn't do it . . . taking care of others right now. I am barely managing myself.
> **Therapist:** Honestly, neither do I.

The work that we mental health care providers do is beautifully complex; it is an honor, for most of us, to stand alongside our clients in their darkest most difficult hours. And, while this often sounds like noble work, the truth is far less altruistic. Characterizing therapists as noble is complicated. It bestows upon us virtues that are sometimes undeserved, and further, it implies that it is unnecessary to adequately compensate therapists for the work we do and the many years of training we have. That may be uncomfortable for some therapists to state, but to be fair, compensation matters within a capitalist system. Perhaps more troubling is when people virtue signal therapists as "noble," they run the risk of diminishing the humanity of therapists. When we therapists are viewed only as noble, then the parts of us that struggle to go to work and hold space for others when we fear for our own health are not acknowledged and the insomnia, depression, and anxiety that some of us struggle with, the same as the rest of the population, go unseen. When virtuous characteristics are bestowed on therapists, we therapists are disavowed of the opportunity to be fully seen and to have our own struggles validated. This is particularly important as we all experience the pandemic. We therapists must be able to acknowledge that we are living through this pandemic even as we support others through it as well.

THE TRAUMA OF IT ALL

It is clear that the events of the past year have been collectively traumatic. Understandings of trauma have evolved in recent years. Trauma used to be thought of only as distinct episodes in which someone feared for their life, experienced particular forms of violence, or witnessed either of these in others. The focus of trauma therapy was primarily on treating the trauma symptoms related to that one event. Consequently, the most studied trauma therapies emerged from this conceptualization. The ways in which we understand trauma have evolved due in part to more holistic and systemic conceptualizations of human experience and suffering, especially experiences of protracted or repeated trauma (Alexander et al., 2004; Herman, 1992). This more expansive conceptualization of trauma led to the introduction of more nuanced ways of thinking about the multiple ways people can experience trauma and the ways it can manifest, such as developmental or complex trauma, historical or intergenerational trauma, cultural or collective trauma (Brave Heart, 2011; Danieli et al., 2017; van Der Kolk et al., 2019). Collective trauma refers to events that are experienced by an entire collective or society that are so impactful as to result in individual distress as well as disruption or reorganization at a societal level (Chang, 2017). For example, in the United States the September 11 attacks on the World Trade Center were widely recognized as a traumatic event for the country. Individuals experienced disparate personal experiences and a range of distress and trauma determined largely by proximity to the attacks, by loss of loved ones, and by membership in particular groups (e.g., Muslims, firefighters). The traumatic effects were more pronounced in the cities and communities in which the attacks occurred. In addition, there were large scale policy changes and legislation following the attacks, for example, the changes made to security in government buildings and travel impacted most Americans. Some of you might recall what it was like to travel prior to 9/11, when nonticketed passengers could meet their loved ones at the arrival gate and full sized toiletries were allowed. In this example, the trauma affected changes not just in the United States but also throughout the world.

While COVID-19 was not a violent attack on society, Americans are undoubtedly experiencing collective distress that is impacting us individually and as a society. The behaviors that are now necessary, such as distancing and mask-wearing, may be in place for some time. Researchers are just beginning to understand the multiple ways in which people are being psychologically affected by this period. Research conducted during the pandemic reveals that frontline healthcare workers are experiencing high amounts of trauma during COVID-19 and are at high risk for traumatic stress responses (Lai et al., 2020). While we don't yet have data assessing trauma outside of a healthcare setting, it is reasonable to believe that the protracted feelings of uncertainty and fear, the disruption to life, and the experience of multiple losses may result in a large number of adults and children manifesting acute and long-term traumatic responses, especially in the absence of preventive measures.

The interrelationship between the health and economic crises caused by COVID-19 is clear. Some people are more vulnerable to and bearing more of the burden of the collective trauma. Racialized people have been disproportionately impacted by COVID-19 in both health and economic consequences (APM Research Lab, 2020). Rates of COVID-19 among Native Americans are estimated to be 3.5 times higher than that of white Americans (APM Research Lab, 2020; Centers for Disease Control, 2020). Similarly, African Americans and Latinx individuals appear to be nearly 3 times as likely to be diagnosed with COVID-19, and they are more likely to die from the condition than their white counterparts (Centers for Disease

Control, 2020). COVID-19 is now the third leading cause of death for African Americans (APM Research Lab, 2020).

The disproportionate economic impact is also uneven across racial groups, with African American and Latinx families being more likely to experience financial instability and food and housing insecurity due to COVID-19 (Ray, 2020). While Asian Americans have been spared higher rates of COVID-19 infection, they have experienced heightened rates of racial stress, discrimination, and violence, much of which has been emboldened by state-sanctioned hate speech. Since the beginning of the pandemic, approximately four out of ten Asian Americans and African Americans have experienced harassment or discrimination (Ruiz et al., 2020). The racial stress and trauma of this period only adds to the layers of collective trauma being experienced.

The relationship between race, racism, and trauma has been made evident (Carter et al., 2020). Racial trauma is a form of race-based stress that can result from the cumulative real and perceived experience or witnessing of racism (Comas-Días et al., 2019). Racial trauma is a distinct traumatic experience, considering the chronic nature of its injuries and the inevitability of being reexposed and reinjured. Given the high rates of discrimination reported among African Americans in the United States, this population is at particularly high risk for experiencing racial trauma. Unfortunately, all racially minoritized groups in the United States are vulnerable to race-related stress (Comas-Días et al., 2019). The Movement for Black Lives has brought increased attention to many of these issues. Some people who experience racial trauma will experience symptoms of PTSD, and some will experience chronic and severe forms of the syndrome (Carter et al., 2020). As therapists on the emotional frontlines, we must be aware of trauma exposure and culturally aligned ways of working with Black, Indigenous, Latinx, and other People of Color.

There are also questions regarding the effectiveness of traditional trauma therapy for racially minoritized populations, which has led to advocacy for more culturally aligned trauma treatments. Recent models, such as that of French et al. (2020), employ an intersectional and liberation focus in concert with Black psychology to increase radical hope and healing, especially in working with African Americans who have experienced racial trauma.

Scholars have also prompted trauma therapists to move beyond a trauma-informed approach to one that has an understanding of the multiple systemic factors (such as oppression) that may contribute to the individual experience and manifestation of trauma (Goodman, 2015). Put together, these approaches illustrate the complexity of the collective trauma(s) being experienced and the particular vulnerability that Black, Indigenous, and other People of Color are experiencing. Therapists practicing today must be aware of these issues and would benefit from additional training on the intersection of race and trauma. As discussed in Chapter 6, therapy can no longer be thought of as racially and culturally neutral space. One could argue that it has never been more important for therapists to be intentional about creating a therapeutic space and to embody an approach that honors the pain and suffering of oppressed people while building on their strengths to help them resist and navigate the oppressions of this moment in history.

Shared Trauma: Seeing Ourselves in Our Clients

Clients are not alone in experiencing these collective traumas. This is a distinct time in which therapists and clients are in it together. Shared trauma refers to times when therapists and clients both share direct exposure to the same, current trauma (Baum, 2010). In addition to their own direct exposure to the traumatic event, therapists experience double exposure (Baum, 2014) as they are also exposed indirectly through sessions with clients. Shared trauma is not completely understood and has received scant attention in the research. More serious exploration of this phenomenon began following the 9/11 World Trade Center attack. Much of what is known focuses primarily on disasters and war zones.

Shared trauma research has suggested the potential for positive gains for therapists as well as ways that therapists are negatively affected. Therapists appear to be at higher risk for PTSD symptoms when they have a greater degree of direct exposure to the traumatic event and for therapists who have their own prior trauma histories (Freedman & Mashiach, 2018). Other research has indicated that therapists can lose confidence in their clinical abilities and effectiveness (Batten & Orsillo, 2002). Indirect exposure also affects therapists, namely, through increased clinical workload; we are more likely to report increased emotional exhaustion and burnout

(Freedman & Mashiach, 2018). Shared trauma can also lead to increased empathy and ability to relate to client concerns, heightened sense of commitment to the work, and increased personal growth (Batten & Orsillo, 2002; Baum, 2014). Some studies reveal that therapists may experience internal conflict and feel forced to choose between professional responsibilities to clients and their own personal/familial needs (Somer et al., 2004). Some therapists may struggle to fully attend to and/or empathize with clients whereas others report difficulty separating their own pain from that of their clients under shared trauma conditions (Lavi et al., 2015; Somer et al., 2004). Similar to what most of us therapists have experienced over the past year, therapists in the research have reported a need to adapt and be flexible with regard to therapeutic setting and physical environment, which may be distressing (Somer et al., 2004). While during the COVID-19 pandemic we therapists are not practicing in a disaster zone—which I have done—the adaptability and flexibility necessary to be effective in both settings are similar.

Notably, there is little known about the impact of shared trauma on the therapy we therapists provide and on our clients (Freedman & Mashiach, 2018). One study with Israeli therapists provides some insight that might prove helpful to the present discussion. These therapists reported a deep identification with their clients, which resulted in trust, intimacy, and a strong therapeutic alliance (Lavi et al., 2015). Most participants reportedly thought of this as a benefit to therapy but acknowledged that it may have also affected clinical decision-making, particularly in their attending more to the trauma than to other areas of the client's life. Consider the following exchange:

Dana: Hey, good to see you.
Me: Hi Dana, good to see you as well. Are you home, in a private space, ready to get started?
Dana: Yeah, I am. How are you? You look a little tired today. Is your daughter staying healthy? I hope that's ok to ask. I've known you for a while now. I know you show up for a lot of people.
Me: You have known me for a while. I am a little tired. The earthquake woke me, and I didn't get back to sleep for a while. But,

I am ok, and thankfully my little one is remaining healthy. I
am glad to be in this space with you. How was the earthquake
for you?

In this exchange, the client asks about the therapist's well-being and
that of my daughter. (As soon as the pandemic began, I informed clients
that I would not be meeting in person due to my daughter's high risk status.) I could have engaged in the usual therapist deflection and ask what
her concerns were about or if she felt a need to take care of me. However,
my experience of her inquiry was that this client genuinely cares and was
able to see me as a full human being. She may have been able to imagine,
or at least appreciate, the challenge of protecting a medically vulnerable
child with high risk factors for COVID-19. She knows that despite whatever
unknown personal challenges I might have, I continue to show up for her.
I saw this as a beautiful reflection of the authentic relationship we share. At
the same time, as her therapist I demonstrated appreciation for her concern
but also provided reassurance. I was able to affirm the relationship and care
extended as well as maintain primary focus on the client. This can be a del-
icate balance, yet it is also important for me to model truth-telling. I *was*
tired, and this *is* a difficult time, and allowing clients to hear and see that
in their therapist can be powerfully affirming for them as well. This may be
of particular significance for Black and Brown women, who are often disavowed of the opportunity to rest or who may internalize shame about the
need for rest and self-care.

Bereavement and Complicated Grief

Another traumatic aspect of this time is the presence of layers of individual and collective grief. Around the world, people have experienced a
range of losses. Grief is hard in normal times; bereavement has become
even more challenging during the pandemic. Family members have been
unable to be with sick or aged loved ones, and end of life traditions and
rituals have been disrupted, if possible at all. Even when families have
been able to hold funerals or memorials, they have often needed to be
smaller, outdoors, and socially distanced, with family members unable

to physically comfort one another or unable to do so without concern regarding COVID-19 transmission. Some families may have been unable to have funerals or other services. The isolation that many people feel is only compounding the grief. Therapists should be particularly attuned to symptoms of complicated grief. Complicated grief refers to intense feelings of grief that are prolonged or that begin to interfere with daily functioning (Goveas & Shear, 2020). It makes sense that many people would be at high risk for complicated grief, especially with sudden losses, the inability to be with loved ones during illness and final hours, and the absence of collective mourning and healing rituals. Research on collective loss following disasters and related events have often resulted in high rates of complicated grief, among other trauma responses (Gesi et al., 2020). Given the continued transmission of infection and lack of clarity on vaccine distribution, therapists likely need to be prepared to work with individuals and families around these grief and bereavement issues for the foreseeable future.

Many people are also experiencing ambiguous loss, which refers to a particular type of grief associated with more intangible losses such as loss of relationships, loss of time with loved ones, missed opportunities for jobs, and lack in other experiences that cannot be resolved easily, if at all (Woods, 2020). COVID-19 has brought with it all of these types of losses, and the inability to discern an end to the pandemic only adds to the weight of the ambiguity. Therapists who are using teletherapy to work with clients that are experiencing complicated grief and ambiguous loss are encouraged to think critically about ways to more explicitly demonstrate empathy and support. Body-inclusive and somatic therapists are well-positioned to work with clients on the ways in which grief and trauma are held in the physical body and to support clients in ways to physically release grief. In addition, there is likely a need and interest in grief support groups for both children and adults. Engaging in grief work and holding the pain of grief and of all the forms of trauma for so many people is difficult work. Therapists engaging in *trauma stewardship* are encouraged to honor and make space for the suffering of others while not taking it on as their own (van Dernoot Lipsky & Burk, 2009).

WORKING FROM HOME AND LIVING AT WORK

Burnout and Compassion Fatigue

It is important that we as therapists honor the emotional burden of holding space and bearing witness to others' pain. Our work can be at once incredibly rewarding and emotionally draining. After months of living through and providing care during one of the most difficult times that many people have ever witnessed, many of us may be burned out or experiencing compassion fatigue. Some of us might have an intimate familiarity with burnout, having already experienced it at some point in our professional lives. While the constructs of burnout and compassion fatigue and their relationship to one another are conceptualized in different ways in the literature, it is helpful to think of burnout, typically, as a cumulative process developing over time. We can experience burnout when we feel overworked and have insufficient internal and/or external resources to engage in the work with integrity or to complete the work to the level expected (Joshi & Sharma, 2020). Burnout may manifest as increased negativity or cynicism about our work and colleagues, or even as irritability with some clients. When we add restricted work conditions, including the blurring of boundaries between the personal and professional as we continue to work from home, we are all prime candidates for burnout.

We therapists are also vulnerable to compassion fatigue, or secondary traumatic stress. Feeling helpless, ineffective, or as if our therapeutic impact is minimal can compound feelings of burnout. This can be even more pronounced when relying on technology and not being with our clients in person. Compassion fatigue is often thought to be more severe than burnout and occurs when therapists (and other human service providers) internalize and take on the pain and suffering of our clients (Joshi & Sharma, 2020; Figley & Ludick, 2017). With compassion fatigue, therapists may experience a loss of meaning in our work and a decreased sense of empathy (Figley & Ludick, 2017). In addition, some people may experience symptoms associated with trauma response, such as emotional numbing, anxiety, sleep disturbance, and intrusive thoughts associated with client experiences. Despite these symptoms, many of us may not be accurate in our assessment of ourselves in real time. Below is a checklist you may find helpful as you check in with yourself about how you are really doing.

Burnout and Compassion Fatigue Warning Signs

☐ I have disturbed sleep, eating, or concentration.

☐ I find myself avoiding or isolating myself from family, friends, and colleagues.

☐ I fail to take regularly scheduled breaks.

☐ I enjoy my work less than in the past.

☐ I find myself bored, disinterested, or easily irritated by clients.

☐ I have recently experienced life stressors, such as illness, personal loss, relationship difficulties, financial problems, or legal trouble.

☐ I feel emotionally exhausted or drained after meeting with certain clients.

☐ I find myself thinking of being elsewhere when working with clients.

☐ I am self-medicating or overusing substances or food, overlooking personal needs, and overlooking my health.

☐ I find my work less rewarding and gratifying than in the past.

☐ I frequently feel depressed, anxious, or agitated.

☐ I enjoy life less than I did in the past.

☐ I am experiencing repeated headaches and other physical complaints.

☐ I sit staring into space for hours and can't concentrate on my work.

(Barnett, 2014)

Barnett, J. (2014, December). Distress, burnout, self-care, and the promotion of wellness for psychotherapists and trainees: Issues, implications, and recommendations. [Web article]. Retrieved from: http://www.societyfor psychotherapy.org/distress-therapist-burnout-self-care-promotion-wellness -psychotherapists-trainees-issues-implications-recommendations

Many of us have experienced one or more of these symptoms. We, as therapists, are at particularly high risk of developing these symptoms right now. We may find that focusing during sessions is difficult or that feeling energized or excited to see clients feels out of reach. In a recent conversation with a couple of therapist friends, we named or admitted things that we have done or that have occurred that are signposts that we need a break or better support. Some examples included: daydreaming about a vacation during a session; chewing gum to keep from yawning throughout the entire session; engaging in yoga to stay awake during a phone session; and lying about the reason for our last-minute cancellation of a session with a client, which in truth was just to take a nap. While some of these signposts might be amusing, they show that therapists' health and well-being matter and can affect the quality of care we provide. Moreover, we often lack awareness of the impact our burgeoning compassion fatigue has on our clients and the care we provide (Pope & Vazquez, 2005). Compassion fatigue could potentially result in us missing something significant in a client's session that may be critical to the client's safety and health. Let's turn to therapist wellness and self-care to discuss things we can do during this time and beyond.

THERAPIST WELLNESS AND SELF-CARE: PRACTICING WHAT WE PREACH

We therapists are notorious for minimizing our own needs, including self-care, in the interest of others. During the pandemic and racial uprisings, many of us may be forgoing or have forgone the usual sources of joy and fun or may have had limited options due to COVID-19 restrictions. Even as many of us become aware of our need for a break or for time off, we often don't take it.

> **Colleague:** I'm taking the week off. The whole week. The entirety of it. Not sure what my clients are going to do, but I can't do it. I don't have it.
>
> **Me:** I completely get that. I trust that they will be ok and that you will be in a better space to show up for them when you get back.
>
> **Colleague:** So, when are you taking some time?
>
> **Me:** What does that even mean these days?. . . I know I need to do that as well or figure out how to get away in a safe way . . . that just sounds like work too.

It is hard to acknowledge that there are limits to our caregiving, as therapists, as parents, as family members, and as friends. We know the sayings: *"You have to take care of yourself first." "Put on your own mask first, then help the people around you."* Self-care is an imperative for therapists during usual times, and during this time of collective trauma, it has to become nonnegotiable. Many of us are hanging on by a thread, perhaps even a tattered thread. If we are not taking care of ourselves, we should be asking whether we are fit to take care of others. Moreover, it is part of our ethical responsibility to be aware of how our physical and mental health may affect our work. (See for example, Section 2g of the American Counseling Association Code of Ethics (2014) and Principle A: Beneficence and Nonmaleficence in the American Psychological Association Code of Conduct (2017a). We can think of self-care as one way in which we practice (and model) wellness and engage in what van Dernoot Lipsky and Burke (2009) call nurturing our capacity to help.

There is a range of ways in which to practice self-care, particularly with the booming wellness industry discussed in Chapter 4. In addition to the personal wellness practices that many of us therapists may support, such as yoga, meditation, and healthy eating, there are specific aspects applicable to how and why we engage in this work that are helpful to consider and potentially to interrupt as we consider self-care. For example, it is important to reflect on reasons for overworking and not taking care of ourselves. For many of us, overworking and self-neglect did not begin during COVID-19, but have been a way of life for a long time. We must question how much of our identity and self-worth is entangled with our work and why. Some of us may believe that our work is to be self-sacrificial martyrs. Some of us may have patterns of unbalanced relationships even in our personal lives, where we have grown accustomed to giving more than we receive. If we are to develop a self-care plan, we must necessarily begin with honest and critical reflection on these questions. We must also consider our point of departure and where we really are in terms of self-care, in our current decision-making, and we must have realistic expectations of our resources and circumstances (e.g., COVID-19 restrictions). In so doing, it is important that we approach these questions and reflection from a place of compassion for, and not criticism of, ourselves. Some additional initial questions recommended by Corey et al. (2018) include:

Pause | Reflect
- What is working and what isn't working in my life?
- Is what I am doing helping or hurting me?
- What is currently dissatisfying about my work or work–life balance?
- To what degree is what I am doing enhancing or harming my relationships?

Your responses to these questions should illuminate areas of your personal and professional lives to which you are not attending. I think it is also important to consider context and the current moment. For example, in reflecting on what is working and not working, what used to work may no longer work for you or your family due to the conditions created by COVID-19. A previously sustainable work schedule may have been fine before you began working from home or balancing work and homeschooling your children. Needs may even have evolved during the COVID-19 pandemic. We may have developed a plan at the beginning of the pandemic, and that plan is no longer working after several months. So many people do not have work–life balance because of the lack of physical separation between work and home life. We must make the necessary adjustments to not only survive this time, but to continue to strive for wellness. Our flexibility and ability to adapt are likely what has kept most of us afloat during the past several months.

Experts in this area advise a number of practices for developing a self-care plan. First, schedule and set aside and protect time for self-care (Corey et al., 2018). This is likely the only way most people will ensure that self-care will happen. Second, develop an action plan that is personal and specifically tailored to your needs and areas for growth. Anticipating challenges and barriers and considering the supports and resources necessary to be consistent and successful with the plan are also critical if one is serious about improving self-care and integrating it as a permanent aspect of one's personal and professional life (Corey et al., 2018). There are many tools that can aid therapists in this work. Norcross and Guy (2007) developed an exhaustive self-care checklist that, while over a decade old, remains relevant for today. Their checklist is organized into multiple sections, which is helpful for mentally and strategically organizing a self-care plan. Below, are some highlights from their checklist, adapted for the present discussion.

Self-Care Checklist

Value the Self
☐ Cultivate self-empathy and self-compassion
☐ Diversify self-care practices
☐ Track, assess, and evaluate self-care
☐ Solicit self-care feedback from loved ones

Refocus on the Rewards
☐ Center personal reasons for entering the field
☐ Create opportunities and pathways for greater freedom and creativity in therapeutic work

Recognize the Hazards
☐ Be realistic about the demanding nature of psychotherapy work
☐ Acknowledge the impact of clinical practice on self and loved ones during this time
☐ Limit exposure to traumatic or otherwise emotionally disturbing material outside of therapy

Mind the Body
☐ Take care of physical self as an aspect of self-care
☐ Track quality and length of sleep
☐ Exercise regularly
☐ Engage in movement between sessions
☐ Maintain a balanced diet and sufficient hydration
☐ Monitor substance use and self-medicating

Nurture Relationships

- ☐ Assess quality of interpersonal relationships
- ☐ Identify three of the most nurturing people in your life and consider increasing time with and support from them
- ☐ Ensure sufficient alone time
- ☐ Procure peer support, consultation, and supervision
- ☐ Evaluate the balance of nurturance you are giving and receiving in relationships
- ☐ Engage in personal therapy for additional support

Set Boundaries

- ☐ Set maximum caseload boundaries: work under maximum capacity to build in time to accommodate emergencies, family demands, and self-care
- ☐ Establish clear boundaries with clients regarding expectations outside of therapy
- ☐ Personalize therapy but have limits
- ☐ Delegate or outsource nonclinical work

Cultivate Spirituality, Mission, and Meaning

- ☐ Identify and connect with your mission
- ☐ Embrace sense of calling as a therapist
- ☐ Cultivate awe and wonder at the human spirit and nature
- ☐ Connect to nature or spiritual sources of hope and optimism about humanity and the world
- ☐ Reflect on intersections of spiritual beliefs and social justice and consider ways to integrate them into personal and professional development

Foster Creativity and Growth

- ☐ Strive for adaptiveness and openness to challenges
- ☐ Engage in the arts and be spontaneous
- ☐ Upload your creativity into innovative therapy

This list provides a number of dimensions of self-care to prompt us to critically reflect on ways to create both boundaries and spaciousness across our practice and personal lives. Boundaries are reported to be the most frequently used self-care strategy employed by therapists (Norcross & Guy, 2007). In addition, spending time with partners and loved ones is often endorsed for therapist rejuvenation. Given the importance of community during this protracted time of social isolation, people are finding new ways to be together and remain connected. Therapists should be encouraged to create a self-care village to help support and sustain us personally and professionally. From a wellness perspective, we must remain centered in the knowledge that self-care is not just about stress reduction or preventing burnout. Rather, self-care is about an investment in our own personal development. As Black feminist scholar and author Audre Lorde reminds us (1988), self-care is not about self-indulgence, it is self-preservation.

CONCLUSION

While writing this book I thought, and perhaps desperately hoped, that by the time I finished writing, COVID-19 would be behind us and significant strides toward racial justice in this country would make some sections obsolete. Unfortunately, it is all still relevant, and the conditions that surround us are likely to remain present in some form for the foreseeable future. We are all living through this time together, therapists alongside clients.

It is a difficult time to be a therapist. At the same time, we therapists are simultaneously living and stewarding people through a historic moment in the history of our world. Some people are getting through this collective trauma only because of the support of a therapist. How we support clients matters, has changed, and will continue to evolve. It should evolve. Anything that is alive and in service of dynamic people living in a changing world must necessarily evolve with the people and the times.

It is not surprising that therapy has increasingly incorporated and relied on technology, given the ways technology dominates our lives. Acknowledging that teletherapy is here to stay opens us to the possibilities that it brings, not just the ways that it differs from in-person therapy. Teletherapy and in-person therapy are not the same, and many of us therapists are coming to realize that in-person therapy had its limitations. It is imperative that we move away from the idea that technology and teletherapy are bad toward a more nuanced understanding and respect for what they offer as well as their limitations. This perspective is liberating because it frees us from a false either/or binary, allowing us to open to the idea that therapy can be more than what we have thus far been providing. We, as therapists, can be more than what we have been. There are healing potentialities in curating a therapeutic experience that includes all the elements and modalities that are in service of client psychological well-being.

Therapy has moved toward centering social justice because it must. The failure of the field as a whole to do this before now is something with which it will have to reckon. Therapists are increasingly aware of the pervasiveness of trauma, in all its forms. And a brave few might be willing to consider the way trauma has begun to be expected and how it permeates every aspect of people's lives as an issue of social justice. We therapists have finally heeded the ancient wisdom and years of research that clearly demonstrate that no one can be well when there is injustice. More therapists than ever before are wellness-centered and taking up a more holistic approach to mental health. With the rise of wellness approaches, it is important that all aspects included in therapy continue to be guided by best practices. Considering the overwhelming empirical support for mindfulness, therapists are likely to see training and competence in mindfulness practices become a requirement for new and seasoned therapists.

With therapy becoming more expansive and flexible in where it occurs— in the office, online, in homes, in communities, and in nature—there is greater commitment to crafting personalized therapeutic approaches that deliver services to the people. I want to revisit the model presented by Mosley et al. (2020), in which they emphasize a need for fostering radical hope. In that model, they posit that a person who possesses radical hope is one who is, in the present moment, aware of and embodying collective memory and faith while simultaneously being oriented to the individual and collective past and future. During this time of collective trauma, continued uncertainty, and ongoing change in the world and psychology, radical hope seems crucial. With radical hope comes the ability to hold on to the good, even as one grieves multiple losses and moves forward to create something better.

Renewal can come from pain and suffering. One of the many devastations Americans have witnessed during this time are the historic fires in the forests and mountains of California. As a native Californian, witnessing the smoke that has surrounded us, (further) contaminating the air and rendering it almost unbreathable, and the loss of historic numbers of trees and wildlife has been heartbreaking. Even as I write this, the forests still burn. I am reminded that though people may witness the metaphorical burning and loss of life as we have known it, there is renewal of life after a burn. Indigenous land scientists, farmers, and people who know the land far better than I do will attest that though some land will be different and perhaps even unbearable after major burns, other land needs to burn in order to renew. What is left will be more fertile and life affirming. As therapists, we are helping people (including ourselves) survive something historic and at the same time reshaping the field. What we intentionally salvage and what we build anew is up to each of us.

Screening for Teletherapy Checklist

Initial Level
- ☐ Client's presenting issues are within my areas of expertise
- ☐ Client's symptoms and health are stable enough for outpatient treatment
  - ☐ If not, what additional support does the client require? _____
  _____
  - ☐ Are these supports available in the home or through collateral care?
    - ☐ If not, refer out for more intensive level of care

Synchronous
- ☐ Qualifies for outpatient treatment
- ☐ Risk for harm to self or others is low
- ☐ Access to and understanding of required technology is present
- ☐ Safe, private environment for teletherapy is available

Asynchronous
- ☐ Client is high-functioning, with no recent or current crises or periods of emotional instability
- ☐ Client is adequately supported
- ☐ Client has access to and understanding of required technology

Areas of Concern: Additional Screening
- ☐ History of emotional instability, aggression, recent hospitalization
- ☐ Severe or persistent mental illness
- ☐ Low cognitive functioning
- ☐ Poor or inconsistent access to required technology

Recommendations
- ☐ Asynchronous stand-alone treatment
- ☐ Adjunctive asynchronous treatment
- ☐ Synchronous treatment. Specify: _____
  _____

Rationale:

Teletherapy Checklist

Getting Started

- ☐ Licensed or legally allowed to practice in client's jurisdiction or state
- ☐ Malpractice coverage that includes teletherapy
- ☐ Research HIPAA compliant and secure videoconferencing platform or comprehensive Practice Management System
- ☐ HIPAA compliant payment options
- ☐ Teletherapy clinical documentation, including informed consent
- ☐ Updated antivirus software, firewalls, and security updates for all devices (computer, tablet, phone)

Equipment & Technology

- ☐ HIPAA-compliant video-conferencing platform or comprehensive Practice Management System
- ☐ BAA for all vendors
- ☐ Secure, password protected computer or tablet
- ☐ High resolution webcam
- ☐ Microphone (internal or external)
- ☐ Noise-reducing headphones
- ☐ High speed internet
- ☐ Ethernet cable (and adaptor if needed)

Online Office Environment

- ☐ Private and secure space to conduct sessions
- ☐ Quiet space with soundproofing or sound machine to reduce external noise
- ☐ Bright and warm lighting
- ☐ Clutter-free background
- ☐ Modern, minimal decoration
- ☐ Comfortable chair with proper back support
- ☐ Camera positioned at eye level
- ☐ Standing desk or shelf at eye level for long days or to integrate movement into session

Remote Therapy Self-Care

- ☐ Schedule intentionally—include breaks
- ☐ Change devices
- ☐ Change locations if possible
- ☐ Alternate between sitting and standing desks
- ☐ Use blue light filtering software
- ☐ Incorporate movement and activity between sessions
- ☐ Engage in end-of-work rituals and wellness practices
- ☐ Use less technology during personal time

Intersectionality & Therapy Checklist

Inclusive Environment & Paperwork

- ☐ Preferred names
- ☐ Gender pronouns
- ☐ Choices in racial and ethnic identities, including self-defined/ write-in
- ☐ Include range of sexual identity options including self-defined/ write-in
- ☐ Relational status options include range of options including different types of relational formations and ethical nonmonogamy
- ☐ Use inclusive language reflective of the chosen terminology of the communities served
- ☐ Land acknowledgment

Intersectional Assessment

- ☐ Ask about multiple intersecting areas of oppression
- ☐ Assess access and barriers to opportunity (e.g., criminal justice system issues, immigration status, economic)
- ☐ Assess sense of community and belonging
- ☐ Spiritual identity, including atheist and agnostic
- ☐ Ask about areas of visible and invisible ability and disability

Therapy

- ☐ Serve as witness to and validate experiences of oppression
- ☐ Affirm and support multiple identities; identify areas of subjugation
- ☐ Avoid assumptions; ask informed questions
- ☐ Identify and interrupt internalized oppression
- ☐ Identify and interrupt microaggressions
- ☐ Connect issues of race, racism, sexual identity, heterosexism, etc. with other areas of client concern

Reflexivity & Professional Development

- ☐ Engage in ongoing self-examination
- ☐ Continue professional development focused on issues of race, sexual identity, and other areas of power and oppression
- ☐ Consult with peers engaged in antiracist, anti-heteronormative, intersectional, and affirmative therapy

References

Accenture. (2019, February 12). *Today's consumers reveal the future of healthcare: Accenture 2019 digital health consumer survey.* https://www.accenture.com/us-en/insights/health/todays-consumers-reveal-future-healthcare

Adames, H. Y., Chavez-Dueñas, N. Y., Sharma, S., & La Roche, M. J. (2018). Intersectionality in psychotherapy: The experiences of an AfroLatinx queer immigrant. *Psychotherapy, 55*(1), 73–79. https://dx.doi.org/10.1037/pst0000152

Alexander, J., Eyerman, R., Giesen, B., Smelser, N., & Sztompka, P. (2004). *Cultural trauma and collective identity.* University of California Press. Retrieved October 18, 2020, from http://www.jstor.org/stable/10.1525/j.ctt1pp9nb

Alper, B. (2015, November 23). *Millennials are less religious than older Americans, but just as spiritual.* Pew Research Center. https://www.pewresearch.org/fact-tank/2015/11/23/millennials-are-less-religious-than-older-americans-but-just-as-spiritual/

Al'Uqdah, S. N., Jenkins, K., & Ajaa, N. (2019). Empowering communities through social media. *Counselling Psychology Quarterly, 32*, 137–149. https://doi.org/10.1080/09515070.2017.1407747

American Counseling Association. (2020, June 6). *ACA Anti-racism statement.* https://www.counseling.org/news/updates/2020/06/22/aca-anti-racism-statement

American Psychological Association. (2003). Guidelines on multicultural education, training, research, practice, and organizational change for psychologists. American Psychologist, 58(5), 377–402. https://doi.org/10.1037/0003-066X.58.5.377

American Psychological Association. (2007). Record keeping guidelines. American Psychologist, 62(9), 993–1004. https://doi.org/10.1037/0003-066X.62.9.993

American Psychological Association Joint Task Force for the Development of Telepsychology Guidelines for Psychologists. (2013). Guidelines for the practice of telepsychology. *American Psychologist, 68*(9), 791–800. https://doi.org/10.1037/a0035001

American Psychological Association. (2015). Guidelines for psychological practice with transgender and gender nonconforming people. *The American Psychologist, 70*(9), 832–864. https://doi.org/10.1037/a0039906

American Psychological Association. (2016). *New APA data show where practitioners work.* https://www.apa.org/monitor/2016/11/practitioners-work

American Psychological Association. (2017a). *Ethical principles of psychologist and code of conduct* (2003, amended effective June 1, 2010, and January 1, 2017). https://www.apa.org/ethics/code/index.aspx

American Psychological Association. (2017b). Multicultural guidelines: An ecological approach to context, identity, and intersectionality. https://www.apa.org/about/policy/multicultural-guidelines.pdf

American Psychological Association. (2018b). *Stress in America: Gen Z.* https://www.apa.org/news/press/releases/stress/2018/stress-gen-z.pdf

American Psychological Association (2020, March). Informed consent checklist for telepsychological services. https://www.apa.org/practice/programs/dmhi/research-information/informed-consent-checklist

American Psychological Association. (2020). *Psychologists embrace telehealth to prevent the spread of COVID-19.* https://www.apaservices.org/practice/legal/technology/psychologists-embrace-telehealth

American Psychological Association, APA Task Force on Race and Ethnicity Guidelines in Psychology. (2019). *APA Guidelines on Race and Ethnicity in Psychology: Promoting Responsiveness and Equity.* https://www.apa.org/about/policy/guidelines-race-ethnicity.pdf

Anderson, O. (2018). *The History and Evolution of the Smartphone: 1992-2018.* Text Request. https://www.textrequest.com/blog/history-evolution-smartphone/

Anderson, K. N., Bautista, C. L., Hope, D. A. (2019). Therapeutic alliance, cultural competence and minority status in premature termination of psychotherapy. *American Journal of Orthopsychiatry, 89*(1):104–114. https://doi.org/10.1037/ort0000342.

APM Research Lab. (2020, Oct 15). *The color of coronavirus: Covid-19 deaths by race and ethnicity in the U.S.* https://www.apmresearchlab.org/covid/deaths-by-race

Association of Black Psychologists (2019). *Ethical standards of Black psychologists.* http://www.abpsi.org/pdf/EthicalStandardsofBlackPsychologists2019.pdf

Associated Press. (2020). *Virus Drives New Demand for Talkspace's Online Therapy.* U.S. News https://www.usnews.com/news/us/articles/2020-05-10/virus-drives-new-demand-for-talkspaces-online-therapy

Babayan, M. (2015). *CAMFT demographic survey: A snapshot of the "typical" California MFT.* The Therapist. https://www.camft.org/Portals/0/PDFs/Demographic-surveys/2015_demographic_survey.pdf?ver=2019-06-23-164118-007

Barnett, J. E. (2014). Renewing one's self-care sensibilities: Distress, burnout, vicarious traumatization, and self-renewal. In R. J. Wicks & E. A. Maynard (Eds.) *Clinician's guide to self-renewal: Essential advice from the field* (pp. 25–43). John Wiley & Sons, Inc.

Barnett, J. E., & Shale, A. J. (2012). The integration of Complementary and Alternative Medicine (CAM) into the practice of psychology: A vision for the future. *Professional Psychology: Research and Practice, 43*(6), 576–585. https://doi.org/10.1037/a0028919

Bashur, R. L., & Shannon, G. W. (2009). *The history of telemedicine, evolution, context, and transformation.* Mary Ann Liebert.

Batten, S. V., & Orsillo, S. M. (2002). Therapist reactions in the context of collective trauma. *The Behavior Therapist, 25*(2), 36–40.

Baum N. (2010). Shared traumatic reality in communal disasters: toward a conceptualization. *Psychotherapy: Theory, Research, Practice, Training, 47*(2), 249–259. https://doi.org/10.1037/a0019784

Baum N. (2014). Professionals' double exposure in the shared traumatic reality of wartime: Contributions to professional growth and stress. *British Journal of Social Work, 44*(8), 2113–2134. https://doi.org/10.1093/bjsw/bct085

Berdahl, J. L., Cooper, M., Glick, P., Livingston, R. W., & Williams, J. C. (2018). Work as a masculinity contest. *Journal of Social Issues, 74*(3), 422–448. https://doi.org/10.1111/josi.12289

Boyd, J. E., Lanius, R. A., & McKinnon, M. C. (2018). Mindfulness-based treatments for posttraumatic stress disorder: A review of the treatment literature and neurobiological evidence. *Journal of Psychiatry & Neuroscience, 43*(1), 7–25. https://doi.org/10.1503/jpn.170021

Boyd-Franklin, N., & Bry, B. H. (2000). *Reaching out in family therapy: Home-based, school, and community interventions.* Guilford Press.

Brave Heart, M. Y. H., Chase, J., Elkins, J., & Altschul, D. B. (2011). Historical trauma among Indigenous Peoples of the Americas: Concepts, research, and clinical considerations. *Journal of Psychoactive Drugs, 43*(4), 282–290.

Brom, D., Stokar, Y., Lawi, C., Nuriel-Porat, V., Ziv, Y., Lerner, K., & Ross, G. (2017). Somatic experiencing for posttraumatic stress disorder: A randomized controlled outcome study. *Journal of Traumatic Stress, 30*(3), 304–312. https://doi.org/10.1002/jts.22189

Bryant-Davis, T., & Ocampo, C. (2005). The trauma of racism: Implications for counseling, research, and education. *The Counseling Psychologist, 33*, 574–578. https://doi.org/10.1177/0011000005276581

Carman, A. (2020, March 27). *Instagram therapists, and their DMs, are open for business.* The Verge. https://www.theverge.com/2020/3/27/21193904/instagram-therapy-live-sessions-covid-19-coronavirus-posts-influencers

Carson, J. W., Carson, K. M., Gil, K., & Baucom, D. H. (2004). Mindfulness-based relationship enhancement. *Behavior Therapy, 35*(3), 471–494. https://doi.org/10.1016/S0005-7894(04)80028-5

Carter, R. T., Kirkinis, K., & Johnson, V. E. (2020). Relationships between trauma symptoms and race-based traumatic stress. *Traumatology, 26*(1), 11–18. https://doi.org/10.1037/trm0000217

Centers for Disease Control. (2020). COVID-19 Hospitalization and Death by Race/Ethnicity. Retrieved October 17, 2020 from https://www.cdc.gov/coronavirus/2019-ncov/covid-data/investigations-discovery/hospitalization-death-by-race-ethnicity.html

Chandra, R. (2019). *6 Problems of "Instagram Therapy."* Psychology Today. https://www.psychologytoday.com/us/blog/the-pacific-heart/201906/6-problems-instagram-therapy

Chang, K. (2017) Living with Vulnerability and Resiliency: The Psychological

Experience of Collective Trauma. *Acta Psychopathologica, 3*(53). https://doi
.org/10.4172/2469-6676.100125

Chao, R. C.-L., Wei, M., Spanierman, L., Longo, J., & Northart, D. (2015).
White racial attitudes and white empathy: The moderation of openness to
diversity. *The Counseling Psychologist, 43*(1), 94–120. https://doi.org/10.1177
/0011000014546871

Cho, W. & Ho, A. T. (2018). Does neighborhood crime matter? A multi-year survey study on perceptions of race, victimization, and public safety. *International
Journal of Law, Crime and Justice, 55*, 13-26. https://doi.org/10.1016/j.ijlcj.2018
.08.002

Clark, P., Friedman, J., Crosson, D., Fadus, M. (2011). Concierge medicine: Medical,
legal and ethical perspectives. *The Internet Journal of Law, Healthcare and Ethics,
7*(1). https://doi.org/10.5580/134f

Clay, R. A. (2020). *CMS recognizes PSYPACT licensure requirements for interstate practice.* American Psychological Association Services, Inc. https://www.apaservices
.org/practice/legal/technology/psypact-licensure-requirements

Collins, P. H. (2000). *Black feminist thought: Knowledge, consciousness, and the politics
of empowerment.* Routledge.

Comas-Días, L. (2020). Liberation Psychotherapy. In L. Comas-Días & Edil Torres
Rivera (Eds.), *Liberation Psychology: Theory, Method, Practice, and Social Justice*
(pp. 169–185). American Psychological Association.

Comas-Díaz, L., Hall, G. N., & Neville, H. A. (2019). Racial trauma: Theory,
research, and healing: Introduction to the special issue. *American Psychologist,
74*(1), 1–5. http://dx.doi.org/10.1037/amp0000442

Cooper, S. E., Campbell, L. F., & Smucker Barnwell, S. (2020). Telepsychology: A
primer for counseling psychologists. *The Counseling Psychologist, 47*(8), 1074–
1114. https://doi.org/10.1177/0011000019895276

Corey, G., Muratori, M., Austin, J. T., II, & Austin, J. A. (2018). *Counselor self-care.*
American Counseling Association.

Crenshaw, K. (1989). Demarginalizing the intersection of race and sex: A black feminist critique of antidiscrimination doctrine, feminist theory and antiracist politics. *The University of Chicago Legal Forum, 140*, 8, 139–167.

Czeisler, M. E., Lane, R. I., Petrosky, E., Wiley, J. F., Christensen, A., Njai, R.,
Weaver, M. D., Robbins, R., Facer-Childs, E. R., Barger, L. K., Czeisler, C. A.,
Howard, M. E., & Rajaratnam, S. M. W. (2020). Mental health, substance use,
and suicidal ideation during the COVID-19 pandemic – United States, June 24–
30, 2020. *Morbidity and Mortality Weekly Report, 69*(32), 1049–1057. https://doi
.org/10.15585/mmwr.mm6932a1

Danieli, Y., Norris, F. H., & Engdahl, B. (2017). A question of who, not if: Psychological disorders in Holocaust survivors' children. *Psychological Trauma: Theory, Research, Practice, and Policy, 9*(Suppl 1), 98–106. https://doi.org/10.1037/
tra0000192

Davidson, R. J., Kabat-Zinn, J., Schumacher, J., Rosenkranz, M., Muller, D., San-
torelli, S. F., Urbanowski, F., Harrington, A., Bonus, K., & Sheridan, J. F. (2003).

Alterations in brain and immune function produced by mindfulness meditation. *Psychosomatic medicine, 65*(4), 564–570. https://doi.org/10.1097/01.psy.0000077505.67574.e3

Davis, D. M., & Hayes, J. A. (2011). What are the benefits of mindfulness? A practice review of psychotherapy-related research. *Psychotherapy, 48*(2), 198–208. https://doi.org/10.1037/a0022062

DeAngelis, T. (2013). A natural fit. *Monitor on Psychology, 44*(8). https://www.apa.org/monitor/2013/09/natural-fit

DeAngelis, T. (2020, July 28). *Are crisis lines meeting new mental health needs?* American Psychological Association. https://www.apa.org/topics/covid-19/crisis-lines-mental-health

DiAngelo, R. J. (2018). *White fragility: Why it's so hard for white people to talk about racism.* Beacon Press.

Dockett, L. (2019). *Walk and talk: Psychotherapy takes a stroll.* Psychotherapy Networker. https://www.psychotherapynetworker.org/magazine/article/2407/walk-and-talk

Dodgen-Magee, D. (2020). *Why video chats are so exhausting.* Psychology Today. https://www.psychologytoday.com/us/blog/deviced/202004/why-video-chats-are-so-exhausting

Drum, K. B., & Littleton, H. L. (2014). Therapeutic boundaries in telepsychology: Unique issues and best practice recommendations. *Professional Psychology, Research and Practice, 45*(5), 309–315. https://doi.org/10.1037/a0036127

Drustrup, D. (2019). White therapists addressing racism in psychotherapy: An ethical and clinical model for practice. *Ethics & Behavior, 30*(3), 181–196. Advance online publication. https://doi.org/10.1080/10508422.2019.1588732

Fanon, F. (2001). The wretched of the earth (C. Farrington, Trans.). Penguin Classic. (Original work published 1963).

Figley, C. R., & Ludick, M. (2017). Secondary traumatization and compassion fatigue. In S. N. Gold (Ed.), *APA handbooks in psychology. APA handbook of trauma psychology: Foundations in knowledge* (pp. 573–593). American Psychological Association. https://doi.org/10.1037/0000019-029

Fischer, L. (2020, Feb 19). The revival of spirituality amongst Millennials and Gen-Z. *Medium.* https://medium.com/futurists-club-by-science-of-the-time/the-revival-of-spirituality-amongst-millennials-and-gen-z-ee00c4f28fc8

Freedman, S. A., & Mashiach, R. T. (2018). Shared trauma reality in war: Mental health therapists' experience. *PLoS ONE, 13*(2): e0191949. https://doi.org/10.1371/journal.pone.0191949

Freeman, D., Sheaves, B., Goodwin, G. M., Yu, L. M., Nickless, A., Harrison, P. J., Emsley, R., Luik, A. I., Foster, R. G., Wadekar, V., Hinds, C., Gumley, A., Jones, R., Lightman, S., Jones, S., Bentall, R., Kinderman, P., Rowse, G., Brugha, T., Blagrove, M., . . . Espie, C. A. (2017). The effects of improving sleep on mental health (OASIS): a randomised controlled trial with mediation analysis. *The Lancet. Psychiatry, 4*(10), 749–758. https://doi.org/10.1016/S2215-0366(17)30328-0

Freire, P. (2000). *Pedagogy of the oppressed* (30th anniversary ed.). Continuum.

French, B. H., Lewis, J. A., Mosley, D. V., Adames, H. Y., Chavez-Dueñas, N. Y., Chen, G. A., & Neville, H. A. (2020). Toward a psychological framework of radical healing in communities of color. *Counseling Psychologist, 48*(1), 14–46. https://doi.org/10.1177/0011000019843506

Gaudiano, B. A., & Miller, I. W. (2013). The evidence-based practice of psychotherapy: Facing the challenges that lie ahead. *Clinical Psychology Review, 33*(7), 813–824. https://doi.org/10.1016/j.cpr.2013.04.004

Geller, S. (2020). *Cultivating online therapeutic presence: strengthening therapeutic relationships in teletherapy sessions.* Counselling Psychology Quarterly. https://doi.org/10.1080/09515070.2020.1787348

Gerber, L. (2007). Social justice concerns and clinical practice. In E. Aldarondo (Ed.), *Advancing social justice through clinical practice* (pp. 43–61). Mahwah, NJ: Erlbaum.

Germer, C. K., Siegel, R. D., & Fulton, P. R. (Eds.). (2013). *Mindfulness and psychotherapy* (2nd ed.). Guilford Press.

Gesi, C., Carmassi, C., Cerveri, G., Carpita, B., Cremone, I. M., & Dell'Osso, L. (2020). Complicated grief: What to expect after the coronavirus pandemic. *Frontiers in psychiatry, 11*, 489. https://doi.org/10.3389/fpsyt.2020.00489

GLAAD (2017). *Accelerating acceptance.* https://www.glaad.org/files/aa/2017_GLAAD_Accelerating_Acceptance.pdf

Global Wellness Institute (2018, October). *Global Wellness Economy Monitor.* www.globalwellnessinstitute.com

Gloff, N. E., LeNoue, S. R., Novins, D. K., & Myers, K. (2015). Telemental health for children and adolescents. *International review of psychiatry, 27*(6), 513–524. https://doi.org/10.3109/09540261.2015.1086322

Glueckauf, R. L., Maheu, M. M., Drude, K. P., Wells, B. A., Wang, Y., Gustafson, D. J., & Nelson, E.-L. (2018). Survey of psychologists' telebehavioral health practices: Technology use, ethical issues, and training needs. *Professional Psychology: Research and Practice, 49*(3), 205–219. https://doi.org/10.1037/pro0000188

Goodman, R. D. (2015). A liberatory approach to trauma counseling: Decolonizing our trauma-informed practices. In R. D. Goodman & P. C. Gorski (Eds.), *Decolonizing "multicultural" counseling through social justice* (pp. 55–72). Springer. https://doi.org/10.1007/978-1-4939-1283-4_5

Gorski, P. C., & Goodman, R. D. (2015). Introduction: Toward a decolonized multicultural counseling and psychology. In R. D. Goodman, & P. C. Gorski (Eds.), Decolonizing "multicultural" counseling through social justice (pp. 1–10). New York, NY: Springer.

Goveas, J. S., & Shear, M. K. (2020). Grief and the COVID-19 pandemic in older adults. *The American Journal of Geriatric Psychiatry, 28*(10), 1119–1125. https://doi.org/10.1016/j.jagp.2020.06.021

Gritzka, S., MacIntyre, T. E., Dörfel, D., Baker-Blanc, J. L., & Calogiuri, G. (2020). The effects of workplace nature-based interventions on the mental health and well-being of employees: A systematic review. *Frontiers in psychiatry, 11*, 323. https://doi.org/10.3389/fpsyt.2020.00323

Grzanka, P. R., & Miles, J. R. (2016). The problem with the phrase "intersecting identities": LGBT affirmative therapy, intersectionality, and neoliberalism. *Sexuality Research & Social Policy: A Journal of the NSRC, 13*(4), 371–389. https://doi .org/10.1007/s13178-016-0240-2

Grzanka, P. R., Frantell, K. A., & Fassinger, R. E. (2020). The White Racial Affect Scale (WRAS): A measure of white guilt, shame, and negation. *The Counseling Psychologist, 48*(1), 47–77. https://doi.org/10.1177/0011000019878808

Grzanka, P. R., Gonzalez, K. A., & Spanierman, L. B. (2019). White supremacy and counseling psychology: A critical-conceptual framework. *The Counseling Psychologist, 47*(4), 478–529. [Invited contribution, 50th anniversary special volume]. https://doi.org/10.1177/0011000019880843

Haddock-Lazala, C. (2020). Urban liberation: Postcolonial Intersectional Feminism and Developing a Socially Conscious Therapeutic Practice. In L. Comas-Días & E. Torres Rivera (Eds.), *Liberation Psychology: Theory, Method, Practice, and Social Justice* (pp. 149–168).

Harvard Health. (2020). *Blue light has a dark side.* Harvard Health Letter. https:// www.health.harvard.edu/staying-healthy/blue-light-has-a-dark-side

Hasbach, P. H. (2013). Moving therapy outdoors: Techniques, challenges, and ethical considerations. *Voices: The Art and Science of Psychotherapy, 49* (1), 37–42.

Health Insurance Portability and Accountability Act. Pub. L. No. 104-191, § 264, 110 Stat.1936 https://www.hhs.gov/hipaa/for-professionals/index.html

Helms, J. E. (1984). Toward a theoretical explanation of the effects of race on counseling a Black and white model. *Counseling Psychologist, 12*(4). https://doi.org/10 .1177/0011000084124013

Herman, J. L. (1992). *Trauma and recovery.* New York: Basic Books.

Hill, C. E., Knox, S., & Pinto-Coelho, K. G. (2018). Therapist self-disclosure and immediacy: A qualitative meta-analysis. *Psychotherapy, 55*(4), 445–460. https:// doi.org/10.1037/pst0000182

Human Rights Campaign. (2020). Fatal violence against the transgender and gender non-conforming community in 2020. https://www.hrc.org/resources/violence -against-the-trans-and-gender-non-conforming-community-in-2020

Hurley, D. (2020). Sleep neurologists call it "COVID-somnia"—Increased sleep disturbances linked to the pandemic. *Neurology Today.* https://journals.lww.com/ neurotodayonline/fulltext/2020/07090/sleep_neurologists_call_it.1.aspx

Jain, R., & Jain, S. (2019). *The science and practice of wellness: interventions for happiness, enthusiasm, resilience, and optimism (hero).* New York: Norton.

Jenkins-Guarnieri, M. A., Pruitt, L. D., Luxton, D. D., & Johnson, K. (2015). Patient perceptions of telemental health: Systematic review of direct comparisons to in-person psychotherapeutic treatments. *Telemedicine Journal and e-Health, 21*(8), 652–660. https://doi.org/10.1089/tmj.2014.0165

Joshi, G., & Sharma, G. (2020). Burnout: A risk factor amongst mental health professionals during COVID-19. *Asian Journal of Psychiatry, 54*, 102300. Advance online publication. https://doi.org/10.1016/j.ajp.2020.102300

King, M. L., Jr. (1968). The role of the behavioral scientist in the Civil Rights Movement. *Journal of Social Issues, 24*(1), 1–12. https://doi.org/10.1111/j.1540-4560 .1968.tb01465.x

Kirkinis, K., Pieterse, A., Martin, C., Agiliga, A., & Brownwell, A. (2018). Racism, racial discrimination, and trauma: A systematic review of the social science literature. *Ethnicity & Health.* https://doi.org/10.1080/13557858.2018.1514453

Lai, J., Ma, S., Wang, Y., Cai, Z., Hu, J., Wei, N., Wu, J., Du, H., Chen, T., Li, R., Tan, H., Kang, L., Yao, L., Huang, M., Wang, H., Wang, G., Liu, Z., & Hu, S. (2020). Factors associated with mental health outcomes among health care workers exposed to coronavirus disease 2019. *JAMA Network Open, 3*(3), e203976. https://doi.org/10.1001/jamanetworkopen.2020.3976

LaRocca, A. (2019). Astrology is serious business, even if it's not real. *New York Magazine.* https://www.thecut.com/2019/03/sanctuary-astrology-app.html

Lassale, C., Batty, G. D., Baghdadli, A., Jacka, F., Sánchez-Villegas, A., Kivimäki, M., & Akbaraly, T. (2019). Healthy dietary indices and risk of depressive outcomes: a systematic review and meta-analysis of observational studies. *Molecular Psychiatry, 24,* 965–986 https://doi.org/10.1038/s41380-018-0237-8

Lavi, T., Nuttman-Shwartz, O., Dekel, R. (2017). Therapeutic intervention in a continuous shared traumatic reality: An example from the Israeli–Palestinian conflict, *The British Journal of Social Work, 47*(3), 919–935. https://doi.org/10.1093/bjsw/bcv127

Levine, P. A. & Crane-Godreau, M. A. (2015). Somatic experiencing: Using interoception and proprioception as core elements of trauma therapy. *Frontiers in Psychology.* https://doi.org/10.3389/fpsyg.2015.00093

Lin, L., Stamm, K., & Christidis, P. (2018). Demographics of the U.S. psychology workforce: Findings from the 2007-16 American community survey. https://www.apa.org/workforce/publications/16-demographics/report.pdf

Lobel, O. (2018). NDAs are out of control. Here's what needs to change. *Harvard Business Review.* https://hbr.org/2018/01/ndas-are-out-of-control-heres-what-needs-to-change

Locke, H. (2020). The psychological impact of video calls: What Zoom is doing to people, meetings and research. *UX Collective.* https://uxdesign.cc/the-psychological-impact-of-video-calls-dbed57aa792b

Lorde, A. (1988). *A Burst of Light: Essays.* Firebrand Books.

Luxton, D. D., Nelson, E., & Maheu, M. (2016). *A practitioner's guide to telemental health.* American Psychological Association.

Lynch, W. R. (2012). Starting and growing concierge psychotherapy and psychiatric practices. In C. Stout (Ed.), *Getting better in private practice* (pp. 253–265). John Wiley & Sons, Inc. https://doi.org/10.1002/9781118089972.ch16

Maheu, M. M., Pulier, M. L., McMenamin, J. P., & Posen, L. (2012). Future of telepsychology, telehealth, and various technologies in psychological research and practice. *Professional Psychology: Research and Practice, 43*(6), 613–621. https://doi.org/10.1037/a0029458

Malott, K. M., Schaefle, S., Paone, T. R., Cates, J., & Haizlip, B. (2019). Challenges and coping mechanisms of whites committed to antiracism. *Journal of Counseling & Development, 97*(1), 86–97. https://doi.org/10.1002/jcad.12238

Martín-Baró, I. (1994). *Writings for a liberation psychology* (A. Aron & S. Corne, Eds.). Harvard University Press.

McCord, C., Bernhard, P., Walsh, M., Rosner, C., & Console, K. (2020). A consolidated model for telepsychology practice. *Journal of Clinical Psychology, 76*(6), 1060–1082. https://doi.org/10.1002/jclp.22954

McEvoy, J. (2020). Sales of "White Fragility"—and other anti-racism books—jumped over 2000% after protests began. *Forbes*. https://www.forbes.com/sites/jemimamcevoy/2020/07/22/sales-of-white-fragility-and-other-anti-racism-books-jumped-over-2000-after-protests-began/#3576a9e5303d

Meyer, I. H. (2015). Resilience in the study of minority stress and health of sexual and gender minorities. *Psychology of Sexual Orientation and Gender Diversity, 2*(3), 209–213. https://doi.org/10.1037/sgd0000132

Miller, P. K. (2017). How white college students enact whiteness: An investigation of the attitudinal, behavioural and cultural components that comprise white racial identity at a historically white college. *Whiteness and Education, 2*, 92–111. doi:1 0.1080/23793406.2017.1327327

Miller, M. J., Keum, B. T., Thai, C. J., Lu, Y., Truong, N. N., Huh, G. A., Li, X., Yeung, J. G., & Ahn, L. H. (2018). Practice recommendations for addressing racism: A content analysis of the counseling psychology literature. *Journal of Counseling Psychology, 65*(6), 669–680. https://doi.org/10.1037/cou0000306

Miu, A. S., Vo, H. T., Palka, J. M., Glowacki, C. R., & Robinson, J. R. (2020). Teletherapy with serious mental illness populations during COVID-19: Telehealth conversion and engagement. *Counselling Psychology Quarterly*. https://doi.org/10.1080/09515070.2020.1791800

National Alliance on Mental Illness (n.d.). *LGBTQI*. https://www.nami.org/Your-Journey/Identity-and-Cultural-Dimensions/LGBTQI

National Association of Social Workers. (2020, March). Telemental health informed consent. https://www.socialworkers.org/LinkClick.aspx?fileticket=fN67-dWQReM%3D&portalid=0.

National Center for Transgender Equality. (2020). *Murders of transgender people in 2020 surpasses total for last year in just seven months*. https://transequality.org/blog/murders-of-transgender-people-in-2020-surpasses-total-for-last-year-in-just-seven-months

Natwick, J. (2018). Counselors are doing what now? Exploring the ethics of complementary methods. *Counseling Today*. https://www.counseling.org/docs/default-source/ethics/ethics-columns/ethics_september_2018_complementary-methods.pdf?sfvrsn=9413542c_4

Nelson, E. L., Cain, S., & Sharp, S. (2017). Considerations for conducting telemental health with children and adolescents. *Child and adolescent psychiatric clinics of North America, 26*(1), 77–91. https://doi.org/10.1016/j.chc.2016.07.008

Norcross, J. C., & Guy, J. D. (2007). *Leaving it at the office: A guide to psychotherapist self-care*. Guilford.

Norcross, J. C., & Lambert, M. J. (Eds.). (2019). *Psychotherapy relationships that work (Vol. 1, 3rd ed.): Evidence-based therapist contributions*. Oxford University Press.

Norcross, J. C., Zimmerman, B. E., Greenberg, R. P., & Swift, J. K. (2017). Do all therapists do that when saying goodbye? A study of commonalities in termination behaviors. *Psychotherapy, 54*(1), 66–75. https://doi.org/10.1037/pst0000097

Owen, J., Tao, K. W., Imel, Z. E., Wampold, B. E., & Rodolfa, E. (2014). Addressing racial and ethnic microaggressions in therapy. *Professional Psychology: Research and Practice, 45*(4), 283–290. https://doi.org/10.1037/a0037420

Panchal, N., Kamal, R., Orgera, K., Cox, C., Garfield, R., Hamel, L., Muñana, C., & Chidambaram, P. 2020. *The Implications of COVID-19 for mental health and substance use.* [Issue Brief]. Kaiser Family Foundation. https://www.kff.org/report-section/the-implications-of-covid-19-for-mental-health-and-substance-use-issue-brief/

Parker, K., & Igielnik, R. (2020). *On the cusp of adulthood and facing an uncertain future: What we know about Gen Z so far.* Pew Research Center. https://www.pewsocialtrends.org/essay/on-the-cusp-of-adulthood-and-facing-an-uncertain-future-what-we-know-about-gen-z-so-far/

Perle, J. G., Langsam, L. C., Randel, A., Lutchman, S., Levine, A. B., Odland, A. P., Nierenberg, B., & Marker, C. D. (2013). Attitudes toward psychological tele-health: Current and future clinical psychologists' opinions of internet-based interventions. *Journal of Clinical Psychology, 69*(1), 100–113. https://doi.org/10.1002/jclp.21912

Pew Research Center. (2019, June 12). *Mobile Fact Sheet.* https://www.pewresearch.org/internet/fact-sheet/mobile/

Pierce, B. S., Perrin, P. B., Tyler, C. M., McKee, G. B., & Watson, J. D. (2020, August 20). The COVID-19 telepsychology revolution: A national study of pandemic-based changes in U.S. mental health care delivery. *American Psychologist.* Advance online publication.

Pope, K. S., & Vasquez, M. J. T. (2005). *How to survive and thrive as a therapist: Information, ideas, and resources for psychologists in practice.* American Psychological Association. https://doi.org/10.1037/11088-000

Presley, R. (2019). *Decolonizing the Body: Indigenizing Our Approach to Disability Studies.* The Activist History Review. https://activisthistory.com/2019/10/29/decolonizing-the-body-indigenizing-our-approach-to-disability-studies/

Prilleltensky I. (2012). Wellness as fairness. *American Journal of Community Psychology, 49*(1–2), 1–21. https://doi.org/10.1007/s10464-011-9448-8

Prilleltensky, I., & Walsh-Bowers, R. (1993). Psychology and the moral imperative. *Journal of Theoretical and Philosophical Psychology, 13*(2), 90–102. https://doi.org/10.1037/h0091122

Ray, R. (2020). *Why are Blacks dying at higher rates from COVID-19?* Brookings. https://www.brookings.edu/blog/fixgov/2020/04/09/why-are-blacks-dying-at-higher-rates-from-covid-19/

Reese, R. F., & Myers, J. E. (2012). EcoWellness the missing factor in holistic wellness models. *Journal of Counseling and Development, 90*(4), 400–406.

Royal Society for Public Health. (2017). *#StatusOfMind: Social media and young people's mental health and wellbeing.* https://www.rsph.org.uk/static/uploaded/d125b27c-0b62-41c5-a2c0155a8887cd01.pdf

Ruiz, N. G., Horowitz, J. M., Tamir, C. (2020). *Many Black and Asian Americans say they have experienced discrimination amid the COVID-19 outbreak.* Pew Research Center Social and Demographic Trends. https://www.pewsocialtrends

.org/2020/07/01/many-black-and-asian-americans-say-they-have-experienced
-discrimination-amid-the-covid-19-outbreak/

Ryu, S. (2010). History of Telemedicine: Evolution, Context, and Transformation. *Healthcare Informatics Research, 16*(1), 65–66. https://doi.org/10.4258/hir.2010.16.1.65

Sammons, M. T, VandenBos, G. R., Martin, J. N. (2020). Psychological practice and the COVID-19 crisis: A rapid response survey. *Journal of Health Service Psychology, 46*, 51–57. Advance online publication. https://doi.org/10.1007/s42843-020-00013-2.

Schalf, S. (2017). Critical disability studies as methodology. *Lateral, 6*(1). https://doi.org/10.25158/L6.1.13

Seppala, E. (2020). *Social connection boosts health, even when you're isolated.* Psychology Today. https://www.psychologytoday.com/us/blog/feeling-it/202003/social-connection-boosts-health-even-when-youre-isolated

Serrano-García, I. (1994). The ethics of the powerful and the power of ethics. *American Journal of Community Psychology, 22*(1), 1–20. https://doi.org/10.1007/BF02506813

Sharf, J., Primavera, L. H., & Diener, M. J. (2010). Dropout and therapeutic alliance: a meta-analysis of adult individual psychotherapy. *Psychotherapy, 47*(4), 637–645. https://doi.org/10.1037/a0021175

Sharma, A., Madaan, V., & Petty, F. D. (2006). Exercise for mental health. *Primary care companion to the Journal of Clinical Psychiatry, 8*(2), 106. https://doi.org/10.4088/pcc.v08n0208a

Shore, J. H., Yellowlees, P., Caudill, R., Johnston, B., Turvey, C., Mishkind, M., Krupinski, E., Myers, K., Shore, P., Kaftarian, E., & Hilty, D. (2018). Best practices in videoconferencing-based telemental health April 2018. *Telemedicine and e-health, 24*(11), 827–832. https://doi.org/10.1089/tmj.2018.0237

Siegel, D. J. (2010). *The mindful therapist: A clinician's guide to mindsight and neural integration.* New York: Norton.

Siegel, D. J. (2017). *Mind: A journey to the heart of being human.* New York: Norton.

Smith, L. C. (2015). Queering multicultural competence in counseling. In R. D. Goodman & P. C. Gorski (Eds.), *International and cultural psychology. Decolonizing "multicultural" counseling through social justice* (pp. 23–39). Springer. https://doi.org/10.1007/978-1-4939-1283-4_3

Somer, E., Buchbinder, E., Peled-Avram, M., & Ben-Yizhack, Y. (2004). The stress and coping of Israeli emergency room social workers following terrorist attacks. *Qualitative Health Research, 14*, 1077–1093.

Spanierman, L. B., & Heppner, M. J. (2004). Psychosocial costs of racism to whites scale (PCRW): Construction and initial validation. *Journal of Counseling Psychology, 51*(2), 249–262. https://doi.org/10.1037/0022-0167.51.2.249

Stephan, S., Lever, N., Bernstein, L., Edwards, S., & Pruitt, D. (2016). Telemental health in schools. *Journal of child and adolescent psychopharmacology, 26*(3), 266–272. https://doi.org/10.1089/cap.2015.0019

Stiles-Shields, C., Kwasny, M. J., Cai, X., & Mohr, D. C. (2014). Therapeutic alliance in face-to-face and telephone-administered cognitive behavioral therapy. *Journal of Consulting and Clinical Psychology, 82*(2), 349–354. https://doi.org/10.1037/a0035554

Stone, M. R. (2013). *Somebody better put their pants on and be talking about it: White therapists who identify as anti-racist addressing racism and racial identity with white clients* [Masters Thesis, Smith College, Northampton, MA].

Stovall, N. (2019). *Whiteness on the couch*. Longreads. https://longreads.com/2019/08/12/whiteness-on-the-couch/

Sue, D. W. (2015). *Race talk and the conspiracy of silence: Understanding and facilitating difficult dialogues on race*. John Wiley & Sons, Inc.

Swift, J. K., Callahan, J. L., Cooper, M., & Parkin, S. R. (2018). The impact of accommodating client preference in psychotherapy: A meta-analysis. *Journal of Clinical Psychology, 74*(11), 1924–1937. https://doi.org/10.1002/jclp.22680

Swift, J. K., & Greenberg, R. P. (2015). *Premature termination in psychotherapy: Strategies for engaging clients and improving outcomes*. American Psychological Association. https://doi.org/10.1037/14469-000

Thompson, C., & Neville, H. (1999). Racism, mental health, and mental health practice. *The Counseling Psychologist, 27*(2), 155–223. https://doi.org/10.1177/0011000099272001

Toporek, R. L., Kwan, K.-L. K., & Williams, R. A. (2012). Ethics and social justice in counseling psychology. In N. A. Fouad, J. A. Carter, & L. M. Subich (Eds.), *APA handbooks in psychology. APA handbook of counseling psychology* (Vol. 2, pp. 305–332). American Psychological Association. https://doi.org/10.1037/13755-013

Trevor Project (2020). *Research Brief: Black LGBTQ Youth Mental Health*. https://www.thetrevorproject.org/2020/02/13/research-brief-black-lgbtq-youth-mental-health/

Truschel, J. (2020). *Top Mental Health Apps: An Effective Alternative for When You Can't Afford Therapy?* PsyCom. https://www.psycom.net/25-best-mental-health-apps

Ugolik, K. (2019). *Is the future of therapy. . . virtual? A look into virtual reality therapy.* Freethink. https://www.freethink.com/articles/is-the-future-of-therapy-virtual-a-look-into-virtual-reality-therapy

United States Association of Body Psychotherapy. (n.d). Definition of body psychotherapy. Retrieved on October 16, 2020 from https://usabp.org/Definition-of-Body-Psychotherapy/

van Der Kolk, B., Ford, J. D., & Spinazzola, J. (2019). Comorbidity of developmental trauma disorder (DTD) and post-traumatic stress disorder: findings from the DTD field trial. *European Journal of Psychotraumatology, 10*(1). https://doi.org/10.1080/20008198.2018.1562841

van Dernoot Lipsky, L., & Burk, C. (2009) *Trauma stewardship: An everyday guide to caring for self while caring for others*. Berrett-Koehler Publishers.

Vera, E. M., & Speight, S. S. (2003). Multicultural competence, social justice, and counseling psychology: Expanding our roles. *The Counseling Psychologist, 31,* 253–272. https://doi.org/10.1177/0011000003031003001

Vidal-Ortiz, S. (2008). People of Color. In R. T. Schaefer (Ed.), *Encyclopedia of race, ethnicity, and society* (Vol. 2, pp. 1037–1039). Sage.

Vogels, E. A. (2019, September 9). *Millennials stand out for their technology use, but older generations also embrace digital life.* https://pewrsr.ch/2A3kD6X

Vogels, E. A. (2020). *59% of U.S. parents with lower incomes say their child may face digital obstacles in schoolwork.* Pew Research Center. https://www.pewresearch .org/fact-tank/2020/09/10/59-of-u-s-parents-with-lower-incomes-say-their-child -may-face-digital-obstacles-in-schoolwork/

Watts, R. J. (2004). Integrating social justice and psychology. *The Counseling Psychologist, 32,* 855–865. https://doi.org/10.1177/0011000004269274

Weinstein, N., Brown, K. W., & Ryan, R. M. (2009). A multi-method examination of the effects of mindfulness on stress attribution, coping, and emotional well-being. *Journal of Research in Personality, 43,* 374–385. https://dx.doi.org/10 .1016/j.jrp.2008.12.008

Weir, K. (2011). The exercise effect. *Monitor on Psychology, 42*(11), 48. https://www .apa.org/monitor/2011/12/exercise

Weise, D. (2014). The pros & cons of concierge medicine. *Health Journal.* https:// www.thehealthjournals.com/concierge-medicine/

Westervelt, E. (2020, September 18). *Mental health and police violence: How crisis intervention teams are failing* [Broadcast transcript]. NPR All Things Considered. https://www.npr.org/2020/09/18/913249469/mental-health-and-police-violence -how-crisis-intervention-teams-are-failing

Woods, S.B. (2020, May 8). COVID-19 and Ambiguous loss. *Psychology Today.* https://www.psychologytoday.com/us/blog/in-sickness-and-in-health/202005/ covid-19-and-ambiguous-loss

Zencare. (2020). *Holistic Therapy.* https://zencare.co/therapy-type/holistic-therapy#: ~:text=Holistic%20therapy%20is%20a%20type,themselves%20on%20all%20 these%20levels

Zur, O. (2007). *Boundaries in psychotherapy: Ethical and clinical explorations.* American Psychological Association. https://doi.org/10.1037/11563-000

Zur, O. (2015). *Beyond the office walls: Home visits, celebrations, adventure therapy, incidental encounters and other encounters outside the office walls.* Zur Institute. https://www.zurinstitute.com/outofofficeexperiences.html

Index

exercise
  in WILD 5 wellness program, 74, 75
experiencing
  somatic, 81
external distractions
  minimizing, 37–38
external therapists
  for collective trauma–related support
    for community, xv

FaceTime, 33
family relationships
  pandemic-related stress and strain
    on, xv
fatigue
  among therapists, 99, 101
  compassion, 180–82
  Zoom, 40–42
fear
  white, 144
  white racialized, 144
federal crisis hotline
  increase in calls to, xiv
fee(s)
  in concierge therapy, 112–14
fee-for-service private practice therapies
  prevalence of, xvii, 96
  reasons for, xvii
fee payment
  in TMH practice, 29–31
flexibility
  ethical issues and, 163–64
Floyd, G., Jr., 120, 141
fragility
  white, 140–49
French, B.H., 175

game-based therapy
  TMH–related, 66–67
gaming apps, 14
gay-affirmative therapy, 136–40
gender
  as independent identity construct,
    150

gender-based violence
  against LGBTQ+ community, 135
gender conforming
  prevalence of, 135
Gen Z
  as allies of LGBTQ+ community,
    135
  healthcare values of, xix
  spirituality among, 86–87
Gerber, L., 170
GLAAD study, 134–35
Google Duo, 33
greening the office
  described, 82–83
grief
  complicated, 178–79
growth
  fostering, 186
Guidelines for Psychological Practice
    with Transgender and Gender Non-
    conforming Persons, 140, 153, 161
guilt
  white, 146

hate crimes
  against LGBTQ+ community, 135
hazard(s)
  recognizing, 185
health
  increased integration of, 71
  telemental see telemental health
    (TMH)
healthcare
  cultural shifts in, xix
  evolving landscape of, xix
  Gen Z thoughts on, xix
  increased consumer choice impact
    on, xix
  Millennials' thoughts on, xix
Higher Power
  belief in, 87
"highly attentive medicine," 95
high-needs clients
  concierge therapy with, 111

trauma
  collective, xv, 173
  COVID-19 pandemic–related, 173–79
  described, 173
  racial, 175
  shared, 172–87 *see also* shared
    trauma
trauma stewardship, 179
trauma therapy
  for racially minoritized populations,
    175–76
traumatic stress
  secondary, 180–82
trust
  in therapeutic rapport, 56–58
two-way interactive video
  benefits of, 8

value(s)
  in social justice–oriented counsel-
    ing, 160
VA systems. *see* Veterans Affairs (VA)
    systems
VC. *see* videoconferencing (VC)
verbal abuse
  against LGBTQ+ community, 135
verification of identity
  for TMH, 52–53
Veterans Affairs (VA) systems
  hub and spoke model in, 4
  VRs within, 14
video-based therapy. *see* videoconfer-
    encing (VC)
videoconferencing (VC), 7–8. *see also*
    TMH practice
  background, 37–40
  benefits of, 8
  clinical effectiveness of, 20–22
  HIPAA–compliant, 32
  lighting in, 38–39
  security considerations in, 31–33
  synchronous, 48, 51
  technology considerations in, 31–33

terminology related to, 31
  two-way interactive video, 8
  uses for, 7–8
videoconferencing (VC) intake ses-
    sions, 52
videoconferencing (VC) platforms
  costs associated with, 35–36
  features of, 35
  requirements for, 35–36
  in TMH practice, 35–36
violence
  gender-based, 135
virtual background
  described, 39–40
virtual environment
  considerations, 36–40
virtual gaming
  multiplayer, 67
virtual office
  attention to, 38–39
  considerations for, 36–40
virtual realities (VRs), 14
  in VA system, 14
virtual therapies (VTs), 1–25. *see also*
    specific types
  clinical issues in, 46–70 *see also spe-
    cific types and* clinical issues in
    TMH
  described, 14
voice
  in social justice–oriented counsel-
    ing, 160
VRs. *see* virtual realities (VRs)
VTs. *see* virtual therapies (VTs)

well-being
  connectome in, 79
  increased integration of, 71
wellness. *see also* wellness approaches;
    wellness-based therapies
  approaches to, 71–93 *see also spe-
    cific types and under* wellness
    approaches

About the Author

Chanté D. DeLoach, Psy.D., is a licensed psychologist in private practice and professor of psychology at Santa Monica College. She has presented at domestic and international conferences and published numerous articles and book chapters focused on trauma, couples therapy, as well as community and liberation psychologies. Dr. DeLoach is a sought-after speaker and leader having served as a previous president of the Chicago Chapter of the Association of Black Psychologists and as volunteer psychologist with the Physicians for Human Rights Asylum Network. A frequent consultant for schools, nonprofits, and professional organizations, she has worked in numerous countries throughout Africa, South America, and the Caribbean. Find her at www.drdeloach.com or on social media @drcdeloach.